The Royal Tantra

on the

Brilliant Diffusion

of

Majestic Space

With Tibetan Text

Translated by

Christopher Wilkinson

The painting on the cover represents the Himalayan blue sheep, or bharal, which is mentioned in the Tantra. It was painted by Tsering Kelsang, a master artist currently has a studio at DoDrupchen Rinpoche's monastery in Sikkim. Tsering Kelsang graduated from the art school at the Tibetan Homes Foundation (VTC) in Mussoorie, India, where he studied under Mr. Ngawang, Mr. Dorjee Tsaktsa, Mr. Dorjee Namgyal, and Mr. Rigzin. Tsering Kelsang has been greatly inspired by the work of Mr. Pema Namdrol Thia. If you are interested in commissioning a Thangka, he may be reached at +918927773342 or on Facebook at: https://www.facebook.com/tsering.kelsang.7

No part of this book may be reproduced in any form or by any electronic or mechanical means including information storage and retrieval systems, without permission in writing from the author. The only exception is by a reviewer, who may quote excerpts in a review.

Published by Christopher Wilkinson

Cambridge, MA, USA

Copyright © 2016 Christopher Wilkinson

All rights reserved.

ISBN: 1534877886
ISBN-13: 978-1534877887

DEDICATION

For all the teachers and students of the Great Perfection.

Also Translated By Christopher Wilkinson

Great Perfection Series:

The Secret Tantras of the Fish Wheel and the Nine Spaces:
Two Ancient Scriptures of the Great Perfection

Ten Early Tantras of the Great Perfection:
A Basket of Diamonds

The Gods and the Demons Are Not Two:
A Tantra of the Great Perfection

The Tantra of Great Bliss:
The Guhyagarbha Transmission of Vajrasattva's Magnificent Sky

Secret Sky:
The Ancient Tantras on Vajrasattva's Magnificent Sky

The Great Tantra of Vajrasattva:
Equal to the End of the Sky

Beyond Secret:
The Upadesha of Vairochana on the Practice of the Great Perfection

Secret Wisdom:
Three Root Tantras of the Great Perfection

Sakya Kongma Series:

Sakya Pandita's Poetic Wisdom

Jetsun Dragpa Gyaltsan: The Hermit King

Admission at Dharma's Gate by Sonam Tsemo

An Overview of Tantra and Related Works

Chogyal Phagpa: The Emperor's Guru

Advice to Kublai Khan: Letters by the Tibetan Monk Chogyal Phagpa
To Kublai Khan and his Court

At The Court of Kublai Khan:
Writings of the Tibetan Monk Chogyal Phagpa

CONTENTS

Acknowledgments — i

Introduction — iii

The Royal Tantra on the Brilliant Diffusion of Majestic Space — 1

1. The Basic Scene — 3
2. No Origins or Applications — 7
3. The Unfathomable Intent — 13
4. Teaching the Heart-Essence of Our Intent — 21
5. The Supreme Inspiration — 27
6. Teaching That Awareness Has No Object — 33
7. A View that Has No Limitations — 41
8. Teaching That Awareness Has No Divisions — 47
9. Teaching the Mandala — 51
10. Setting the Measure of Our Practice — 55
11. Cutting Through Exaggerations from Within — 59
12. The Two Accumulations Are Perfected in Ourselves — 63
13. Teaching That The Bodhicitta Has No Basic Root — 69
14. Teaching The Significance of Equanimity — 79
15. The Non-Conceptual Is Not To Be Meditated On — 83
16. Teaching That There Is No Going To Or Coming From This Dominion — 87
17. The Self-Liberation of the Vehicles — 93
18. Untying the Knots — 97

19	The Secret Great Bliss	101
20	Teaching That the Awareness Is a Golden Vase	107
21	Revealing Our Field of Practice	113
22	Making Our Ideas Real	117
23	Unpolluted Perfection	123
24	The Meaning Does Not Move	129
25	The Secret Liberation of the Sky	135
26	Revealing the Three Embodiments to Myself	141
27	Refuting Cause and Result and Recognizing the Three Embodiments	145
28	Teaching the Way That We Are Gathered into this Dominion	151
29	There Is No Break In the Continuum	157
30	Teaching Dhyāna Meditation	163
31	Teaching That the Unborn Cuts Through to the One	167
32	Teaching That the Characteristics of the Bodhicitta Have No Birth or Ending	171
33	Our Own Power of Awareness	175
34	The Occurrence of Miracles	179
35	Decisive Contemplation	185
36	Teaching That We Have Received the Empowerment from the Beginning	189
37	Teaching the Specifics on Empowerment	195
38	Samaya Are Not to Be Numbered or Protected	197
39	Teachings on Touching and Meeting with the Three Embodiments	201
40	There Are No Applications for the Six Collections	207

41	The Supreme Practice	213
42	Teaching the Transmission than which There Is No Higher	219
43	Recognition of the Five Embodiments and the Five Greatnesses	225
44	Everything Is Perfection Without End	231
45	Teaching That there is One Characteristic	239
46	The Misunderstanding of the Great Perfection	245
47	Presenting the Entourage with Advice	253
48	The Entourage Rejoices in the Teacher	255
	The Tibetan Text	257
	About the Translator	345

ACKNOWLEDGMENTS

First and foremost, I wish to thank my root teacher Dezhung Rinpoche for constantly bringing out the best in me and encouraging me to pursue a comprehension of every branch of Buddhist learning. It was he who introduced me to Dilgo Kyentse Rinpoche, and through his recommendations enabled me to receive full empowerments, transmissions, and permissions in the areas of Mahā, Anu, and Ati Yogas. With the highest regard I wish to thank Dilgo Kyentse Rinpoche, Khetsun Zangpo Rinpoche, Nyoshul Khen Rinpoche, and Khenpo Palden Sherab for their kind instruction and encouragement in my effort to translate the literature of the rDzogs chen. There are many individuals, too many to name here, that have helped me over the years to become a qualified translator, in many ways. At this time I want to remember the kindness of Ngawang Kunga Trinlay Sakyapa, Jigdral Dagchen Sakya Rinpoche, Dhongthog Rinpoche, H.H. Karmapa Rangjung Rigpay Dorje, Kalu Rinpoche, Chogyam Trungpa Rinpoche, Geshe Ngawang Nornang, Carl Potter, David Ruegg, Turrell Wylie, Gene Smith, Karen Lang, Richard Solomon, Jack Hawley, David Jackson, Cyrus Stearns, Herbert Guenther, Eva Neumeier-Dargyay, Leslie Kawamura, Robert Thurman, Paul Nietupski, Lou Lancaster, David Snellgrove, Jean-Luc Achard, Steve Landsberg, Tsultrim Alione, Carolyn Klein, Rob Mayer, Jonathan Silk, David White, Mark Tatz, Steve Goodman, and Kennard Lipman. I want to make special thanks to Marcos Gonzalez Pardo for proofing the manuscript and to Robert J. Barnhart for his generous support. I also want to offer a very special thank you to Tsering Kelsang, who painted the wonderful image of the blue sheep in the mountains for the cover of this book. The many people who have contributed to my understanding and ability to do this work cannot be counted. I wish to thank everyone that has taken a kind interest in these translations, however slight, for your part in making this work a reality.

INTRODUCTION

The Great Perfection, also known as the Atiyoga or Dzogchen (*rDzogs chen*), is a tradition of esoteric Buddhism that upholds instantaneous enlightenment. The literature of the Great Perfection has been divided up into three groups or sections: The Mind Section (*Sems sde*), the Space Section (*kLong sde*), and the Upadeśa Instruction Section (*Man ngag sde*). The Royal Tantra on the Brilliant Diffusion of Majestic Space is the King of the Space Section Tantras, and is here translated in full for the first time.

The Space Section transmission is known as the Vajra Bridge (*rDo rje zam pa*). It is said that Vairochana, a famous translator who was active during the Eighth Century of the Common Era, received the texts and instructions for the Space Section from his teacher Śrī Singha, and then passed them down to his student Mipham Gonpo. It is said that for five generations of this lineage every master achieved a rainbow body at the time of his passing away.

I have previously translated and published several of the Space Section Tantras. The Great Tantra of Vajrasattva: Equal to the End of the Sky is a Root Tantra of the Space Section. The Nine Spaces of the Ocean of the Bodhicitta, contained in The Secret Tantras of the Fish Wheel and the Nine Spaces, is also a Root Tantra of the Space Section. The Tantras on Secret Wisdom, contained in Secret Wisdom: Three Root Tantras of the Great Perfection are also Root Tantras of the Space Section. It has been a great pleasure to translate the King of the Root Tantras of the Space Section: The Royal Tantra on the Brilliant Diffusion of Majestic Space. I hope that you enjoy it.

I have included images of the Tibetan manuscript to help preserve this important literary tradition and for your convenience.

Thank you,

Christopher Wilkinson

June 2016

The Royal Tantra on the Brilliant Diffusion of Majestic Space

THE ROYAL TANTRA
ON THE
BRILLIANT DIFFUSION
OF
MAJESTIC SPACE

In the Indian Language:

　Maṇḍala Dadu Bhihase Yaya Rāja Tantra Nāma

In the Tibetan language:

　kLong chen rab 'byams rgyal po'i rgyud

In the English language:

　The Royal Tantra on the Brilliant Diffusion of Majestic Space

THE BASIC SCENE

I bow to the Blessed One, the All Good One!

On one occasion I heard these words myself:

Being indivisible from the bodies, speech, minds, virtues, and good works of all the Sugatas of the ten directions and the three times, and dwelling in an identity that does not move from out of the state of being a single circle, everything is one in the space of equanimity, but in an effort to realize the meaning of this and to make it public, in the abode of Akaniṣṭa, on a field that is indistinguishable from the foundation of the three realms, to an entourage that was indivisible and appeared from out of myself, in which the Buddhas of the three times and the sentient beings of the three realms are not different, and in which those of the world and those who are beyond the world are in a single company, where I myself and my true nature are indivisible, and where from my essence and my true nature an unbroken river of manifestations appear to work for the benefit of living beings, I spoke with a melodious voice that purported the roar of a lion, and brilliantly explained the meaning of this royal and brilliant diffusion of the majestic space of the mind itself:

All the enumerations of names for the Dharma,
However many there may be,
Lack, from the beginning, any basis for their attribution
And are one in that space.

In a single majestic space,
Samsara and nirvana may arise as anything,

According to conditions,
And therefore the Dharma on the surface
Is like the clouds in the sky
And like the rainbow colors in the sky.

Awareness dawns on us,
So the state of our dominion
Is a self-awareness that is unobstructed.
It has no faults.
It has no borders or limitations.

The precious wisdom that possesses no ideas
Has no true nature,
So it may appear to be anything.

Everything is a space for the Bodhicitta.
The mandala of the Victorious Sugata
And the reverted ideas for imparting empowerments
That use ignorance and delusions
Grow larger,
And are the Dharmas of samsara.

All the Dharmas,
However many there may be,
Are one in Buddhahood,
So ideas about both their existence and their non-existence,
And views about both their goodness and their badness,
Are mistaken.

Where there is a single equanimity
We cling to extremes
Selves and others appear to be separate
Due to conditions.
When we engage our intellects in the existence
Of things that are non-existent,
We are led by our yearnings,
And we appear to be in bodies.
On account of the sorrows of clinging to a self,
We are not aware of the purpose that dwells within us.

In the proper truth,
There is no happiness or sorrow.
We cling to a vesture of emptiness

As if it was a real entity.
When we investigate,
There is no real entity.
A thing that does not exist
May appear to be anything.

In the space of self-awareness
There is no emptiness or entity.
When we understand that they are not there,
We are liberated from the path of samsara.
This is the inspiration of the finest of those who have understanding.

The true nature of a single characteristic
Appears in all of them.
The totally encompassing embodiment
That has no demarcations
Arises from its dominion as the body of the Victorious One.

All things, none excepted, arise in a single dominion,
In a totality,
Without any creator.
As they are not entities,
They may appear to be anything.

The dominion of the Dharma appears as the many things,
But its true nature is without essence.
The Bodhicitta, the continuum of which is unceasing,
Has no characteristics.
It has no position.

All things are naturally indivisible as Dharmas.
Anyone who would cling to them
Would be viewing them in terms of positions.
Their mind would be deluded.
For the correct meaning,
They would use their deprived intellects.
They would be clenched by the fetters of the noose of their clinging.

So he spoke.

From the Royal Tantra on the Brilliant Diffusion of Majestic Space, this is chapter one: The Basic Scene.

The Royal Tantra on the Brilliant Diffusion of Majestic Space

NO ORIGINS OR APPLICATIONS

Then again the Blessed One spoke:

Those who desire to dry out
This great ocean of samsara
Must look for the heart of the Dharma
In themselves.
We must reach to the way it is
With each and every thing,
Whether external of internal,
For selves and others are non-dual.

Our bodies, speech, and minds are one in the soul.[1]
Dharmas that are made out to be other than the soul
Do not exist,
Even in the smallest part.
The bounteous enumerations of all things
Are also not visible in the way things are.
They are like illusions,
So the intellect that understands them
Makes our senses flow out into their objects.
It does not send them into the abode of blissful awareness,
So its significance is the same as if it surely did not exist,
But we get the sorrow of seeing it as if it existed.

---

[1] Tibetan: bDag, Sanskrit: Ātman

However it may be evident,
The space of reality is self-originating.
Its true nature is the domain of the sky.
Those that are beyond this world,
And also those manifestations of methods and compassion
Who are of the world,
Are the miracles of the dominion of wisdom.
They are the heart of the Dharma.
They are its own grace.

The three horrible existences and the Buddhas
Absolutely do not live separately or apart.
The self is an attribution of our intellects on the way things are.
When we understand this,
It is the finest inspiration.

Buddhahood is not to be sought from an other.
In the reality of primordial Buddhahood
What would be the benefit of cleansing our spirits?
What would we achieve by abandoning things,
Or by taking them up?
Even the heaps, domains, and generative forces
Are not divisible from the Buddha Fields and the virtuous Dharmas.
They are a space of primordial equality.

The four kinds of birth[2] of the six classes of living beings
Are entries into the primordial path of enlightenment.
There is nothing that is called "a sentient being"
That is anything other than the dominion of the Dharma.

We are not present in any one.
We encompass them all.
We use the way of attachment to remain in equanimity.
We are neither close to nor distant from anything,
So we dwell forever in the space of non-duality.

There is nothing that is not subsumed within this.
All things are perfected in the one,
So this is the highest pinnacle of the vehicles.
It is an overarching adornment.

---

[22] From a womb, an egg, moisture, or miraculous birth.

The Great Spirit[3] is a glory that is inclusive of all things.
It is the highest inspiration of the Victorious Ones.
There are no Dharmas other than this,
So what will we analyze?
What will we engage in?
Who will be of benefit to whom?
Who will inflict harm on whom?

In the samadhi that has no origin or application
We have entered into equanimity from the beginning.
That is why we have nothing to visualize,
And nothing to join with or to part from.

The Bodhicitta has no true nature.
It is like a precious jewel.
It may appear as anything.
It is not contrived by anyone.
It is inherently pure.

Names and Dharmas that cling to conventionalities
Are all naturally indivisible.
Self-originating wisdom has its own space.
Happiness, sorrow, and even equanimity
Are clearly self-arising and self-pacifying.
In their own space they are totally pure.
In the way things are there is no contrivance.

From the unborn the many things are born.
They are not born in any true birth.
There is not even an atom that will demarcate them.
There is no movement in any true motion.
They do not become anything.
They are unborn.

The heart of a vajra has its own grace.
It is neither stained nor destroyed by anything.
The heart of a lotus is our own body.
It has no exterior or interior.
It is thusness.

---

[3] Tibetan: bDag nyid Chen po, Sanskrit: Mahātman

THE UNFATHOMABLE INTENT

Then again the Blessed One spoke:

If we do not know
That the transcendence of the world
And each and every designated name and enumeration
For the different worlds
Are of a single true nature,
When we talk about their enumeration,
We fail at what they mean.

Through attributing names, conceptualizations are born.
Through holding onto objects, a yearning attitude emerges.
Through being lead to the results that we yearn for,
They appear to be heaps, domains, and generative forces,
To be objects, times, and positions,
To have colors and shapes.

In the dominion of equanimity there is nothing at all.
It is based on the differentiation of subtle and coarse ideas
That we talk about the enumerations of the vehicles,
But we do not understand equanimity,
So there will be problems.

The true nature of the Dharma is non-dual.
To say: "This" is to have a deluded intellect.
The Vinaya, Sutras, and Abhidharma
Are attributed to be Three Baskets,

But this is only a name.
It does not exist in any significance.
This is why when a teacher attributes something
To be the Dharma,
He is exhausted.

The true nature of the dominion of the Dharma
Is not a field of practice for words.
Those who are deluded cannot understand.

The Buddhas of the past,
Those who have not yet passed on,
And all the Victorious Ones who will come later on
Are indivisible from the All Good Vajra,
The god of the gods,
And they are present as one.

For this reason,
We do not move from our natural purpose.
Everything that appears among the Dharmas of the many things
Is divided into an enumeration
From the one.
The totality of the Dharmas is without divisions.
When we know one,
We also know them all.
When we understand one,
We also understand all of them at one time.
The totality of them is indivisible.
They are the state of the sky.

It is because we are free from all grasping to a self
That we do not envision an understanding
Or one who understands.
It is because all the Dharmas appear
Within this thusness that is not an entity
That it is the foundation for all samsara and nirvana.

Further,
The true nature of our dominion
Is a true nature that manifests in this way,
So it is like the sky blazing in light.
Liberation through the dawning of the base
Is a treasure of portent.

When we are naturally present,
That is the space of our contemplation.
To possess a meaning
Is the space of ideas.
To have honesty is an unmistaken path.
When we have no contrivance,
We are present in our own way.

No matter what physical practice we may do,
We have no real yearning for our bodies.
All the paths of practice for our speech and our minds
Are remiss at what makes us happy,
So without any real yearning,
We are present with what happiness there is.

There is no contrivance in the sky.
Just so, we also do not have bodies.
There is no one who owns the Dharma.
All the fields of practice for our bodies, speech, and minds
Are like illusions.
They have no true nature.

The body does not give birth to the mind.
There is no basis for that,
So there have been no subjects or objects
Since the primordial.
Great and small are indivisible.
There are no material things.
From the beginning,
There has been no clinging to any idea
Or to its decay.

We are in a search for what is or is not to be visualized
In the sky which has no demarcations,
But our mind is itself like the sky,
So when we settle our intellects,
Which are like the sky,
We are one in a natural dominion.

The clingings of our minds
To a body and a speech
Are not to be sought for here,

So no matter how they appear to us,
There is no referent for our visualizations.

There is nothing to dwell on in this,
So however things are,
We do not contemplate anything else.
We must also not think about what we do not contemplate.

To be naturally present
Is the space of our inspiration.
In the dominion that is not to be thought of
Inconceivable wonders appear.

All the Dharmas, none excepted,
Are inconceivable.
Self-awareness is beyond all speech and thought.
There is neither non-conceptualization nor any meaning to it.
Anything other than it also does not exist.

The dominion of the Dharma is not to be contemplated.
There is not even an atom to be contrived by any remedies.
However all these things dawn on us,
That is the dawning of our natural base.
Do not make them out to be levels of the Dharma!

To remedy what we do not accommodate is a conceptual attitude.
Truth and untruth are grounds for doubts.
Faults and virtues are causes for taking things on and throwing them off.

The dominion of equanimity has no truth or lies.
In its significance there is no motion.
If we do not move away from what this means,
That is the yoga of yogas.
It is brilliantly majestic.

The virtues of dwelling one-pointedly,
And the understanding in which we think for only a moment
Are one in their natural dominion.
This is why in majestic equanimity
They are alike.
They are alike.

We say: "In thusness it is so,"
For they cannot be estimated through any measure.
They are difficult to fathom,
Extensive in depth,
And spacious in being doors,
So they are not fields of practice for the critical
Who are deluded.

The mind itself is a majestic enlightenment.
There is nothing on which to make attributions
That it exists or that it does not exist.
The Bodhicitta appears to be existent,
But it does not negate entities in any way,
So the Bodhicitta appears to be non-existent.

It inherently pacifies our demarcations,
So we are present in a liberation
From the extremes of existence and non-existence.

Our attachments and our five kinds of emotional problems
Blaze,
While we absolutely do not move.
This is the effulgence of self-originating wisdom.

There is nothing to attribute,
So this is the cause of the self.
Reality appears from out of ourselves.
Our emotional problems,
And even the five unpardonable deeds,
Are ornaments for the dominion of the practice of our desires.

We are not empowered into them.
They are our own conditions.
They manifest as our playfulness.
Through the delusions of ignorance,
We see them as being problems.
We obstruct them as being some other,
And we reject them,
But here we do not reject them.
We will understand them by settling into them.

Liberation is the heart of empowerment,
So we do not reject it.

Here, we understand it by practicing it.
Union is a practice of methods,
But we do not dwell on it.

Wisdom is the path of great bliss.
We do not cling to any other being on our side,
While we do not separate ourselves.
This has been revealed to be a life of acceptance.

In this life of the Bodhicitta,
We are not overwhelmed by the hosts of the four Maras.
We are not killed by the three kinds of enemies.
We do not fall into the six crevasses.
We do not fail at the river of effortlessness.

When we look for something higher than this objective,
The reward for being a Buddha,
It is nowhere else.

This is effortless and has no limits.
It is the dominion of the Dharma.
Great compassion does not create emptiness.
Lust and hatred are pure in their abodes,
So the mind that puts things together
Has no apparent feelings.

No matter what kinds of miracles may arise
From out of our dominion,
They may rise up.
They may be pacified.
They have their own grace.
They are like precious jewels from the ocean.
Their wonders are not to be sought out anywhere else.

The spells of essential compassion
Are apparent within our five emotional problems,
Without being sent forth,
But because they are objects to be taken in by compassion,
They encompass everything,
Without being equanimities.

Self-originating wisdom has no rise or fall.
There are analogies and validations for this.

Self-origination is not something that can be fathomed.
It shines in the dominion of majestic knowledge.

The Bodhicitta is a precious jewel.
It is the base from which all virtues emerge.
It is the great circle that subsumes all things.
It is present it its own way of being,
Without our searching for it.

The Bodhicitta is primordial Buddhahood.
It is spontaneously realized from the primordial,
So without rejecting anything,
We are liberated into our own place.

The Bodhicitta is positionless.
Its true nature is indefinite,
So it is not present as a unity.
It encompasses all things.

The Bodhicitta is not something to search for.
Its virtues are perfected in itself,
So it arises everywhere,
Without having a location.

There is no practice of the Bodhicitta.
Everything is subsumed within it,
So it is the spontaneously realized reward
That we do not work toward.

So he spoke.

From the Royal Tantra on the Brilliant Diffusion of Majestic Space, this is chapter three: The Unfathomable Intent.

TEACHING THE HEART-ESSENCE OF OUR INTENT

Then again the Blessed One spoke out unmistakably on the intentions of his heart:

From out of the essence of the single circle
There are none who have or have not become Buddhas.
We are one.

We may make an attribution that Buddhahood is a result,
But the virtues there are in attaining it
Are not anywhere else.

The mind itself is a majestic space.
By force of this,
Sentient beings may appear to be causes,
But the grim prospects of samsara
Are not anywhere else.

The effulgence of this effortless and majestic space
Is a reality that has no cause or result,
So Buddhas and sentient beings are indivisible.

There is nothing that I have contrived from this.
We may attribute causes, conditions, and results,
But we would be teaching with interpretable intentions,
And fail.

We are present without any mistake.
We are clear without any effort.
Unceasingness is, in fact, the space of wisdom.

In this abode of thusness
There is no distraction or non-distraction.
There is no motion or non-motion.
For this reason,
There is no other inspiration of the Victorious One
Than this.

To understand that causes and results are material things
Within this completely pure reality,
Is to be ensnared by bad philosophical conclusions.
We are deluded,
So our purpose is reverted.

That is why this is most difficult to teach
Or to talk about.
From out of the sky's dominion of swirling majestic space
This is the majestic abode for everyone,
So to practice on objects and to completely fade away
Are delusions.
We deviate in our purpose.

When we destroy things with logic,
They are not destroyed.
Majestic space is liberated by its own grace.
When we determine the limits of our thoughts
They are not determined.
Majestic space is determined by its own force.

When our own minds have the resolve of logic,
That is the *swastika* of the changeless intent.
The sentinel over the meaning of scripture and reason
Smashes our stupid and reverted ideas into atoms.
The transmission of the intent that does not turn back
Is not sent out to any extremists.
We retain it.

Peerless knowledge is the measure of our awareness.
We do not practice on any object.

This is the mind of equanimity.
This is not something that is entirely common.
This is not something to be sought after or worked on.
It is not necessary to do anything for this.
We do not need austerities or difficult practices.
This is not something to purify or to travel over.
Our non-contrivance is clear to us in our own place.

To have power is to have no object of attachment.
There is no result to be obtained by voyaging over a path.
There are no attributions that would signify
The meaning of this effortless primordial wind
In words.

There is no referent for a visualization
That we might use as an object.
It is not necessary to work on chants for our samadhi.
What would we work on?
Where would we abide?

The significance of effortlessness is not to be praised.
The Dharma as it appears and is well known
Comes from ourselves.
It is our own adornment.

To hold onto it as being some other
Is an attitude of conceptualization.
To yearn for this is to have a deluded mind.

There are no subjects or objects.
If we do not know that the path of liberation
Is our own mind,
We will not succeed in seeking it
Through any other majestic methods.

If we do not know that the teacher is us,
There will not be any All Good One anywhere else.
If we do not know that the teaching is us,
There will be no enumerations of the vehicles anywhere else.
If we do not know that the entourage is us,
We will give birth to a consciousness that there is some other object.
If we do not know that the time is us,
We will not cut through the rope of our hoping.

In this way the significance of our presence
Is a non-duality of bondage and of liberation.
The limitations of words
That would introduce us to something to be measured
Are objects to be visualized,
While they are not to be thought of or examined.

We hold onto our mental practices as meaningful,
But even in the count of a hundred ten-millions of eons
We will not meet with the meaning of effortlessness.
The majestic path of purity is the source of all things,
So the doorway of birth is also not to be halted.
The unhalted is the space of the Bodhicitta.

The Bodhicitta has no birth.
It also does not sever the pathway of death.
The unsevered is the space of the Bodhicitta.
The Bodhicitta has no death.
This ambrosia has no birth or death.
It is present within us,
So we do not need to search for it.

It is through distinguishing existence and non-existence
That the grounds for deviation of permanence and annihilation
Come about.
The two extremes are not present in our dominion,
So our non-conceptualization melts into the space of our wisdom.

When we find the body of self-originating wisdom
We will not fail due to any of these extremes.
The precious jewel of the banner of victory
Is especially noble.
It is the supreme pathway.
It is the heart of the unsurpassed Sugatas.
It is the body of the Bodhisattvas on the ten levels.
It is the body of the sentient beings who are in the six classes.

There is no great treasure other than this one.
The true nature of all things
Is one in this.
We are, however, not sure that we are alone,
While we are beyond all positions.

The Royal Tantra on the Brilliant Diffusion of Majestic Space

This encompassing space that is like the sky
Melts into the dominion of the nameless.
The space of the dominion of the heart of the Dharma
Is the precious jewel that is the origin of all things.
The wind of our awareness is not to be travelled over,
And is beyond argument.

The mind itself has no base or root,
So we cannot even apprehend a color or shape for it.
It does not depend on an object or a place.
It gives birth to all things,
So it is the mother of the Victorious Ones of the three times.

All things abide where there is no abiding.
All things also depend on something that is not dependable.
No matter where we may go,
Travelling the highlands and surrounding them with arrows,
We do not move away from the space of our own minds.

This is the domain of the great charnel ground
That is for everyone.
Our demarcations are pure in this dominion,
So it is a majestic purity,
A space of delightful experience.
It brings together every wonder,
So it is a gathering of piles of precious jewels.

There is no object or anyone who keeps any object,
So this is an inconceivable body, speech, and mind.
All of the Victorious Ones understand this,
So this is the most outstanding of all of their inspirations.

The six classes of living beings are deluded,
So they do not understand.
They abide as one with this,
But they do not recognize it.

Those with small intellects do not understand,
So they are liberated through the extremes
Of permanence and annihilation.
Then there are a few who have intellects
Who do not look at anyone else,

The nameless must not be meditated as being a name.

We are eternally present, from the beginning,
Without any contemplation.
Our dominion is not to be contemplated.
This is why we are beyond the bases
For contemplating any objects.

Thusness has no base,
So the river of consciousness has no characteristics.
Because it has no demarcated cause,
It is the dominion of the Dharma.
This is beyond the limitations of any visualization.

What will we find by searching on a path?
To have no conventionalities is Buddhahood.
There is nothing to search for except Buddhahood.

Buddhahood is called: "Buddhahood."
It is nowhere other than the Bodhicitta.
The Bodhicitta is Buddhahood.
Buddhahood is also the Bodhicitta.
The mind and Buddhahood are indistinguishable.
There are no classes of samsara or nirvana.
This is the nature of everything.

This is also lacking any objects for our conceptualizations.
There is no place that we must yearn for.
Awareness that is without objects
Is a class in itself.

The six classes of birth and death do appear,
But it is through looking at things in terms of
Our yearnings for subjects and objects
That we hold the noble Dharma to be a self.

It is because we have made a unanimous decision
Regarding our dominion
That by the power of our delusions
We wander through samsara.
This is described as the grounds for deviation of impurity.

The Royal Tantra on the Brilliant Diffusion of Majestic Space

When we hold to any position as an object,
With the exception of positionless spontaneous realization,
We make a unanimous decision regarding our domain,
So this is described as the grounds for deviation of purity.

The true nature of the Bodhicitta
Has neither purity or impurity.
Unchanging non-duality is the dominion of the Dharma.
This dominion has no grounds for deviation.
It is just like moving over the earth.

With the exception of the dominion of the Dharma,
Which is non-dual and is beyond our thoughts,
There are no objects that appear to be dual
That we must engage in or that will make things happen,
So the embodiment of the Dharma is alone.
It is brilliantly secluded.
It has no position,
And is expansive like the sky.

It has no object to be negated,
Nothing to be proven,
And nothing to take up or reject.
Effortless majestic space is spacious from the beginning.

The six classes and five lineages of sentient beings
Are like the deceptive wheels of an illusion.
They are generally encompassed by reality,
So objectless awareness is primordially majestic.

The true nature of our minds is indefinite.
It does not penetrate the doors of the external or the internal.
It has no mouth or bottom.
It is primordially clear.

Samsara, from the beginning, is nirvana.
Sorrow manifests as the Bodhicitta.
There is nothing that we must attain,
Or that we must engage in.

There is no division between objects and minds.
When we attribute something to be a miracle of the mind,
Which is not attributable,

It is essentially our mind,
But there will not be even an atom to visualize.
For this reason,
This is beyond any basis for attribution.

To see this is to directly perceive the Buddha.
To meditate on this may be a ground for deviation
Through demarcating things.
When there is nothing to meditate on,
We seek to wander,
Which is like looking for a golden ladder into the sky.
When we seek some Dharma that is other than our mind
We are like the deer who are tortured by optical illusions.
We will not meet up with our objectives.

When we know the true nature of our minds,
We know the true nature of the Dharma.
When we know one thing,
We also know them all.
When we are aware of one thing,
We are also aware of them all.

In the space of self-awareness
There is no ignorance.
Ignorance and wisdom are a pair
That are attributed to be separate,
Without any root or basis for this.

Further, ignorance is a deluded mind.
To have nothing to think about and to do dhyāna meditation
Are a pair that is definitely one,
But it is divided into separate things.

Further, the inferior have deluded intellects.
Having nothing to meditate on and doing meditation
Are a pair that is definitely one,
But is divided into separate things.

Further, there are intellects that understand their subjectivity.
With regard to the essential and correct meaning,
What would we meditate on?
What would we contemplate?
In our contemplations,

We are beyond the limitations of visualizations.
In our meditations,
We are beyond any object that would distract us.
Using the way of this intent,
There is nothing to exemplify.

So he spoke.

From the Royal Tantra on the Brilliantly Diffuse Majestic Space, this is chapter five: The Supreme Inspiration.

TEACHING THAT AWARENESS HAS NO OBJECT

Then again the Blessed One spoke, without any extreme or middle, on the intent that is neither to be hindered nor worked toward:

Limitless space is without position,
And is spontaneously realized.
We are brilliantly diffused within the dominion of wisdom.
Our indefinite playfulness is like the sky.

We brilliantly teach great miracles.
We are beyond the extremes
Of "This is it" and "This is not it."
We are beyond all the conventionalities of names and words.
We are beyond things that must be exemplified.
We are beyond limitations.

We have no diffuse existence or diffuse non-existence
To hinder or to work toward.
We are beyond any objects that may be visualized,
So we are beyond any measure.

This is the space of enlightenment.
It is like a water moon from the dominion of the ocean:
A reflection appears,
But it has no true nature.
A diffuse appearance diffuses from out of the dominion of emptiness.

This has nothing to do with any object.
It is beyond any base or root.
Each and every thing in the external or the internal,
In the vessel or in its contents,
Is the heart-essence of the Dharma:
The Bodhicitta.

It may appear to be anything.
It has no characteristics.
The spaciousness of this space is beyond any measure of its vastness.
Without hindrance,
We practice whatever pleases us within this vastness.

This reality is beyond any limitations.
It is beyond any objects that might be a basis for examination.
Awareness has no object,
But it manifests as an object.
It is the true basis for all things.

So without abandoning any of our clingings to positions,
We diffuse within positionless space.
Because we do not limit its vastness or fall into any position
We are beyond real entities,
As is the dominion of the sky.

We do not hinder or yearn for the four extremes,
So we do not have any visualization of any object.
This is unchanging and spontaneously realized.
It is a majestic pervasion.
It is a spacious space
That is obviously without any measure for its vastness.

From the center of the space
Of a single majestic space,
There arise all the bounteous sub-spaces,
But they are spontaneously diffused,
And are at peace within unchanging space.
They are all diffuse,
And in this they are one.

All things are present in a state of equality.
In a reality of motionlessness
We do not move away from the significance of equality.

Inequalities do appear,
But they are one within equality.
They are diffuse within a dominion
In which we do not reject or accept anything.

Entities that appear to be diffusely existent
Diffuse,
And everything is born from them.
This is why non-entities
That are empty and diffuse in their non-existence
Diffuse.
They have no characteristics,
So on the other shore from both entities and non-entities
There are not even any names to call samsara and nirvana.

By rejecting samsara and nirvana,
We do not reject anything.
The two of them are one in our dominion,
So we are beyond the limitations of any pair of Dharmas
To be looked at.
There is nothing to which we may attribute existence or non-existence.

This self-arising playfulness is indefinite.
It emerges from our own dominion.
Because it is self-arising, it does not set.
We diffuse into the domain of great wisdom.
Awareness has no external or internal.
It is a majestic pervader of all our fields of practice.

It divides things clearly,
For there is nothing to take up or to cast off.
This is why within the space of equality
We have no positions or preferences.
We do not move away from this single majestic space,
So bounteous sub-spaces diffuse everywhere,
But they are indefinite.
They diffuse into unchanging space.
This total diffusion has no "This is it."
It is a state that we do not search for by saying: "This."

We do not move away from what there is.
We diffuse into thusness,
And so we understand what it means

Not to be anything.

The indefinite diffusion of space
Has no exterior or interior.
In this indivisible and unattached reality
The thing we meditate on and the act of meditation are non-dual.
Duality and non-duality are a dominion of equality.
They are not separate,
So they must be equal.

From the center of the space of a single equality
Bounteous sub-spaces that are not equal arise.
Due to the differences in their being similar or dissimilar,
They may be anything.

This dominion has no separation of good and evil.
When they are similar they diffuse into similarity,
But even when they are dissimilar
They are totally diffused.

There is no separation or disclosure of them.
The Dharma is not exemplified by the Dharma.
We do not abide in any dominion
That is an object that is like this.
What it is
Is not in contradiction to what it is.
This is the essence of all our philosophical conclusions.

In the absence of any contradiction or non-contradiction,
We are one.
There is nothing whatever that does not diffuse into this dominion.
For this reason,
It is the pervasive space of the All Good.

We are spaciously present,
For all things are equal.
We search with conceptualizations,
And meditate on non-conceptualization,
But where there is nothing to search for,
Everything is the same.

Our non-dual nature diffuses into space.
Both of them are just our own minds,

The Royal Tantra on the Brilliant Diffusion of Majestic Space

So there is nothing whatever that appears as an entity.
The reality which has nothing at all
Is entirely lacking in any good or evil,
And in any taking things up or rejecting them.

In our natural dominion we are one,
So we are inherently free from the complications of demarcation.
In the true nature of the unborn mind
This kind of essence is not present.
There is nothing that we must stop or must work on,
And nothing that we must reject or acquire.

Disagreement and its remedies are indivisible,
So they brilliantly melt into a space of unity.
In the majestic space of the effortless mind itself
We totally reject all searches.

In an uncontrived state,
We are spontaneously realized.
Our problems and virtues,
Happiness and sorrow,
And the Dharmas of samsara and nirvana
Are like clouds in the atmosphere of the windy sky.
They are self-originating,
And are liberated into the space of their own peace.

The attribution of being liberated is a conventionality.
It falls into the position of liberation,
So it is large in the disease of grasping and conceptualization.
It holds the single space of liberation and non-liberation
To be a duality,
And it is diffused within them.

In the significance of equality there is no delusion.
The great circle is the embodiment of the Dharma.
In the true nature of the Bodhicitta,
We do not reject anything.
This is the majestic rejection.
We do not dwell on anything.
We are pure,
So we are liberated into a space that is beyond limitations.

The Royal Tantra on the Brilliant Diffusion of Majestic Space

We abide in the state of a majestic pervasiveness.
We are alone and do not depend on anything.
We have no objects.
We have no preferences.
We have no position.
We have no abode.

For these reasons our own space was not created by anyone.
It dawns on us clearly,
So it has no outside or inside.
It has no preceding cause.
It has no support,
So it has no subsequent presence,
And has no objects.

There is no basis for us to put down our habitual tendencies.
This is why the basis of all things has no objects.
It is a pristine space.
It is like the pathways of the birds
In the domain of the sky.
There are no trails.

This is beyond having any problems or virtues.
The Dharmas of samsara and nirvana
Have no cause or conditions.
They come from themselves.
It is because they have no characteristics
That they diffuse into space.

We have no hopes or fears,
So we are luminous in our dominion.
Our dominion dawns on our dominion.
This is the Bodhicitta.

Subjects who do not understand
That the mind and space are a unity
Are not made of any material stuff.
There is nothing that is separate from us
That would appear to be an other.
It is by the power of our understanding
That we attribute them to be others.

The Bodhicitta has no outside or inside.

The Royal Tantra on the Brilliant Diffusion of Majestic Space

Within objectless space there is a total diffusion.
This is a reality that has no base or root.
It is from out of a state of total purity
That the dependent connections of the playfulness of illusion arise.

The dawning of the base is a self-liberation
That is self-evident,
So without any effort,
We diffuse into limitless space.

So he spoke.

From the Royal Tantra on the Brilliant Diffusion of Majestic Space, this is chapter six: Teaching that Awareness has No Object.

A VIEW THAT HAS NO LIMITATIONS

Then the Blessed One spoke earnestly to those below him:

The Auditors are deluded about the meaning.
They hold that objects and the mind are a duality.
They are mistaken.

The Private Victors are deluded away from the meaning.
They conceive of the force in the twelve dependent connections.

The Bodhisattvas of small intellect
Cling to the way of the two truths.
Whatever may appear
Is the self-evidence of the mind itself,
So to seriously think about some other side
Is a deluded intelligence,
For equanimity is not to be conceptualized.

The *Kriya* meditate on the gods of the three families,
So they have rites and works
By which they seek within their bodies and their voices.

The vehicle of the Tantra of Both[6]
Is like entering onto a pathway of vocal jealousy.

---

[6] Sanskrit: Uba. This refers to the Upa Yoga system.

Yoga has mantras and mudras,
But it is just like doing the dances of the madmen.
No matter what appears,
It is self-awareness,
So there is nothing that is not the Bodhicitta.
To view it as anything else
Is to have a deluded intellect.

With the *Mahā* we are indivisible from great bliss.
This is a view that is beyond any field of practice,
But it clings to methods and wisdom as being meaningful.

The view of the *Anuyoga*
Is that wisdom appears forcefully in its own dominion,
But non-dual Bodhicitta is a great bliss.

We use the four kinds of yoga as a basis,
But no matter how we view them,
They are the dominion of the Dharma.
We do not move into anything else,
So we diffuse over all the vehicles.

Without there being any higher or lower,
Majestic space is like a king.
It bestows empowerment on each and every one.
It brings all the kingdoms together into one.
It neither works on nor abandons the two extremes.

There is no turning away from the space of reality.
Extensive happiness is the dominion of the Bodhicitta.
It subsumes all things,
So we are one in its circle.

From the beginning,
The embodiment of the Dharma is unborn.
If it were born,
It would be a diffuse birth
Into a birthless state.
If it died,
It would be a diffuse death
Into a deathless state.

In the state of the circle

The Royal Tantra on the Brilliant Diffusion of Majestic Space

There is no birth or death.
Samsara is diffuse.
Nirvana is diffuse.
Indivisibility is diffuse.
Virtue is diffuse.
Evil is diffuse.
Non-rejection is diffuse.

In the state of the circle,
Samsara and nirvana,
Virtue and evil,
And cause and result
Are primordially absent.

If there is permanence,
It is diffuse permanence.
If there is annihilation,
It is diffuse annihilation.
In the state of the circle,
Permanence and annihilation are absent.

Equality has no preferences.
It is primordially expansive.
Appearance is diffuse.
Emptiness is diffuse.
Indivisibility is diffuse.

A single circle is both apparent and empty
Because it has been absent from the beginning,
It is a state of equality.
The circle of equality is spontaneously diffuse.

Both external and internal appear to be non-dual.
The totality of appearance has no preferences.
It is the dominion of the Dharma.
However it may appear,
The appearance is itself diffuse.

In the spontaneous diffusion of the nameless circle,
Both external and internal are a non-dual emptiness.
The totality of emptiness is pervasively encompassing.
It is the dominion of the Dharma.
However we may be empty,

We diffuse into this dominion.

In the spontaneously diffuse circle of luminous unity,
Both external and internal are a non-dual awareness.
The totality of awareness has no objects.
It is the dominion of the Dharma.
However we may be aware,
That is the dominion of our awareness.
In the circle that has no rising or falling,
Both external and internal arise as non-dual.

Everything arises pristinely.
This is the dominion of the Dharma.
However it may arise,
Wisdom is diffuse.
In this spontaneous realization that does not pass away or change,
Both the external and the internal are present in non-duality.

Everything is present without change.
This is the dominion of the Dharma.
However it may be present,
Spontaneous realization is diffuse.
In the circle that has no birth or ending,
Both the external and the internal are liberated into non-duality.

Everything is liberated in a single solitariness.
This is the dominion of the Dharma.
However it may be liberated,
This is the space of the embodiment of the Dharma.
In this majestic diffusion of space,
No matter what may be created
Through all the aspects of the three times,
That is our own reality.

The space of reality has no demarcations.
All the dharmas,
Including those that exist and those that do not exist,
Are unborn from the beginning,
And have no basis,
So whatever they appear to be
Is an appearance that has no demarcations.

The Royal Tantra on the Brilliant Diffusion of Majestic Space

It is not necessary to do anything about
Their state of being contrived or adulterated.
This was neither contrived nor created by anybody.
Its natural state is like the sky.
Dharmas on the surface: Rainbow colors and masses of clouds,
And the occurrence of thoughts and feelings,
However many there may be,
Are just the sky.
We do not need to clarify it.

They are purified in the space that is self-arising and self-purifying.
They diffuse into a place where there is nowhere to go.
They arise within a place where there is nowhere to arise.
In this same way,
The vessel and contents of samsara and nirvana
Are self-arising and self-pacifying.
This is the space of reality.

There are no dharmas that we may view as being something else
After they are pacified within the Bodhicitta,
So in the Bodhicitta there is no birth or death.
The body of the Victorious One does not pass away or change.
It is a state of clarity that has no exterior or interior.
It is the state of the heart of self-originating wisdom.

The miracle of birth is the Victorious One's speech.
The undivided three bodies are a spontaneously realized space.
After we are pacified within the Bodhicitta,
We do not move away from the dominion of unity.
Our bodies, speech, and minds arise as our own effulgence.

In the space that is beyond deeds
There are no divisions.
Like the clouds in the sky,
We diffuse into space.
We do not move from the dominion of wisdom,
But through the compassion of the self-originating Victorious One,
All of his disciples, with no exceptions, are trained.

The mudra of playfulness is like a constellation of stars.
The miracle of their unity is not to be estimated.
In this dominion differences are entirely absent.
The dharmas that arise out of

The sky-space of self-originating wisdom
Are all attributed by our grasping at being separate,
But in this dominion there are no distinctions.
This total perfection has no confusion.
It is the ornament of our dominion.

The space of this dominion liberates us into our own place.
We do not move away from this single majestic space.
Bounteous sub-spaces will all arise,
But they are the spaces of
The four kinds of natural and spontaneous realization.
Their essence is the space of self-originating wisdom.
Their significance is the space of unborn non-duality.
In this reality that has no beginning or end
This itself is the space where our rewards are primordially realized.

The many things are condensed into four,
But they arise from the one.
There are innumerable miracles from the one.
They arise from the one,
And they diffuse into the base.

So he spoke.

From the Royal Tantra on the Brilliant Diffusion of Majestic Space, this is chapter seven: A View That Has No Limitations.

TEACHING THAT AWARENESS HAS NO DIVISIONS

Then again the Blessed One spoke on his own inspiration without error:

In the reality of unified reason,
There are no characteristics for enlightenment or non-enlightenment.
The true nature of the ultimate and the relative is one.
It is non-dual.
It is beyond our thoughts.
It has no birth or ending.

The sentient beings of samsara's three realms,
And all the pure realms where the three bodies are arrayed,
Are from the beginning single in essence.
They are indivisible from the beginning,
So there are no remedies to be used
For purifying the façade of filth.

The darkness of our limitations is cleared away in a single moment.
Unlimited diffuse space is spontaneously realized.
The space of the embodiment of the Dharma may be present
As anything at all.
The manifest embodiment is naturally indefinite.
It may appear as anything at all.
It may shine as anything at all.

The Royal Tantra on the Brilliant Diffusion of Majestic Space

Because they have no birth,
Our pleasures are perfected.
The embodiment of pleasure may be anything at all.

The vajra body has no beginning and no end.
The vajra body has no destruction or separation.
It is indivisible,
And is beyond birth and death.
It is, in fact, the body of real enlightenment.

Reality is one,
But it appears in five embodiments.
A variety of appearances may arise in any way,
But they do not move away from the space of the five bodies.

Even the suffering of heat and cold in hell
Diffuses within our own space of reality.
There is nothing that is separate from us,
So in the space of our three bodies,
We are primordially Buddhas.

Even the sufferings of being put into service of the animals
Diffuse within our own space of reality.
There is nothing that is separate from us,
So in the space of our three bodies,
We are primordially Buddhas.

The humans, gods, asuras,
And the rest of the six classes of living things,
Do not have sorrow in their own spirits.
They too diffuse within the dominion of the Dharma.
There is nothing that is separate from us,
So in the space of our three bodies
We are primordially Buddhas.

The specifics on the vehicles,
However many there may be,
Are said to be eighty-four thousand,
But they are the virtues of a single majestic space.
This is exhausted as it is taught to our disciples.

There are absolutely no causes or results
Which may be attributed to anything other than this.

The space of reality has no cause,
From the beginning.
It has no conditions.
It is a space of playfulness, from the beginning.

Our result is a self-originating wisdom,
But this is beyond all the causes and results that we demarcate.
From the beginning,
Our three bodies are liberated into space.

There are no Dharmas that are not subsumed within this.
The five corruptions are, in fact, abodes that possess happiness.
Our objects and the good things we desire
Are primordial Buddhahood.

The root of all the dharmas is the Bodhicitta.
There do not exist any dharmas that are extraordinary
In that they do not arise from the space of the mind.

So he spoke.

From the Royal Tantra on the Brilliant Diffusion of Majestic Space, this is chapter eight: Teaching that Awareness Has No Divisions.

TEACHING THE MANDALA

Then again the Blessed One spoke on his own inspiration without mistake:

A mandala is called a "mandala."
It is because it subsumes all things and perfects them
That this is the mandala of the Bodhicitta.

It is because it is beyond any piercing
Of the doors of the external and the internal
That it is the mandala of equanimity.

It is because there is no duality of extremes and middles
That this is the mandala that has no border or center.

It is because it has no samsara or nirvana above or below it
That it is the mandala that has no high or low.

It is because it is beyond the two obstructions
That it is the mandala that shines without being displayed.

It is because our awareness has no outside or inside
That it is the mandala of indivisible pristineness.

It is because it is beyond both stopping and working on
That it is the mandala of the Mahamudra.

The Royal Tantra on the Brilliant Diffusion of Majestic Space

It is because we are liberated into our own places
Without rejecting anything
That it is the supreme mandala of naturally spontaneous realization.

This space is also pervasively encompassing
In bringing everything together.
It is generally encompassing,
A space that subsumes the ten levels.
It is because we discriminate divisions from the one
That there is the wonderful apparition of the ten levels.

They are subsumed into the one,
So there is no high or low.
Because there is no high or low,
There is no wide or narrow.
Because it is beyond extremes and middles,
It has no outside or inside.
Because this has no birth or ending,
It has no three times.
Because it has no three times,
It has no birth or death.
Because it is not compounded,
It is the body of the Victorious One.

In the equanimity of my contemplation,
I am one.
The practices of the Victorious One's contemplations
Are vast beyond thought,
But self-originating wisdom is a space of unity.
There is not even an atom that moves into something else.

Uncontrived contemplation is a supreme state.
The Buddha's enlightenment is our own mind.
The sentient beings of the six classes are our own body.
Total purity is the body of enlightenment.

It is because there is nowhere to search for it
That this is the majestic transmission of the unerring mind.
One who abides in this field of practice
Dwells in an intent that has no position.
In this world,
The gods and the humans are shaken.
On the level of Buddhahood,

The Royal Tantra on the Brilliant Diffusion of Majestic Space

This is the best of principles.

It is not necessary to travel, search, and purify
Our paths, levels, and supports.
From the beginning,
We are not attached to anything,
So why would we depend on anyone else?

The mind itself is the great perfection,
So we have nothing to meditate on or to visualize.
Non-meditation is the equivalent of being a Buddha.
For this reason,
We do not meditate on the meaning of this non-meditation,
And because we are not free from being scattered,
We are equal in being without any meditation or non-meditation.

There are no analogies for the sky.
We do not abide in meditation.
The mind that clings is not to be meditated on.
Existence and non-existence are one in this dominion.
There is nothing to doubt about this.

The true nature of entities,
Both external and internal,
Appears to us by the power
Of our reverted perception of their existence
And the intellect that uses bad philosophical conclusions
To perceive their non-existence.

The Dharmas of perceiving both existence and non-existence
Are perceptual Dharmas that are pure in their own dominion.
This is how we are liberated
From the extremes of both permanence and annihilation.

The intellect that would meditate
Does not understand what this means,
And so it deviates from the meaning of equanimity.

So he spoke.

From the Royal Tantra on the Brilliant Diffusion of Majestic Space, this is chapter nine: Teaching the Mandala.

SETTING THE MEASURE OF OUR PRACTICE

Then again the Blessed One spoke on the meaning of the contemplation of these things without error:

The true nature of the majestic space that subsumes all things
Is a Dharma that is neither good nor evil.
What would there be to practice about this?
Is there anything to experience?
What would it be?

There is nothing whatever that goes beyond this.
We do not transcend it.
We do not crave for it.
It is a river of the sea.

The objects of our visualization are like the sky.
The measure of their subtlety is that they are equal to atoms.
The measure of their stability is that they are like Mt. Meru.
They are spacious.

This is the space of the sky and of the ocean.
This is the true nature of the All Good Mother.
She is equal to the purity of the nameless sky.

We may talk about the enumerations of the Victorious Ones,
Living beings,
And all the rest,
But our true minds have the purity of majestic space.

We will not find them by searching for them.
This embodiment of the Dharma is not to be sought,
But this body of bodies is apparent to everyone.

What is this?
It is Buddhahood!
I seek for myself,
But I am nowhere else!

The diffusion of thusness is a total diffusion,
But when we seek it in an object,
We do not find it.

Noble enlightenment is not in some other.
If we desire enlightenment,
That is a non-virtuous karma.
If we settle our intelligence on objectives,
Practicing to be great,
We may kill due to our lack of compassion,
We may rage due to our being without fear,
We may do all kinds of things that are inappropriate,
The things we practice may be harmful to others,
We may be lifeless and devour those who live,
We may be concerned due to a lack of compassion,
We may do the ten non-virtues in our bodies,
We may guide sentient beings to the abodes of their deliverance,
We may turn out to be evil takers of lives,
But if we had been annihilated from the beginning,
Who would there be to be evil?

This being so,
A path to freedom that is close to here
Does not exist.
When we settle our intellects on a path to freedom that is close,
We will not need to be concerned about its essence.
When we have graspings toward anything,
Then even if a higher consideration dawns on us,
We will be obstructed.

We may not worship the Buddha.
We may blame our instructor.
We may do any common behaviors,

But we will do what is meaningful,
So there will be no contradiction.

This intent is not to be carried in words.
It is something to be applied to our core resolve.
In an inferior body there is a holy mind.
It is the only child of the Buddhas of the three times.

Even the entirety of the eight divisions of gods and demons,
Who are chained to this world by their own cruelty,
Are to be carried in the way of lords.
Their contemplations are equal to those of all the Buddha.

In the sky itself,
We play in the sky.

So he spoke.

From the Royal Tantra on the Brilliant Diffusion of Majestic Space, this is chapter ten: Setting the Measure of Our Practice.

CUTTING THROUGH EXAGGERATIONS FROM WITHIN

Then again the Blessed One spoke on his own inspiration without mistake:

In the pristine reality of the basis of all things,
Our skull-jump[7] awareness blazes and beams out.
We completely understand what we did not understand.
Wisdom blazes in the space of understanding.

In samsara, in fact, there is no samsara.
In the wheels of delusion themselves
There is nirvana.
Wisdom dawns on the wise ones.
Things appear to be dark for those who are not wise.

If we throw this off,
There is no ambrosia anywhere else.
It has no birth or death,
So it is not compounded.

From the beginning,
The body with the heart of a vajra
Has come forth without a cause or a result,
So from the beginning,

---

[7] Tibetan: Thod rgal

It is a state that is like the sky.

This transmission of my unerring intent
Is taught to be the best of methods,
Without our searching for it.
Whoever we teach it to
Will have no tasks and no impermanence for themselves.

This destroys the extremes of existence and non-existence.
It is not to be understood by logic.
It is not to be destroyed,
So it is a vajra mind.

The deluded look for the extremes of existence and non-existence.
This is like a rainbow at the roof of the sky.
It will not be set in order by our awareness.
As the extremes are not liberated into their own places,
And objects are not gathered into themselves,
Those who wish that the Buddha would appear
Look and look,
But they are deceived by their own attributions.

We are contaminated by our cravings for causes and results.
A Dharma of the Buddha that is other than this
Will not be proven through either causes or conditions.
Both causes and conditions are adventitious Dharmas.
If these two exist, birth and destruction exist.
If these two do not exist, there is no birth or destruction.

The absence of birth and destruction is the correct path.
It is present within us.
So there is nothing to search for.
This is a reality that is naturally present.
We must not attribute anything at all to it.
It is completely beyond the limitations of practices.

This reality is not to be designated and not to be practiced.
We are not separated from it for even an instant.
It is present in everyone.
It is a pervasive space.
This is the true nature of the seven.
It is the heart-essence that is the source of all things.
It is the best of the vehicles.

The Royal Tantra on the Brilliant Diffusion of Majestic Space

In the majestic space of total purity
There is, from the beginning, nothing to fathom or to visualize.
However, there is also nothing to look at as being holy.
The view of non-existence is a space of holiness.
This is the true nature of all things.
It is a field of practice that has no position.
It is primordial Buddhahood.

In this we absolutely do not have any position.
In this there are no obstructions to remove.
In this there is no need to speak out any praises.
This is the reality of emptiness.
It has no basis.

Some see it as the way of the king.
Some see it as being like the public,
Or like an entourage.
Some see it as being correctness itself.
There are inconceivable ways of seeing this,
But just as we see it, it is our own true nature.

When we do not give birth to ideas
We will see it correctly.
When we are not devoured by doubts,
We are liberated into our dominion.
Through liberation there are especially noble virtues.

As for the Buddhas,
Their attachment is great.
Throughout the three times,
They continuously crave for their dominions.

As for sentient beings,
Their ideas are great.
Where there is a single self-evidence
They understand there to be others.
They are free from attachment to their dominions,
So their attachments are great.
In their effort to unify with an intent that is non-abiding,
They brilliantly illuminate what is spacious and vast,
So they quickly see the butter lamp of shining space.

The seeing that has no seeing
Sees the meaning of emptiness.
After we have eliminated our habitual tendencies,
There is no seeing.
This is the seeing of the meaning of the continuum that is unbroken.
There is no seeing after our obstructions have been exhausted.

After wisdom dawns on us,
There is seeing.
The heart-essence of the effortless Dharma
Is not to be exemplified with words and leaves.[8]
It is not to be destroyed by grammar or by designations.

Shapes and colors are not to be seen.
Due to conditions, anything at all may appear.
Therefore, we do not spend our intellects
On the Dharmas of appearance and of repute,
So our minds are not attached to the stuff of material entities.

There is nothing on the other side of any other conditions,
So we ourselves practice our own Dharmas.
This is beyond all vision and hearing,
So we sever the basic root of the mind from inside.

This is the majestic path of yoga,
So it cuts through our doubts
About whether the motion is dense or subtle.
This is beyond measure,
So we do not throw it into the mouth of subtle experiences.

So he spoke.

From the Royal Tantra on the Brilliant Diffusion of Majestic Space, this is chapter eleven: Cutting Through Exaggerations from Within.

---

[8] Before paper was invented, the Dharma was written on leaves.

THE TWO ACCUMULATIONS ARE PERFECTED IN OURSELVES

Then again the Blessed One spoke on his own inspiration without error:

The cave that is the spirit of my inspiration
Is a cutting through to my objectives.
Except for this,
No one will seek the path of liberation anywhere.

Those who are darkened do not understand,
And they seek for some meaning.
They are like the congenitally blind
Who seek for light in a visualization.
They use the analytics of the navel
For determinations of their own intellects.
They seek for a meaning that has been present from the beginning.
They are like those who are from the islands of jewels
That look for rocks.
By mixing gold with brass, it becomes adulterated.

Taking in and holding on are the cause of samsara.
To designate them to be the Dharma is a sorrow.
An excess of listening and contemplation is a cause of distraction.
Meditation and practice are attitudes of works and deeds.
The Three Jewels is a designated name.

There is no other than this one that is supreme.
This very absence is the path for everyone.
The mind itself is a majestic space.
We have nothing to take up or to reject.
We have no extremes,
And we also have no middle.
In the reality in which there are no extremes or middles
There is nothing to negate or to prove,
So the unborn totality of emptiness is a spacious space.

The samsara and nirvana of each and every dharma,
None excepted,
Are pure in a space that is effortless from the beginning.
The way that awareness dawns on us
Is like the sky or like a miracle.
We do not divide it into sections.

All of samsara and nirvana,
And all happiness and sorrow,
Abide as one in the mandala of expansive space.
Self-awareness is self-evident.
It has no roots.

Awareness may appear to be anything within our dominion.
When we look at it this way,
Even the pure realm of the Victorious Sugata
Has come forth from delusions that are reverted ideas.
Everything from the great abode of hell on upward may appear,
But it will have a single cause:
The space of reality.

There is one equanimity.
It may dawn on us as anything.
It is not to be stopped.
It is a majestic vastness.
It is not to be sought.
It is majestic from the beginning.

To impart empowerment on the mind itself
Is the Dharma of samsara and nirvana,
While the totality of everything is not to be visualized.
The unborn is the dominion of the All Good One.
It has no position,

The Royal Tantra on the Brilliant Diffusion of Majestic Space

But due to conditions it may be evident as anything.
It brings forth everything that we want,
And exhausts our vision.

In the purity of the liberation of our knowledge,
Our objectless awareness shines through space.
The entity that understands itself is pacified within the sky.
Although we may attribute it to be an entity,
It is a space of emptiness.

In what we do not, from the beginning, grasp,
What would we conceive to be emptiness?
Through planting the seeds of samsara
We deviate into the place where causes and results have outflows.

Samsara and nirvana appear to be a duality,
But there is no King of Equality other than this.
Through their thusness, samsara and nirvana are pure.
The pure and the impure appear from the one.

There is no essence to our yearnings for objects that appear.
Those who hold to a position on emptiness
Will thereby go on to the Maras of yearning.
By holding onto our own characteristics
And turning away from holding onto entities,
We designate them to be "empty,"
And so we are exhausted.

In the essence of this single awareness
There are no exaggerations of things as being empty
Or as being entities.
At times when we are afflicted by harsh sorrows,
When we dwell within the prisons of samara,
The true nature of the Bodhicitta
Has no characteristic of this suffering,
Nor any reason for happiness to appear.

It is gathered together by the power of our self-awareness,
And we are proud to possess self-originating wisdom,
So everything is the majestic path of total liberation.

By just going into the one,
We may be sure,

This is a path that has no high or low,
And it is also an abode that has no good or evil.
Everything melts into this,
So the crevasse of samsara is the Bodhicitta.

In this dominion there are not grounds for deviation,
So from the beginning we have no characterization
That would conceptualize a self.
We are totally liberated into the state of the sky,
So this is like a pure sky or like a miracle.

Our understanding emerges from our lack of characterization.
The assumption of what we must know
Is a self-originating true nature.
We are inherently liberated.
This is an effortless space.

The many things appear,
But they have no creator.
The many things arise from the one,
Therefore we are alone.

We look at our own face.
These are the instructions for a non-dual encounter.
I am sticking my fingers
Into the contemplations of the Buddhas.

There is nothing other than
The single space of the mind,
So there is nothing besides the Bodhicitta.
The way of being of the mind is primordially realized,
So there is no reality remaining to be worked on.

It is like the sky.
It is established from the beginning.
The Ati is beyond deeds and searches,
So we do not depend on any other result.

The way it arises is as a clarity,
Like the light of the sun and the moon.
It is not to be hindered.
It is our own grace.

The Royal Tantra on the Brilliant Diffusion of Majestic Space

A clear vision of wisdom purifies our emotional problems.
It cuts through the grounds for deviation
That there are in joining and separating the vehicles.
It is free from the insertion of crevasses into our dominion.

The way that it is
Is not to be visualized,
So the cavernous space that is for entities
Turns our understanding away from emptiness and entities.

This is real,
And it has been determined to be great.
This is primordial,
And its greatness is beyond any object that we might search for.

This cuts through words.
We do not dwell on any object that might be characterized.
The continuity of our way of liberation is unceasing,
So the equanimity of the equality of time has no birth or cessation.

Everything is a space for primordial Buddhahood.
There is not even a name for birth, death, passing on, or changing.
The entire totality of all the Dharmas,
Both external and internal,
Is not in a duality with our selves,
So the space of the circle of unbiased equality
Is the dominion of the totality of the Bodhicitta.

We do not move away from our single true nature.
It is unchanging, just as it is:
A space of great bliss.
We abide at our base.

It is not necessary to seek for primordial liberation.
No matter how we may meditate and search,
Doing things strenuously,
We will fail in our power.
Where there is no crevasse,
A ground for deviation appears.
This is indeed the erroneous pathway of the lowly.

Those who turn the advantage from themselves to another
Pollute their own reality by themselves.

They are like the deer that are tortured by optical illusions,
Or like blind people who scrutinize the sky.

They want to find it,
But they do not find it.
Their result is an accumulation of wisdom,
But it is just their mind.

Merit and wisdom are perfected in the Bodhicitta.
We do not do anything by practicing.
We do not accumulate anything that does not fade away.
The spacious space of the sky is like an ocean.
The two kinds of majestic accumulations are perfected in ourselves.

The way that awareness dawns on us
Is such that it certainly does appear
As if there were a world and something beyond it,
But both of these are unborn.

There is no samsara.
There are no wheels of delusion,
So there is no diffusion.

The base of the Bodhicitta is like the sky.
We have been present, from the beginning,
In a space that is stable and unchanging.
The unborn is beyond any objects,
So it is beyond the limitations of speech, thought, and ideas.
It is not present in any individual characteristics.
It is like a space of illusions,
So we have no recognition.

So he spoke.

From the Royal Tantra on the Brilliant Diffusion of Majestic Space, this is chapter twelve: The Two Accumulations Are Perfected in Ourselves.

TEACHING THAT THE BODHICITTA HAS NO BASIC ROOT

Then again the Blessed One spoke out unmistakably. He gave instruction on his contemplations:

The dominion of the Dharma has no extremes or middle.
When we exemplify things with names,
There are extremes and middles.

The dominion of the Dharma has no self or others.
When we divide things by their objects,
There are selves and others.

The dominion of the Dharma is not to be visualized.
When we attribute things to be others,
There are visualizations and abodes.

The dominion of the Dharma is not to be sought.
A thing that is not to be sought is naturally present,
So it is the way things are.

There is no one whosoever that contrives this,
So likewise we abide in equanimity within this uncontrived state.
This is the palace of all the Sugatas.
This is the majestic pathway of nirvana.

The dominion of the Dharma appears as the many things.
There is not even an atom of a method
That would move it somewhere else.

We are totally pervaded by the playfulness of its unmoving method,
For this is the dominion of equality.
We do not move anywhere beyond the space of the mind.

To begin with,
We have no basis for our birth.
In the Bodhicitta, there is nothing to seek.
Samsara and nirvana are not brought forth,
For they are self-originating,
And they arise from the base.

In the interim,
We have no object on which to dwell.
All things abide in the space of our awareness.

In the end,
We have no object for our liberation.
All things are liberated in the state of our dominion.

In this, we do not purify our own spirits,
For even if we search for it from someone else,
We will not find the Dharma.

The space of our contemplation has no going or coming.
To dwell within it is a state of understanding.
All of the Dharmas that are present in the three realms
Are Buddhas from the very beginning.
In the immediate present they are not transformed by any conditions.

We do not separate the level of Buddhahood and the abode of hell
According to any preference.
In the Bodhicitta they are one,
So a division into two does not exist.
All things exist in equality,
So to be without clinging to any position is a space of happiness.

Even the crevasses of samsara's six classes
Are present within ourselves.
We cut through them within ourselves.

The Royal Tantra on the Brilliant Diffusion of Majestic Space

There are no sentient beings that are off to the side.

The things we must know fall into our own realities.
There is no cause to give birth to attachment or hatred for them.
Entities are not present as any kind of object.
Because there are no entities,
There is nothing to see as an object,
Be it great or small, or an attribution.

Even the contemplations of the Victorious One
Are united in the dominion of equanimity.
Anything may arise out of the dominion of equality.

This wonderful treasure of precious jewels
Was not given birth to by anyone.
It does not diminish, nor is it suppressed.
It has no augmentation or detraction,
And has no passing on or changing.
It is beyond our clingings to existence and non-existence.
It is indivisible from the beginning,
A pristine space.

Everything is self-originating and self-apparent,
So we are beyond the limitations of great uncertainty.
In this, there is no samadhi to be sought.
Our practice is beyond happiness and unhappiness.
We are naturally unmoving,
So our view is designated to be the majestic space of the sky.

Everything is born from an unborn dominion.
The miracle of birth is an ornament of the unborn.
We do not move away from thusness,
So our playfulness appears to be like the unborn.
Because we do not pass away or change,
We are without birth.
Because we are not destroyed or divided,
This is the space of the vajra.

We are not destroyed by anything.
We do not join with or part from anything.
Because we do not join with or part from this dominion,
We have no outside or inside.
We have no rise and fall.

There is no real basis for this,
So there is no samsara or nirvana.

Because there is no cause or result,
There is no virtue or evil.
This being so,
The Dharmas that are demarcated as being virtuous or evil
Are adventitious,
So they have no meaning.

The indivisible cause and result is a great circle.
The Bodhicitta has no roots.
Everything is our own minds:
The ornament of our awareness.
This single correct pathway is a supreme bliss.
There is no entering or leaving the path of great bliss.

Our dominion arises within our dominion.
This is the power of awareness.
To meditate on non-conceptualization is a good idea.
It is no different than a conceptualization.
Both of these are the same in having no good or evil.
This is also the power of awareness itself.

In this there are no meditations, non-meditations,
Or views about non-duality.
This is the happy condition of non-dual self-liberation.
Everything in the apparent world of the three realms
Is truly of the nature of the mind.
We are liberated in the space of the Bodhicitta.
We are inherently present within a space of equality.

All these entities that appear like this
Are not dharmas that have material substance.
They are the play of the Bodhicitta.
The mind is an unborn self-awareness.
It is beyond the limitations of objects and those who have objects.

The unborn dominion has no final exhaustion.
There is no touching of the dominion of the sky.
Our taking things in and holding onto them
Do not beam out into any objects.

The Royal Tantra on the Brilliant Diffusion of Majestic Space

In the unborn dominion, conclusions are severe.
They are beyond our thoughts,
So they are clear without our having any objects.
The Dharmas of place, time, object, and sense
Are equal from the beginning
Within spontaneously realized space.

We do not divide the single circle into sections.
We do not divide the single majestic space into sections.
Within the true nature of the single majestic space,
Bounteous sub-spaces will all appear.
They are totally round,
So there are no clear divisions.
Through them, each and every living being
Has the majestic path that is the space of the Bodhicitta.

In the majestic space of the Bodhicitta,
A basis for designation is not established in any area,
But because the things that we attribute to it are not negated in any way
They appear just as we designate them.
This is called: "A dominion."

We make designations about a thing that is baseless,
So how could there be any final exhaustion of it?
As it is with a jewel treasure that is like the sky,
By the force and power of its essentiality,
It may appear to be anything,
While it has no true nature.

It is not to be visualized,
And it is beyond any objects.
It has no field of practice,
And there is nothing that is like it.
It is not to be taught,
And not to be practiced.
It has no birth or ending,
And there is nothing to say about it.
It is beyond any limitations,
And it has no true nature.

The endless space of the Bodhicitta,
From out of the center of the space of self-originating wisdom,
Imparts the empowerment into the Dharmas of the many things.

All the attributions that make up a perfect store
Of teachers, teachings, entourages, times, and places,
Arise from the beginning out of our own grace.

Even the teachings on the nine vehicles and the three bodies
Appear through the wonders of the single Bodhicitta,
According to the differences in the intelligence of our disciples,
As being divided into nine or into three.
There may be differences in the intellects of our disciples,
But the fields of our disciples, the act of training them,
And the remedies that are subtle and coarse wisdoms
Are an enumeration of eighty-four thousand vehicles.

We do not move away from the space of equality
And being that there are no differences,
We are one in our dominion.

There are the Sutras, the Vinaya, and the Abhidharma.
There are the Three Baskets, and all the rest.
They are teachings that are brilliant, average, or base,
But to designate them as being on a side
Is a cause for delusions.

However it may appear,
There is no changing from the dominion of the Dharma
Into something else.
Everything is created by a single dominion.
The creator has no real basis for his being.
He does not create anything at all.
This is the space of the awareness.

The space of creation and non-creation
Does not envision the duality of equality and non-equality.
In thusness there are no objects.
There are no subjects that are made of material matter.
The many kinds of Dharmas are individually ascertained.

Reality is alone.
It is secluded from the beginning.
Appearances and everything in the world,
The three realms, and all these many things,
Emanate from out of the Sugata's Bodhicitta,
But there is nothing that emanates out from the Bodhicitta.

The Royal Tantra on the Brilliant Diffusion of Majestic Space

All things are the space of a single circle.
The majestic space of the circle is pervasive,
So there appear four majestic spaces that are subtle.

The way of being of the Bodhicitta
Is that it may be present in anything at all,
And that it may be visible in anything at all.
Our view is a majestic space that has no location.

The way of manifesting of the Bodhicitta
Is that it may manifest as anything,
And it may be practiced as anything.
Our practice is indefinite.
It is a majestic space.

The way of existing of the Bodhicitta
Is that it may be anything.
It may meditate on anything.
Its meditation is without visualizations.
It is a majestic space.

The way of liberation of the Bodhicitta
Is that it may liberate anything.
It may realize anything.
We do not work toward a result.
This is a space of primordial realization.

From out of the one there appear the four.
This is the virtue of being self-originating and self-evident.
From out of the space of the one,
Everything arises,
So we are gathered into a single indivisibility.

This is why we are exhausted
Within the space of dualistic clingings and differences.
The establishment or non-establishment
Of our bodies and our minds
Has no previous or later,
But from their equality the unborn is considered to have been born,
Without any basic root.

There is no basis for an abode of attachment
In which our habitual tendencies are gathered up or not gathered up.
So they are self-appearing,
In the way of the sky.

We do not use any visualized referent
By which we would say: "This"
For what we mean.
That is certainly true,
But all the Dharmas that appear and are well known
Are self-originating.

Emptiness is majestic as an ornament of our dominion.
There are inconceivable events and feelings,
But they are indivisible from our dominion,
So they are self-originating and self-pacifying.
They have their own grace.

This being so,
We cannot fall away from them.
There is no movement toward this intent,
So one-pointed settling is Buddhahood.
There is no going,
For this is primordial Buddhahood.
In it there is no moving or quaking,
So we are naturally present on the level of the Buddha.

The conventionalities of movement and non-movement
Are attributions that are mere exemplifications.
Our own essence is beyond any talking.
It is extremely deep and far.
It is difficult to fathom.
In its spaciousness it is profoundly deep.
It is the space of the sky.

The space of the sky has no mouth or bottom.
Self-luminescent awareness has no outside or inside.
Just as it has no real basis,
It is exemplified by analogies,
So in the majestic element of the sky
There is nothing to designate as "existent" or "non-existent."

This reality that is beyond exaggeration and depreciation

Is beyond the sicknesses of both good and evil.
It is high,
So in the sky of the mind itself
We are free from the limitations of existence and non-existence
And from the objects of visualization.

We have no object,
And in this we have no absences.
We settle into our natural space without searching.
We melt into the state of an effortless dimension.

There is no difference between settling and not settling.
We do not contemplate.
We do not think.
In our own way,
We may give birth to any ideas,
And we do not hinder them,
So our method of settling is to have no settling.
Not settling,
We have no going or coming,
So we hold our awareness in its own place.

This is the method of meditation in which we have no meditation.
We are not devoured by dualistic thoughts of doubt.
This is a method of contrivance in which we do not contrive.
This is our meeting with the reality that is our own mother.
This is the penetration into the core of the unchanging.

Inconceivable appearances appear within this.
They appear here,
And are not to be seen anywhere else,
So our virtues are perfected within ourselves.
There is not anything that is other than this.

We do not look for meanings that do not exist.
Looking and not looking are non-dual.
When we are liberated into our own place,
That is the space of reality.

So he spoke.

From the Royal Tantra on the Brilliant Diffusion of Majestic Space, this is chapter thirteen: Teaching that the Bodhicitta Has No Basic Root.

The Royal Tantra on the Brilliant Diffusion of Majestic Space

TEACHING THE SIGNIFICANCE OF EQUANIMITY

Then again the Blessed One spoke on the intent of his contemplations without error:

Thusness is not to be visualized,
And is not to be sought.
When we do not change from this into anything else,
We will not be stained by the problems of clinging attachments.

In the holiness of our knowing awareness,
We will have no objects that are associated with planetary referents,
So attitudes of either lust or hatred will not be born.
We will be free from having any object to our thinking,
And because we will have no meditation or non-meditation
We will not fall from our space of understanding.

The subject and its reality are one,
And it has no divisions or clarifications,
Nothing to take up or to reject,
So we do not follow on the trails of delusion.

We do not have any objects that we must work on visualizing
In meditations that have signs or have no signs,
So we have nothing to distinguish or to clarify
In our understanding or non-understanding.

We have no cause to take things seriously,
So we have no objects that we must throw off.

We also do not work within the lazy mouth of equanimity.
Even our lust, hatred, and stupidity
Are the ornaments of great bliss,
So we do not cut off our lusts and hatred at the root.

Liberation and non-liberation are attitudes.
Our graspings are our ideas,
So when we have nothing to take in or to hold onto,
We have no bondage or liberation.
The enemy of our holding on
Is majestic liberation.

When we are liberated by liberation,
We are ourselves.
Even non-liberation may be understood as liberation.
Holding onto dualities is a particularity of our understanding.
It arises due to the power of a single self-evidence.
This is because there is liberation through understanding.

Through misunderstanding there is also liberation.
Clinging to dualities is a particularity of our understanding.
It occurs through the power of a single self-evidence.
We are liberated by our understanding,
So our view is simply self-evident.

The Bodhicitta has no bondage or liberation.
Bondage and liberation are equivalent Dharmas.
There has been no understanding or misunderstanding
From the beginning.
As an enemy of equanimity,
Understanding is great.

Misunderstanding is seen as a problem,
So we fail at what it means to have an unbiased equality.
Even when we take things into our experience,
Our thoughts are active.
When we settle down without taking them in,
We have an intellect that understands.

No matter as what or how our intellects arise,
They seem to be in the positions of good ideas or bad ideas.
We contrive our bodies and contrive our minds
To support our experience.

We contrive this to be equanimity,
As if we were contriving the sky by building it.
As our enemy is our own clinging to duality,
It is great.

Even with the views and meditations of the eight stages,
We work at striving and searching,
And then we desire Buddhahood.
In the equanimity of the contemplations of the Buddha,
To conceive of the inconceivable is to take it as our enemy,
And so we fall into the extreme of equanimity.

This is why we enact the karma of killing our enemies.
All the Dharmas that are subsumed into either problems or virtues
Are gathered into the totality of a majestic equality.
In the space of self-awareness,
We cut through to the core.

Until we recognize the meaning of the unborn,
We have no attachments or hatreds
Toward our enemies and companions.
In the Bodhicitta,
We are all one.
Our enemies and our children are equal.
Wherever we may seek them,
Gold and rocks are equal,
So we do not move from what it means to be equal.

Because we do not move from what it means to be equal,
There is no good or evil in this,
So everyone is a Buddha,
And there is no one who is not a Buddha.

However we look at it,
We are one in having no birth or ending.
We appear to be different,
But we are unborn,
And there are no clear distinctions in the space of the unborn.

Everything is a single majestic space.
It manifests as the real basis for each and every thing.
Without rejecting any kind of grasping at a position,
We arise in a totality that has no position.

This is pristine,
So it is evident to everyone.
It has no borders or limits,
So it is the dominion of the Dharma.
The vastness of self-originating wisdom is not limited.
Beyond a single self-nature that has no limits,
The vastness of the Bodhicitta is not limited.

We are not attached to the position of non-existence,
So we make emptiness into a view.
We are naturally without any passing on or changing,
So a clinger to emptiness is a word for a fool.

Those who cling to entities have perverted desires.
There is neither anything to be seen nor anyone who sees it.
In the space of non-dual equality we are liberated.

If we make up a view out of equanimity,
We will reject non-equanimity,
Which is a reverted idea.
Further,
To have a dualistic vision is a deluded mentality.

We do not hinder anything at all.
We have no position.
We are liberated from the extremes of equality and inequality.
It is through the taking in and holding on
Of our delusional non-awareness
That we practice the extremes of clinging to positions,
But we will not find any,
So once we cut through the grime,
We will be beyond all the fields of practice that involve searches,
For they will not be visible as objects for our thoughts.

So he spoke.

From the Royal Tantra on the Brilliant Diffusion of Majestic Space, this is chapter fourteen: Teaching the Significance of Equanimity.

THE NON-CONCEPTUAL
IS NOT TO BE MEDITATED ON

Then again the Blessed One gave his entourage instruction on the unerring significance of his contemplations:

We make attributions about the majestic space
Of the bliss of enlightenment
With the delusion of our reverted ideas,
And then we understand that there is a meaning of cause and result.
In our correct abode,
We do not fabricate them.

We are like those who see an objective,
But then turn away from the path.
We do not understand our own appearance,
So we are obstructed even more than those
Who have no causes or conditions.

In our true natures, we have no moving or quaking,
And so we are present in this way,
But no matter how we are present,
There is not even an atom of our own minds
That appears as something else.

We will not seek out anything at all
On the side
That is something other than ourselves.

The intellect of emptiness and the signs of demarcation
Are eternally indivisible through time,
So there is no place to put emptiness
That is on the side.

When we meditate on the meaning of non-dual awareness
With intellects that either accept or do not accept duality,
We do not turn back the winds of demarcation.
If we are to set them down into their natural bases,
Then what are the Buddhas proving?

When we have nothing whatever to visualize,
What would sentient beings use
To take things up or to reject them?

When we have no attachment to the taste of our samadhi,
We will not be born from out of an abode of lust or hatred,
So our true nature will come forth from our understanding.

Buddhas and sentient beings are not a duality,
So we do not divide samsara and nirvana,
Or good and evil.
These things come forth from their own state or force.
Even though we do not travel over the levels and paths,
We do not move from thusness,
So whatever we do,
We emerge from that which has no outflow.

This does not appear to be anything at all.
It is not to be visualized.
We do not see anything at all.
We do not meditate on anything.
When we look beyond the things that are sure,
This will be clear.

The philosophical conclusions of the Buddha
Have an intent that is without birth or ending.
The majestic path of all the Victorious Ones
Is that the Buddhas absolutely do not have
Any contemplations other than this.

Everything comes out from this contemplation.
It clarifies even the nations and abodes of the noble ones.

The Royal Tantra on the Brilliant Diffusion of Majestic Space

Even the bodies and habitual tendencies of sentient beings
Are visible in that they depend on this.

The specifics on the vehicles,
However many there may be,
Come forth by the grace of this.

This is subtle in its peace.
It is difficult to describe.
It does not constitute an object
For our visualizations and contemplations.
Everything that is in the mouth of meditation and practice
Comes from the state of our minds,
Without our thinking about it.

It is not necessary to work on self-originating wisdom.
There is nothing to be made from the space of the sky.
The children of the Victorious Ones abide with me,
So they do not attain any result other than this.

There is no other essential meaning,
So it is not necessary to enter onto a path of total liberation.
This comes about by the force of compassion,
So we do not need to seek it on the pathway of hoping.

This is not more noble then the abodes of attachment and hatred,
So to desire a reward that has no position
From a journey of taking things in and holding onto them,
Is like an old dog barking at a bird.
The profound inspiration will not occur to us.

We seek for the meaning of the non-conceptual,
Then we throw what appears to us onto the cotton,
Then we look with our mouths in the direction of emptiness,
And so we enter onto a path of which we have no knowledge.

By going to the right,
We twist to the left.
By desiring non-conceptualization,
Our path becomes conceptual.
We wander through the dense prisons of samsara.
This is difficult to contrive,
So the fall is a big one.

This being so,
We must not meditate on anything at all.

So he spoke.

From the Royal Tantra on the Brilliant Diffusion of Majestic Space, this is chapter fifteen: The Non-Conceptual is Not to Be Meditated On.

TEACHING THAT THERE IS NO GOING TO OR COMING FROM THIS DOMINION

Then again the Blessed One spoke to the entourage on the topic of his unmistaken contemplations:

Without any visualization that says: "This,"
This reality that is like the sky
Is beyond any object that we may demarcate.
It is an equality that shines on everyone.
The light of the sun and the moon
Clears away the darkness of stupidity.

The Bodhicitta is a lamp.
It is the key that opens up
This terrible and dense iron door,
And once this door of miraculous secrets is open,
The treasury of the three bodies that is a treasure of jewels
Is revealed.

Seeing them,
We are the equals of the Victorious Ones.
This majestic space that brings forth total liberation
Is the supreme inspiration.
It is profound.

The vehicles of the inferior do not see this.
The supreme vehicle is an extremely expansive Dharma.

It is profound,
And is not to be taken hold of.
By grabbing it we do not hold it.
It is like a water-moon.

This total equality that brings forth all things
Is the space of the sky.
The great perfection is beyond deeds.
It is an expansive Dharma.
Through the state of this heart-essence,
We are freed from deeds and searches.

The purity of our own minds
Is the space of the dominion of the sky.
Those who see its characteristics
Are the children of the Victorious Ones.

Everything is a space for the All Good One.
Whatever appears, it is the sky of the All Good One.
In the center of the space of the pure dominion of the sky
There is a place to go for both samsara and nirvana.

We are perfect.
We are perfect.
In this we are perfect.

We are gathered.
We are gathered.
In this we are gathered.
The outer and inner samsara and nirvana are gathered into this.

The Victorious One might search for
A Dharma that is more profound than this one,
But he will not find it.
Sentient beings are not aware of this.
When they have joined with the mind of ignorance,
They will be liberated.

The majestic path for living beings
Is a space that was left behind by the Rishis.
The expanse of the sky-space is All Good.
When everyone understands that this is so,
They will, from the beginning,

The Royal Tantra on the Brilliant Diffusion of Majestic Space

Have attained the supreme path that we do not take up.

When we investigate well,
The mind of itself is the source of origination
For the awareness of equanimity.

All the Victorious Ones of the three times,
None excepted,
Do not leave for anywhere.
This is it.
They do not abide anywhere.
This is it.
They do not arise from anywhere.
This is it.

Our base is placed into our dominion.
There is not even an atom of Buddhahood other than this.
The pure realm of nirvana
Is the prison of the sentient beings of the three realms.
The majestic space that brings us together in non-duality
Is a source of motion that is equal for us all.

There is nothing that exists besides this for us to reject.
There is nothing to look for that is not this.
This majestic space is not to be thrown off or to be separated from.
It is a palace that we do not enter or leave.
It is the reality of the Bodhicitta.
It abides in each and every thing.
It abides continually, without moving.
It abides continually, within a natural purity.
It abides continually, without any exemplification.

We do not conceptualize any color or shape.
We do not visualize our own characteristics.
We do not go beyond the intent of knowing this.
Our virtues are spontaneously perfected,
So with the exception of our own minds,
There do not exist, from the beginning,
Any other Dharmas on the side.

This has no outside or inside.
It is not divided into two.
The external and the internal

Are naturally one as our All Good Mother.
We do not see any hither side or thither side,
So we abide in equality
Within the space of the two extremes.

Beyond this single equanimity
There are not two.
In our indivisibility we are one
In the body of the Victorious One.

It is unnecessary to meditate on any object
Other than the body of the Victorious One.
It is unnecessary to keep to any remote place that is isolated
Other than our own senses and those of others.

Our objects and our minds are one in space,
So there is no exhaustion to be seen in the external.
All of the Dharmas of the path and of the result
Are, from the beginning, not to be exemplified,
So it is not necessary to travel to the level of total liberation.

The heart-essence of the teachings is ourselves,
So while the eight divisions of gods and demons are most powerful
They do not cross over the heart of the Buddha.
There is no one who contrives this.
There is no one who transcends this.

What will we meditate on?
Based on who's inspiration?
Without meditating,
Our demarcations are liberated into their own place.
Through the karmas of doing and not doing things
There will not be the least bit for us to hold onto.

Non-action is, from the beginning, the level of Buddhahood.
It is pure from the primordial.
It is the supreme center.
We do not use any difficult practices or austerities.
We abide happily in the space of enlightenment.

One who does not need anything at all
Is pure from the beginning and has no problems.
He goes to the level of the noble ones without any travelling.

The dominion of the Dharma is the abode of all the noble ones.
The totally pure basis of all things is the Bodhicitta.

I say that there is nothing but the mind,
So however the mind itself may be present,
It will be accommodated.
Whatever it may arise as will also be accommodated.

It is self-originating as a heart of playfulness,
So it is the origin of everything, both external and internal.
This heart, from the beginning, has no basic root.
Anything at all may emerge from nothing at all.

Those who are fortunate will understand.
Those who have no fortune are not going to understand.

So he spoke.

From the Royal Tantra on the Brilliant Diffusion of Majestic Space, this is chapter sixteen: Teaching That There Is No Going to or Coming from This Dominion.

THE SELF-LIBERATION OF THE VEHICLES

Then again the Blessed One spoke on the meaning of his unmistaken contemplations:

When we are beyond all positions and preferences,
We do not visualize any extremes or middles.
We have no exaggerations or depreciations,
So we absolutely do not have anything to accept or to reject.

This is beyond all causes and results,
So from the beginning we are not born into conditions.
The reality that is beyond causes and conditions
Is a view that is beyond the extremes that the Tirthakaras,
Whose views are bound into knots,
Use for the evil practices of both permanence and annihilation,
So they do not understand.
Yearning for duality is the demon of holding onto a position.
The view of the Atiyoga does not limit the vastness of reality.
Both of them are self-evident and self-liberating,
So we do not reject the Tirthakaras.
They are ornaments for the great perfection.

The views of the Auditors are bound into knots.
They view a single instant,
And that there is no connection between objects and the mind.
They believe that a reality
In which existence and non-existence are equal
Does not exist.

This is the demon of clinging to a position.
In the reality of the Atiyoga,
Both of them are self-evident and self-liberating,
So we do not reject the Auditors.
They are an ornament for the great perfection.

The views of the Private Victors are bound into knots.
They direct their consciousness onto a single empty object,
And work on applications and reversals
For the twelve dependent connections.
They believe that a reality in which origins and applications are equal
Does exist.
This is the demon of a position and a preference.
In the equanimous reality of the Ati,
Both of them are self-evident and self-liberating.
We do not reject the Private Victors.
They are an ornament of the great perfection.

The Mind Only view is bound into knots.
Self-luminosity is free of subjects and objects,
But they view their own door as being happy.
They comprehend a way in which a hollow crystal is pure,
So they believe in two kinds of selflessness.
This is the demon of clinging to a position.
In the reality that may resemble anything at all,
Both of these are self-evident and self-liberating.
We do not reject the Mind Only.
They are an ornament for the great perfection.

The view of the Middle Way is bound into knots.
Awareness has complications in the relative reality,
But in the ultimate we encounter a state that is uncomplicated.
Their view is a belief in the intent of there being two truths.
For a reality that is non-dual and equal,
They view there to be a duality.
This is the demon of clinging to a position.
In the reality that is non-dual,
Both of these are self-evident and self-liberating.
We do not reject the Middle Way.
It is an ornament of the great perfection.

The view of the Kriya is bound into knots.
They view relative appearances as being of three classes,

The Royal Tantra on the Brilliant Diffusion of Majestic Space

While the ultimate is beyond the extreme of purity.
They do not make their view
As being in the way of a lord and his servants.
They cling to reality, in which good and evil are equal,
As being a duality.
This is the demon of clinging to a position.
In the intent of an equanimous reality,
Both of these are self-evident and self-liberating,
So we do not reject the Kriya.
It is an ornament for the great perfection.

The view of the Both[9] is bound into knots.
They follow along the trails of a higher and lower view and practice.
They view one thing,
And they practice one thing.
Their angry mouths cling to duality.
This is the demon of clinging to a position.
In the way of both we do have views.
In the reality in which the high and the low are equal,
Both of them are self-evident and self-liberating,
So we do not reject the Upa.
It is an ornament of the great perfection.

The view of Yoga is bound into knots.
The appearance of the ultimate has no true nature.
The relative is a deity with the blessings of purity.
In the reality of their equality,
Which has no demarcations,
Appearing to be a god is the demon of grasping at a position.
In the reality that may resemble anything,
Both of them are self-evident and self-liberating,
So we do not reject Yoga.
It is an ornament of the great perfection.

The view of the Mahā is bound into knots.
After we enter the door of methods and wisdom,
Truth is indivisible and we are beyond any fields of practice.
For this intent, which is the equality of realities,
We are beyond any fields of practice.
This is the demon of clinging to a position.
Both of them are self-evident and self-liberating,

---

[9] gNyis ka, is Uba in Sanskrit, and refers to the Upa.

So we do not reject the Mahā.
It is an ornament of the great perfection.

The view of the Anu is bound into knots.
Once we have entered the door of our dominion and wisdom,
Both the All Good One and the All Good Mother are non-dual.
They are the gods of great bliss.
In the reality where existence and non-existence are equal,
To fall into the position of non-duality is a demon.
In the reality where our vastness is not limited,
Both of these are self-evident and self-liberating,
So we do not reject the Anu.
It is an ornament of the great perfection.

Everything is perfected in a state of effortlessness,
With no confusion.
This is the ornament of our complete perfection.
Without rejecting anything,
There is a space where we are liberated into our own place.

The bodies of the Buddhas,
And the bodies of sentient beings,
Are ornaments of our dominion,
However they may appear.

So he spoke.

From the Royal Tantra on the Brilliant Diffusion of Majestic Space, this is chapter seventeen: The Self-Liberation of the Vehicles.

UNTYING THE KNOTS

Then again the Blessed One spoke on the intent of his unerring contemplations:

All living things are Buddhas,
From the beginning.
Emotional problems are the ambrosia of wisdom.
The crevasse of samsara is the Bodhicitta.
The three poisons shake out the teachings on the three bodies.

Cutting through the roots of birth and death,
The total liberation of the three realms,
Burning up the pair of subjects and objects,
And each and every vision of a deed and a doer:
I myself am clinging to myself,
And I am doing it.

The root of it is the space of the Bodhicitta.
The Bodhicitta is the embodiment of the Dharma.
It is present as wisdom,
So it is no one else.

The Victorious Ones are also the body of this.
Even the supreme vehicles of the outer, inner, and secret,
As many as there are taught to be,
All of them being famous,
Are just the mind.

Its virtue is that there is no Dharma other than the mind.
A so-called "Buddha" is nowhere else.
The mind itself may not be liberated into space.
We may not understand that it is within the state of realty,
And we may have attitudes that cling to duality:
We throw our knots into the space of the sky,
For they are the knots of a mind that clings to a position.

There is nothing to criticize,
But a critic emerges.
We do not see this by looking.
It is not to be contemplated.
The Ati view has no position or preference.

Even if we look at it,
It is not stained by having any problems.
When we do not look,
These demarcations are liberated into their own place.

The view of non-dual self-liberation
Is a view of both existence and non-existence,
So it unties the knots there are in clinging to a position.

The meditation of the Ati has no perceptual referents.
Even if we meditate,
We are not stained by any problems.
A self-originating playfulness dawns on us.
The demarcations of non-meditation are liberated into their own place.
Through a self-originating non-dualistic meditation,
We untie the knots of clinging to positions,
Of there being or not being anything to meditate on.

Our practice has nothing to be taken up or to be abandoned,
So even if we practice,
We are not stained by problems.
This is the way that self-originating wisdom arises.
The demarcations of non-practice are liberated into their own place.
Through the practice of non-dual self-liberation
We untie the knots of intentional searching.

The result of the Ati has nothing to reject or to achieve.
We may work on it,
But we are not stained by any problems.

Self-originating virtues arise within us.
The demarcations of not working toward anything
Are liberated into their own place.
Through the result of non-dual self-liberation,
We untie the knots of our hopes and fears.

As for the samaya that have no borders to protect,
We may protect them,
But we are not stained by any problems.
Self-originating playfulness is our adornment.
The demarcations of non-protection are liberated into their own place.
The samaya of non-dual self-liberation
Untie the knots of the separation of faults and virtues.

As for the good works that have no deeds or searches,
We may do searches and practices,
And there is not any problem.
They are the playfulness of our self-originating wisdom.
The demarcations of non-action are liberated into their own place.
By the good works of non-dual self-liberation
We untie the knots of clinging to positions.

The levels and paths are not to be studied or to be traveled over,
But if we study them or travel over them,
There are no problems.
Self-originating playfulness manifests as levels and paths.
Non-study and non-travel are liberated into their own places.
By the levels and paths of non-dual self-liberation
We untie the knots of intentional travels.

So he spoke.

From the Royal Tantra on the Brilliant Diffusion of Majestic Space, this is chapter eighteen: Untying the Knots.

THE SECRET GREAT BLISS

Then again the Blessed One spoke to his entourage:

The vastness of majestic space has no position.
It unties the knots of the existence in which we cling to positions.
It cleanses away the knots of the two kinds of bondage,
And the darkness of the two kinds of obscurations.

The precious lamp that clears away the darkness
Shines in the Buddha fields
Of the six kinds of living beings.
Every position, border, high, low, superior, and inferior
Is equally present in the vastness of a single circle.
It is obvious that the Buddha is not above us.
It is obvious that samsara is not below us.

Samsara and nirvana,
Causes and results,
Are ourselves.

The sorrows of the six classes of living beings
May be liberated in this,
But in the Bodhicitta there is no self or other.
In the meaning of equality,
There is no superior or inferior.
The absence of a high or low is the sky of equality.

Awareness is the pervasive space of reality.
It encompasses all things,
So it is the majestic pervader.
It has no duality,
So it does not pass away or change.
It is unchanging and stable,
So it is the vajra self.

Our true nature has been present from the beginning.
This is the fortress of the vajra sky.
With the weapon of objectless awareness,
We are from the beginning liberated in this way.
Because the things that we desire may appear to us as anything,
This is the precious jewel of wonder.

From the beginning, we have dwelt within its essence.
In this, there is no birth or death,
And there is no passing away or changing,
So this is called our reward.
When we understand that we are our own rewards,
Where will there be any grounds for deviation or crevasses?
Even if there are any,
We cut them off with our force,
So what would it be that is called a "crevasse"?

A crevasse is itself the Bodhicitta.
Those who have not untied the knots in their minds
May seek for a noble path that is off to the side,
But they are like prisoners who have gotten out of a pit:
They hope to be free,
But they are not free.

When we desire,
The thing we desire is a limitation.
When we desire existence,
We are fettered by the extreme of permanence.
When we desire non-existence,
We have an attitude of annihilation.

Yogins are bound in the knots of these two:
Permanence and annihilation.
These are the bonds of their actions.
How will we untie their knots?

The Royal Tantra on the Brilliant Diffusion of Majestic Space

When we use the paths of the lowly,
Or any other paths,
To untie them,
They are not liberated,
For they are enmeshed by the ropes of their yearnings.

The secret to the untying of the knots is like this:

We do not look at the extremes as being problems.
We do not differentiate being bound and being liberated.
Without rejecting the two extremes, we are self-liberated.
We also do not dwell on any mere non-duality,
And although we may look at both of them,
They appear by themselves.

The depression of the four extremes is the space of the sky.
Bondage and liberation are non-dual.
We are happy in our own places.

One is happy.
Two are happy.
Everyone is also happy.
All the sentient beings in the three realms are also happy.
The Buddhas of the three times are also happy.

They are happy to be in the space of
The self-evident embodiment of the Dharma.
The embodiment of the Dharma does not pass away or change.
It dwells within all the Dharmas of samsara and nirvana,
And we are happy in every way.

There is no fixed certainty in this,
So we do not hinder any deeds or practices of any kind.
We practice whatever happiness there is in this space.
We do not hinder any fields of practice at all,
So we do not have any anxiety about anything at all.

We have no reservations about anything at all,
So who is it that is ensnaring whom?
Bondage and liberation themselves are also the Bodhicitta.
A person who understands that things are so
Will practice without any limitations on their field of practice

And on who is practicing what.

This is a reality that has no I or self.
It is inherently present without contrivance and without adulteration.
In a reality that is certain to be there,
There arises an intent that is certain to be without mistake.

As our intellects abide happily within space,
The embodiment of the Dharma,
Which has no birth or ending,
Is unborn,
And therefore it does not end.
It does not rise,
And therefore it does not fall.
It is not created,
And therefore it is not destroyed.

It is not visible as some real entity.
It is beyond positions.
It does not appear,
And therefore it does not move.
It is present from the beginning,
Without any coming or going.
It encompasses all things,
And has no obscurations,
So the embodiment of wisdom that is like the sky
Is beyond the names for existence and non-existence.

The embodiment of the Dharma is not to be exemplified.
It has no form that may be measured or estimated,
Great or small.

The embodiment of the Dharma has no real base.
It is beyond the objects that we demarcate.
Therefore the embodiment of the Dharma has no conventionalities.

An object and one who has the object are not established,
So the embodiment of the Dharma has no view.

It is beyond the two kinds of real yearnings,
So the embodiment of the Dharma is not to be apprehended.

It has no analogy.
It is beyond analogies.
It has no measure.
It jumps over measurements.
It is beyond the extremes of our exaggerations and depreciations.
Without limits,
Without space,
And without positions,
We are happy.

So he spoke.

From the Royal Tantra on the Brilliant Diffusion of Majestic Space, this is chapter nineteen: The Secret Great Bliss.

TEACHING THAT THE AWARENESS IS A GOLDEN VASE

Then again the Blessed One spoke:

The embodiment of the Dharma is not to be conceptualized.
The embodiment of pleasure is not to be measured.
The manifest embodiment is inconceivable.
This is the place of origin for all of them:

Everything is the majestic self-origination of everything.
From the blazing great hammer of emptiness
The meaning of self-originating wisdom appears.
It is pervasive,
And has no outside or inside,
So the totality of everything is neither to be taken up nor rejected.

E Ma!
This is a marvelous secret.
Holy people will understand this.
In the past,
This kind of thing was not understood,
And the seeds of samsara came from that.

The wandering Buddhas are greatly astounding.
The Buddhas of the past also saw
The purpose that we do not reject or accept,
And that the enlightenment of our emotional problems

Is not to be taken up or to be rejected.
The thing that is the true nature of our emotional problems
Emerges without any basic root,
So self-originating wisdom is self-evident.

Further,
There is no opposition to it.
The true nature of the Bodhicitta
Has also arisen without anything preceding or following it.
Self-originating wisdom is self-arising.
It also does not fall.

If we understand this with certainty,
There is nothing but this.
If we see this well,
We will not need to contrive anything.
If we cut through our doubts,
We will have resolve.

There is no other holiness of the mind than this.
The true nature of the mind is spontaneously realized.
Characteristics for our minds are not born.
We dwell in what pleases us within the space of what is.

Our root is our mind itself.
It is a majestic space.
We cannot determine it definitively to be one.

The experience of contemplation is a majestic space.
We do not move from a state of equality,
So we are beyond the extremes of settling or not settling.
We find this to be a certainty.
It is the supreme purpose.

The thing that is most difficult to find
Is a resolute understanding.
Those who are not fortunate will not find it.
This is a field of practice for fortunate people.
There are those who do not see the basis of this contemplation,
But look for it elsewhere.

What hope is there?
They are deluded.

The Royal Tantra on the Brilliant Diffusion of Majestic Space

A multitude of deeds and tasks
Is the cause of samsara.
A multitude of agendas and prospects
Is an obstacle on our path.
A multitude of expansions and contractions
Is a torture for our minds.
Those who follow on the trails of demarcations
Have fields of flesh.
When this happens,
They think about the meaning of this.
This is also the door that lets them be born.
This is also the door that lets them die.
This is also the path that makes them die.
This is also the ground where they let out a great sigh.

From the beginning, we are the equal of the Buddhas.
We are indeed great.
This is a glory that subsumes all things.
A heart of glory is a space that is beyond deeds.
The sun of self-originating wisdom
Removes the cataracts of our ignorance,
And we see.

We see our individual teachers in this.
We see our individual entourages in this,
We see our individual teachings in this.
It appears in all things,
So it is a majestic and pervasive encompasser.

We also see the levels of all the Buddhas.
We make our own companions in virtue.
We also make our own entourage of auditors.
We also make our own karma of teaching.

There is no sure teaching of the unsurpassed secret mantra
Other than this one.
There is no exhaustive end to interpretable endings.
Interpretable meanings are mouths of word-leaves.
The definitive is a vehicle of certainty
It cuts through doubt.

After we have sought out a pathway
That is difficult to travel over,

The Royal Tantra on the Brilliant Diffusion of Majestic Space

We will see a meaning that is difficult to see.
To make its meaning into something real,
We will look for its cause,
Or we will not look for it.
We will attain its result,
Or we will not attain it.
We will conceptualize an object,
Or we will not conceptualize it.
We will purify a vessel,
Or we will not purify it.
We will be imparted empowerment,
Or it will not be imparted.
We will be educated in the things there are to know,
Or we will not be educated.

This majestic space does not depend on anything.
Extreme yoga[10] is the transmission of the great perfection.
Some describe it to be primarily a blessing.
The blessings of this are propounded unto everyone.
The wonders of the ordinary are inconceivable.
In particular, they are the majestic status of the supreme ones.

Some believe that this is to be obtained from someone else.
There is no getting or losing of this,
So the fruits of this ripen for everyone.
We do not disregard the results of karma.
The wonders of the ordinary are inconceivable.
In particular, they are an abode of supreme status.

Some study or do not study.
This is not to be studied by saying: "This."
All those who do not study know from the beginning.
It is not necessary to listen to, explain, or hear about this.
Our demarcations are self-liberating.
This is especially noble.

Some visualize or do not visualize.
There is no visualization or materialization of this.
This is totally clear to those who do not visualize,
For it is without obscurations or coverings,
So it is especially noble.

---

[10] Atiyoga.

Those who come out to look for these special qualities
Do not need to elicit compassion from others.
It is not necessary to disregard the results of karma.
It is not necessary to make the unclear clear.

When we see the meaning of not seeing,
Everything will be clear
Within the changeless dominion of the Dharma.

So he spoke.

From the Royal Tantra on the Brilliant Diffusion of Majestic Space, this is chapter twenty: Teaching That the Awareness Is a Golden Vase.

The Royal Tantra on the Brilliant Diffusion of Majestic Space

REVEALING OUR FIELD OF PRACTICE

Then again he spoke:

In the bliss of our own experience
We do not have marks or exemplary features.
This is certainly true,
But our own appearance is clearly an embodiment of pleasure.
We are visible to the faces of the Bodhisattvas.
Our compassion encompasses everyone.

It is certainly true that we have no subjects or objects,
But our own appearance manifests as a manifest embodiment.
We are visible to the faces of the sentient beings of the three realms.

The embodiment of the Dharma has no characteristics.
It has no family or class.
This is certainly true,
But it is pervasively present throughout samsara and nirvana.

The embodiment of pleasure has marks and exemplary features.
The manifest embodiment dwells among those
Who understand the Dharma.
The embodiment of the Dharma has nothing to do.
It neither has marks nor does it not have them.
It has neither knowers of the Dharma nor non-knowers.
It has neither closeness to nor farness from anything.
It is equanimously present,
Like the end of the sky.

Everyone may investigate it,
But they will not see it.
The Buddhas do not see this,
So all the world, including the gods, may inquire into this,
But they will not see it.

Even the bounteous holy pure lands
Arise by the grace of this thing that is not to be visualized.
Even the numberless Victorious Ones
Are manifestations of this thing that is not to be visualized.
This being so,
All things occur within this dominion.

The majestic space of effortlessness
Is the basis of everything.
It has been left behind for everyone,
For it is the most excellent life.
We may elucidate this to anyone who understands it,
For due to its special qualities,
Their understanding will open up.

Samsara and nirvana will all be instantaneously clear.
This pierces the hearts of all the Victorious Ones.
It even rises upon the sun that makes things shine.
The sentient beings of the three existences
Also rise up from out of the space of the sun of wisdom.
Even the division of benefits and damages
Is the majestic power of the grace of self-originating wisdom.
Even the pure land of Sukhāvatī
Is the grace of self-originating wisdom.

Each of these has their own virtues,
But their majestic power is the effulgence of self-originating wisdom.
The worldly who dwell on their levels,
And those of the levels who dwell on their paths,
Are there by the power of the knowledge of self-originating wisdom.
Their statements on listening and explaining,
And the totality of everything they enjoy,
Are deeds and practices of the dominion of the Dharma.

The true nature of all things is effortless.
Even the Dharma is a Dharma that has no tasks.

The Royal Tantra on the Brilliant Diffusion of Majestic Space

In the way of the unborn, we are primordially Buddhas.
We may practice, but it is a practice without deeds.
It is the enjoyment of profound meanings.

Everyone indeed enjoys this dominion.
Everyone has come forth from the state of this dominion.
They emerge from this dominion,
And they abide in this dominion.
This dominion dwells in this dominion.

This is not to be visualized.
Its abiding throughout all samsara and nirvana is not to be visualized.
Even lust, hatred, stupidity,
Pride, jealousy, and all the rest:
The five poisons and the five families
Are present in this dominion without differentiation.
In thusness we are one,
And so there is the pleasure of a non-dual dominion.

In the same way,
The Buddhas and sentient beings,
And the things that are generated by karma and by compassion
Have no origins or applications in their classifications,
So the mind itself has the power of this majestic space.
Without the grace of this majestic space,
The conventionalities that we designate,
Their existence or non-existence,
And the existence or non-existence of the things we see,
The clarity or non-clarity of the things we look at,
Whether we are stuck or are not stuck in the prison of samsara,
Whether we go or do not go to the level of the Buddha,
Even the Buddhas of the three times
Have not taught these things to anyone else in the past.

This being so,
It is sure that the grace that is here,
Whether we are set or are not set on the level of enlightenment,
Whether we dwell or do not dwell on the meaning of the heart,
Whether we conceptualize or do not conceptualize
The uniqueness that there is,
Whether we understand or do not understand the correct meaning,
Whether we engage in or do not engage in the correct meaning,
Whether we hear or do not hear

The teachings of the definitive transmission,
It is not the case that these are anywhere else.

Everything is an ornament for the dominion of totality.
This dominion has no basic root,
So everything is in the state of being unborn.
This dominion is not to be hindered,
So all of these things are not to be hindered.
Awareness that has no birth or ending is thusness.
It is uncontrived.
It is the unerring path.
It is unadulterated.
It is the dominion of the Dharma.
It is inconceivable.
It is the correct conclusion.
It is emptiness.

In this way,
It is the profound.
It is difficult to analyze.
In this way,
It is expansive.
It is majestically vast.
Those who abide in this way
Will have an uninterrupted stream of the highest view.
They will abide where there is no birth or ending.

So he spoke.

From the Royal Tantra on the Brilliant Diffusion of Majestic Space, this is chapter twenty-one: Revealing Our Field of Practice.

MAKING OUR IDEAS REAL

Then again the Blessed One Total Awareness[11] spoke on some other things:

The three times have no birth or ending.
The objects of our vision also have no birth or ending.

To be without a cutting off of our continuum
Is the best view.
The abodes of our meditation also have no birth or ending.
To be without a cutting off of our continuum
Is the best meditation.
The doors of our practice also have no birth or ending.
To be without a cutting off of our continuum
Is the best practice.
The results of our realization have no birth or ending.
To be without a cutting off of our continuum
Is the best result.

Our encompassing compassion is not cut off in its continuum.
The good works that we seek are not cut off in their continuum.
The wonders that we work for are not cut off in their continuum.
The blessings that we dedicate are not cut off in their continuum.
The samaya that we protect are not cut off in their continuum.

---

[11] Kun rig

The Royal Tantra on the Brilliant Diffusion of Majestic Space

We are together in the absence of a birth and an ending,
So we pierce the window of a secret dominion.
When we understand that this is the true nature of our continuum
We abide in it with no break in our continuum.
This is our dominion.
Because there is no break in its continuum,
We are liberated.

This is our space.
The Dharma of samsara also has no break in its continuum.
Nirvana also has no break in its continuum.
This is the same as our searching for a path.

There are no secret Dharmas in this.
Their essence is not to be visualized,
So there are also no written Dharmas in this.
The three times are not separated in their continuum.
They are invisible.
There is only one.
It may appear as anything.

We do not see them.
We are one.
We may see anything.

We do not hear them.
We are one.
We may hear anything.

Whatever we see,
Whatever we hear,
Whatever appears,
In does not manifest as anything other than our own dominion.

Those who understand
Are great people with their own grace.
Throughout all time they are present in this.

Everyone is liberated with this space.
We do not visualize any demarcations for this.
The saying: "Pacify your own spirit" applies to this.

If we do not understand the pacification of our own true nature,

The Royal Tantra on the Brilliant Diffusion of Majestic Space

We may pacify our own minds
For a hundred thousand ten-millions of eons,
But they will not be cleansed.
Our natural filth is not purified by washing it.
Just so, we may wash the sky,
But it will not be cleansed.

It is unnecessary to wash our natural filth.
We do not conceptualize it to be an entity,
So the saying: "Not to be hindered or worked on" applies to this.

If we do not understand natural blockages,
We may stop something for many ten-millions of eons,
But it will not be blocked.
This is our own mind,
So there is nothing to block.
It is not necessary to block self-originating demarcations.
We do not look at them as being problems.
The saying: "Without accepting or rejecting" is exactly this.

If we do not understand their natural indivisibility,
We may take things up or reject them
For a hundred ten-millions of eons,
But we will not succeed.
They are our own minds,
So we do not touch them.
Self-originating wisdom has no limits,
So it is not necessary to rely on antidotes for discord.
This being so,
In the space of just an instant
We understand the characteristics of this dominion,
And we are indubitably on the level of Buddhahood.

For this reason,
Totality is an unborn dominion.
This is ascertained in enlightenment itself.
The fortunate will ascertain this without a doubt.

Those who use this to understand
Dwell in the heart of enlightenment.
However everything may appear,
It is alright.
However we may understand everything,

It is alright.
However everything may be,
It is alright.

Moving, sleeping, eating, and walking:
These are the four paths of practice.
Whatever they appear to be,
And whatever we may do,
There is no clinging in our dominion.
For this reason,
The unoriginated and unborn
Is the king of utterances.

The invisible river of the embodiment of the Dharma
And the compassion of the visible embodiment of form
Appear with no interruptions in their continuum,
So they are like the space of the sky,
Or like miracles.

Being self-originating and self-pacifying,
Their continuum is unbroken.
Their heart-essence is the space of the Bodhicitta.

For fortunate people
This is, from the beginning, their golden vase,
So we must not visualize that it is in any position.

Whatever we see,
We see it as a holy thing.
Seeing the one,
We see all.
We are not devoured by doubts,
So we see the intentions of all the Buddhas.

When we thoroughly understand these things
We will understand the purposes of all living things.
The awareness that understands this has no position.
Unspeakable self-awareness arises in our experience,
So self-originating wisdom does not rise or fall.
It does not harbor the darkness of the extremes.
It shines on everything,
Without any exterior or interior.
It does not harbor the darkness of the deeps,

The Royal Tantra on the Brilliant Diffusion of Majestic Space

So it is not necessary to decimate ignorance with any remedies.

It shines on everything,
Without having any mouth or bottom.
There is no penetrating the doors of any outside or inside,
So this is called: "The transmission of what actually appears."

This is the majestic path of purity,
So it is called: "The unmoving wind of understanding."
This is beyond the limitations of visualizations.
It is the true essence of the non-abiding embodiment of the Dharma.
It is self-originating, without causes or conditions,
So it is the majestic sky of self-originating wisdom.

Everything is subsumed within this,
So it is the circle ornament of unadulterated total perfection.
It is beyond utterances, speech, and thought,
So it is the Bodhicitta that is beyond any measure.

Its natural characteristic is to be one,
But by the power of its virtues,
It may appear to be anything.
It is naturally without characteristics,
But by the power of our prayer
Anything at all may be realized.

People who have no fortune
May search in the direction of this
For an eon or for their lives as humans,
This is certainly true,
But they obscure themselves with their own energy,
Then they see things revertedly,
So they may dwell on this for however many hundreds of years,
But they will not recognize it.
They will search far away for what is near,
So it is not likely that this will appear to the unfortunate.

The fortunate have pure intellects.
Without covering anything up,
They pervade.
Without any great or small,
They see.
Without any good or evil,

They practice.
Without any high or low,
They penetrate.
Without any wide or narrow,
They contain.
Without any cause or result,
They accept.
Without any male or female,
They practice.
Without any darkness or visibility,
They see.
Without any earlier or later,
They go.

Whether things are accomplished or not accomplished by karma,
Whether they accumulate or do not accumulate any maturation,
Whether there is or is not any birth,
Whether there is or is not any ending,
All these things are instantaneously clear.

Further,
In our dominion the power of awareness appears as our own miracles.
Those that do not see this for themselves
Do not understand.
These unfortunate people do not know this.

Everything is self-evident in this true nature,
But the reverted do not know this.
It exists in everything,
But what is close
Is also far.

So he spoke.

From the Royal Tantra on the Brilliant Diffusion of Majestic Space, this is chapter twenty-two: Making Our Ideas Real.

UNPOLLUTED PERFECTION

Then again the Blessed One spoke on his contemplations without error:

Spontaneously realized reality
Has the reward of being an inexhaustible treasure.
All samsara and nirvana come from it.
Everyone who appears and is known to us practices it.

This is an effortless state that we do not search for.
Like the space of the sky,
It is spaciously encompassing.
Like the substance of gold,
In shines forth in unity.

It manifests in differences,
But is perfected in its unity.
Its root is unchanging.
Its result is unity.

All the Dharmas that come from this
Are unchanging in my essence.
There is nothing whatsoever that appears to be anything else.
The uncomplicated encompasses all things.
It is a majestic pervader that has no outside or inside.

The Buddhas that dwell throughout the three times
And all the sentient beings of the three realms of samsara,
In the essence of their vajra hearts,

Are in the reality of being primordial Buddhas.

All of us abide in this,
So we are, from the beginning, liberated.
The majestic liberation of everyone
Is the space of my view.

Self-originating wisdom is not to be sought,
So in the absence of any intentional striving,
We have succeeded from the beginning at our great purpose,
Without a hassle.

Those who do not reject any problems or virtues at all
Do not look to either accept things or to reject them.
They are liberated into their own place,
So they are settled into purity.

In the absence of any settling or non-settling
We are liberated in the space of reality.
We are inherently without divisions, clarifications,
Rejections, or acceptances.

This is not to be sought,
And not to be worked on.
We are surely liberated without any planetary referents.
We are spontaneously realized,
Without any positions or preferences.

The fortunate who understand that things are so
Have no meditation or non-meditation.
They liberate demarcations into their own place,
So the Bodhicitta,
Which is non-dual:
This reality that is the Bodhicitta,
Is none other than enlightenment itself,
So in this there is no liberation or non-liberation.

No matter what we may do,
We do not go beyond this.
It is a majestic space that has no birth or ending.
There is no place for it to arise as anything else,
So I have no position or preference about myself.
I do not limit my vastness or fall into a position,

So everything abides in a non-dual space.

My view has no position.
It is a space of self-liberation.
It is like a golden island.
It has no divisions or clarifications.

My meditation has no position.
It is a primordial space.
It is like the wind from a bird.
It melts into its dominion.

My practice has no position.
It is a self-evident space.
It is like a river of water.
It is smooth and easy.

My result has no position.
It is a primordially realized space.
It is like the wind in a valley.
It is clear and unpolluted.

In the unified circle of samsara and nirvana,
Our seeking minds,
Which are our own dispositions,
Look for a view, meditation, practice, and result,
Which is like a mixed material of gold with silver,
But this is not polluted.
We are ornamented by a single comprehensive perfection.
This turns out to be special.

It is the fortress of the Ati.
Through destroying it,
It is not destroyed.
It is a vajra castle.
It has no birth or ending,
So it is a sky-like reality.

Anything we do in the space of the sky
Is happiness.
Anything that appears in this spontaneously realized space
Is liberated.

When we cut through to a single awareness of samsara and nirvana,
The equal and the unequal will not be divided or clarified
By the power of our minds.

This is the space of the one.
We make a determination about the nets of dualistic extremes,
And so we use proofs that it is unparalleled
And that it has no position.
To be completely free from yearnings
For a visible object,
We have no position or classification.

This is a primordially majestic pervasion.
Its meaning does not change.
We have struck to the core.
Positionless awareness uses an open mouth
To cut through all the complications there are
In clinging to extremes.

We have nothing to negate or to prove,
So we are equanimous from the beginning.
The object and the mind are not divided into categories.
Objectless awareness is self-evident,
So after the depths of our yearnings for proofs have emerged
There will be no causes or results.

Reality is majestic.
Those who desire to seek a position for this
Will have no grounds for deviation in its being pure or impure,
Which would be an obstacle for the path of the eight stages.[12]

Belief is a transmission for both ourselves and for others.
Doubt is a ground for deviation.
We cut through it with force.
The clear light that has no outside or inside
Purifies the darkness of our extremes into space.

Causes and conditions are not removed by remedies.
The embodiment of the Dharma has no destruction or separation.
The space of wisdom has no ignorance.
The space of the sky liberates everyone.

---

[12] Probably referring to the first eight vehicles of the nine vehicle system.

So he spoke.

From the Royal Tantra on the Brilliant Diffusion of Majestic Space, this is chapter twenty-three: Unpolluted Perfection.

THE MEANING DOES NOT MOVE

Then again the Blessed One spoke. He gave instruction on samsara and nirvana with these words:

When there is no motion,
We do not conceptualize.
The idea of a true self
Does not appear within our intellects.

If we want to engage in non-conceptualization,
We are planting the seeds of conceptualization.
We may see the meaning of non-conceptualization,
But this is not non-conceptualization.
It is an intellect that is making thoughts.

Subtle movements are obstacles for samadhi.
Regarding this root Bodhicitta,
To designate it as existent is the extreme of it being an entity.
To designate it as non-existent
Is to have an empty intellect.

We have a grasping of this empty intellect,
So we are not always in the extreme of it being an entity.
All entities are impermanent.
This being so,
The grim prospects there are in our demarcations
Are small.

People who are fortunate
Do not work on engaging in the meaning of non-conceptualization.
Their intellects do not dwell on the meaning of emptiness.
They do not look for a place to put their experience.
They do not dwell on objects for their yearnings and attachments.
They are not tied down by the ropes of their memories.
Stakes put down to hold onto things are not for them.
Everyone is a Buddha,
So they do not visualize an object or an abode for their compassion.

The space of non-conceptualization
Is also the embodiment of the Dharma.
We do not see it by looking for it.
It is clear when we settle ourselves.
Everyone and everything is clear,
So we abide from the primordial
Where there is no rising or falling.

This encompasses everything and everyone,
So we have dwelt, from the beginning, in spontaneous realization.
We do not conceptualize anything,
So, from the beginning, we have gone beyond
The dharmas of demarcations.

Everything is the compassion of enlightenment,
So the emptiness of the embodiment of the Dharma
Is nowhere else.
It is due to the equality in all our fields of practice
That our fields are totally pure.
They have been like this from the beginning.
So to whom would we ask why or what?

There are no analogies to be used to make exemplifications,
Nor are there any words to be spoken.
This is certainly true,
But in our effort to make an approximate teaching to start out with,
The Bodhicitta that pervades all things,
Without any extremes or middles,
Is like the sky.

Because it is beyond the two kinds of entities,
The Bodhicitta is beyond exaggerations and depreciations.
It brings us everything we desire,

The Royal Tantra on the Brilliant Diffusion of Majestic Space

And does not reject any of our methods,
So the Bodhicitta is like a precious jewel.

It is totally illuminating without any outside or inside,
So the Bodhicitta is like a lamp.

Without moving or quaking, it appears in everything,
So the Bodhicitta is like an ocean.

It is beyond contrivance and adulteration.
It is not to be transformed,
So the Bodhicitta is like molten gold.

There are bounteous nouns used to exemplify it,
But there is only one thing that they reveal.
No matter what enumerations of names we may attribute to it,
There is only one essence of meaning.
For each analogy there is a meaning,
A symbol for exemplification.
Names, nouns, and words of exclamation,
Grammar, conventionalities, and dharmas that are demarcated
Are realities that have no real basis.

What are we to conceptualize?
What are we to practice?
There are no objects that we must seek for.
There is nothing to be said
In words that exemplify through analogies.

This itself and what is not this,
As it is and other than this,
The unerring and the deluded,
The uncontrived and the contrived,
What is not something else and what is itself,
The one who has the thing and the thing itself,
The dominion and the entity,
And all the rest:
All of these divisions of the differences
Between good and evil
Are by their own natures delusions of the intellect.

In the Bodhicitta there are no differences.
This majestic space is the heart-essence of emptiness.

The Royal Tantra on the Brilliant Diffusion of Majestic Space

By merely understanding it for an instant,
We go there:
To the space of enlightenment.

This does not depend on the dharmas that we demarcate.
Space does not dwell within the dharma of emptiness.
Anything at all may appear from out of nothing whatever.

This is totally clear without even looking.
When we analyze it we do not find it.
It may appear as anything.
It is an essence that emerges from out of an absence of entities.
It has no true nature,
While it encompasses everything.
It has no true basis,
While it brings forth all things.
It is not to be worked on,
While it may realize anything at all.
It does not rest in equanimity,
While it is present within itself.
It has no desire,
Yet it fulfills our every purpose.
It fulfills all our wishes,
Yet it is not necessary to seek it.

The sun of wisdom arises on itself.
It is the basis for the generation
Of all the intents of the Secret Mantra.
It is the field of training for all of our disciples.
It is the true self of everyone,
The space of enlightenment.
It does what has not been done,
And we reach the end.

So all the good works that have been done
By all the Victorious Ones of the three times,
Whatever they may be,
Were done by this,
And all the deeds that have been done
By all of the sentient beings of the three realms,
Whatever they may be,
Were done by this.

There is no creator of me whosoever.
Without any creation,
All my purposes are realized,
So this precious jewel that brings forth what we wish for
Is a base from which come forth great miracles.
This is the way to turn the wheel of the Dharma.

From the Royal Tantra on the Brilliant Diffusion of Majestic Space, this is chapter twenty-four: The Meaning Does Not Move.

THE SECRET LIBERATION OF THE SKY

Then again he spoke out on the significance of his unerring contemplations:

For so long as they exist,
The root of each and every dharma
Is our own Bodhicitta.
It arises throughout all the enumerations of its branches.

The mind itself is unborn from the beginning,
So samsara and nirvana are unborn.
They are perfected in a single instant.

Our emotional problems,
Our happiness and sorrow,
And all the rest,
Are not to be rejected.
This is what we ourselves are.

There is nothing other than the Bodhicitta,
So the unborn is perfected as our own ornament.
The dhyāna meditations of virtue,
Holidays,
The Dharmas that are visible to our faces,
Our fields of practice,
And also the true nature of every substance
Are the Bodhicitta itself.
They are the ornaments of our happiness.

We have all the ornaments.
We are completely perfected.
The great perfection is an indivisible Dharma.
For some it is there.
For some it is not.

We are all similar,
So we are completely perfected.
The differences that are enumerated by the lowly
Do not exist.

From the reality of the unborn
There is the reality that has no cause or conditions.
In the absence of causes and conditions
Anything at all may arise.
It is the same way as with an assortment of jewels.

As things are for everyone,
Everyone seems to be a Buddha.
We have no going or coming.
We are the equal of the sky.
We have no engagement or reversal.
We are liberated in our dominion.

Our causes and conditions are exhausted,
So our emotional problems are cleared away.
We have no bondage or liberation,
So we are free from hindering or working towards anything.
We have no beginning or end,
So our continuum is not broken.

Those who think that there are three times
Deviate from the purpose of their equanimity.
In the reality where there are no three times,
We make attributions,
Saying: "They have no basic roots."

The Dharma of the base has no referents and is free from any position.
Making attributions about it is only a delusion.
There is no base to work on,
And nothing is sure.
There is no being or non-being,

The Royal Tantra on the Brilliant Diffusion of Majestic Space

But everything appears.

There is no good or evil,
But everyone is liberated.
There is no high or low,
But everything is clear.
There are no differences,
But we are liberated.

When we seek out a visualization
For a purpose that is correct,
There is no: "This is the cause and the condition."

There is no abode for lust and hatred.
This is the path of enlightenment.
There is no birth.
There is no ending.
This is the ornament of our view.

The ambrosia of wisdom overcomes samsara.
It lands on top of it.
It suddenly penetrates it.
It emerges in force.
It arises in space by itself,
And systematically overcomes the cities
Of the six classes of living beings.

It has no birth or death,
So it decimates illusions.
It thoroughly liberates everyone in the three realms.
Regarding this,
The dharmas that are subsumed within duality
May appear to be anything,
But there is no benefit or harm in them.
We are merely attributing names to the three existences.

Reality is primordially a possibility.
It is not possible that it be born.
For unhindered awareness,
Anything is possible.
The fields of the Buddha, however,
Have no birth.

The Royal Tantra on the Brilliant Diffusion of Majestic Space

The many things that are unborn are the souls[13] of everyone.
They have been present since the beginning,
So everyone is unborn.

In the reality of the unborn,
Anything we look at as being either a cause or a condition
Is uncompounded,
So our orientation is backwards.
We put exaggerations and depreciations onto the correct intent.
We deceive ourselves by ourselves.
What a pity!

This is the field of the Buddha.
Sukhāvatī is not anywhere else,
But if we do not reject suffering,
And if we are not equanimous about anything,
We will not succeed.

We do not desire and are not attached to happiness,
And we systematically do not develop lust or hatred,
So while we have no remedies,
We are free in our dominion.
There is nothing whatever that is not pure within our dominion.
There is nothing whatever that is not liberated into space.

Through attributions,
Even our delusion is thrown into our dominion.
Even the Dharmas of samsara are thrown into our dominion.
Nirvana melts into space.
The Dharmas of samsara also rise up out of our dominion.
Nirvana comes forth from out of space.
Our dominion is manifest in space.
This is most astounding.

In the beginning,
It did not come from anywhere.
It is present in the base.
It does not pass away or change.

In the present,
It does not abide anywhere.

---

[13] Tibetan: bDag. Sanskrit: Ātman

It is indefinite.
It is beyond deeds and searches.

In the end,
It does not go anywhere.
Except for being a single circle,
The three times do not exist.

Because there are no three times,
There is no birth or ending.
Awareness that has no birth or ending
May arise as anything.
It is pervasively encompassing.
Because it is pervasively encompassing,
Its vastness is not limited.

We do not fall into any position,
So who is benefiting whom?
Who is inflicting harm on whom?
Who is creating causes and conditions?

There is no previous or later,
So there are no causes or results.
Because there are no causes or results,
There is no samsara or nirvana.
Because there is no samsara or nirvana,
There is no enlightenment.

Anyone who desires a reward in this
Has turned their back on the correct meaning.
A previous or a later beginning or end is not born,
So even our abode dwells in the unborn.

Even our arising rises up in the unborn.
Even our being is unborn.
Even our liberation is liberated into the unborn.

Those who exaggerate their birth into this
Do not know their own faces.
What a pity.

If there were a birth,
All the sentient beings that are given names

Within the three realms,
None excepted,
Would gather up their flesh and bones,
But would still have space in their mouths.
They would be liberated into the dominion of the unborn,
So the majestic pathway for living beings
Is the dominion of the sky.

We may practice anything
Within the state of the sky.
We will rise up without hindrance.
We are self-originating and self-pacifying.
We have no birth or ending.
We cut through to the one,
So we have no applications or reversals.

You may say:
"Well then,
From what causes and conditions
Do these kinds of appearances arise?"

They are self-originating,
So they have no causes or conditions.
The sky will not become an entity.
In awareness that has no birth or death,
The opportunity to destroy it without demarcations does not exist.
All the Dharmas that appear in this way
Are self-arising from an essence that is nothing at all,
But they may appear to be anything.
We are without the exaggerations and depreciations
Of permanence and annihilation.

So he spoke.

From the Royal Tantra on the Brilliant Diffusion of Majestic Space, this is chapter twenty-five: The Secret Liberation of the Sky.

REVEALING THE THREE EMBODIMENTS TO MYSELF

Then again the Blessed One, the King of Teachers, gave instruction on the correct meaning:

The things that are designated to be dharmas
That have changed from something or have not changed,
However many there may be:
For what reason and by who were they so designated?
Who is the maker of this designation?
What is the basis for the designation?
On what are its object and place dependent?

If they have changed from something,
They have changed from themselves.
Even if they have not changed,
They are themselves.

We must know our own faces,
So we give ourselves names.
We ourselves are the makers of the designations.
We designate a thing that has no basis for designation.
We become attached by our natures,
And we look at this with force,
Then we made a variety of demarcations into something grand,
And so a nameless woman turns out to have a name.
Where there is no object, we attach the name of "object."

Where there is no place, we attach the name of "place,"
While the object and the place are the same.

Karma and habitual tendencies appear to be different.
We designate our own selves to be causes and results.
Through placing our yearnings on a cause,
We make the result into a demarcated object.
We turn away from what it means to have no cause or result.

A cause and a result are the same reality.
The cause itself is self-evidently the result,
So we have no yearning for a cause,
So we are perfected in the result,
Which is to be without yearning.

It is also unnecessary to depend on an object.
This is beyond the objects we may search for in a place.
Everything happens through a method.
This is the direct result of reason.

Because things happen methodically,
They are self-originating.
Self-origination does not refer to any method.
It also does not refer to any effulgence in our knowledge.
It is naturally without contrivance or transformation.

This is what it is to dwell in an uncontrived result.
The contrivances of our awareness are absent in this.
Knowing awareness does not become an object.
We are without ignorance and unknowing,
So ignorance and the embodiment of the Dharma
Have different names,
But have the same meaning.

Sentient beings that emerge out of karma
Are designated to be ignorant.
The Victorious Ones who are realized out of wisdom
Are designated to be embodiments of the Dharma.
Karma and compassion have no division.
Ignorance and the embodiment of the Dharma are of one nature.
Buddhas and sentient beings are significantly one.

The Royal Tantra on the Brilliant Diffusion of Majestic Space

What becomes a cause and what becomes a condition,
What becomes a result and what becomes a condition,
What becomes a result and the force to be a remedy,
What is designated by karma and what is designated by our ideas,
What is designated by a name and what is designated by a power,
What is designated by the karma of sentient beings,
And what is designated by our ideas about the path:
These are designations made in the name of the Buddha.

The thing that is designated is also an idea.
No matter what we do we will have a grasping attitude.
The reality that is beyond ideas and practices
Is present in equality,
Like the space of the sky.

Just as the sky has no end,
Reality is beyond the objects of our thoughts.
Just as the sky has no center,
Reality is liberated from the extremes of our practices,
So it is a force of power.

The space of the mind is its power.
Its not leaving anything behind is its playfulness.
Its not changing from this is its practice.

Its presence as a single true nature,
Its presence as a single essence,
Its manifestation in different characteristics,
Its emergence as wonders that have no position,
Its manifestations being spread out in every way,
Its way of seeing knowledge appearing in any way,
And its lack of any birth or ending
Are its force.

That majestic space has no attachment
Is its own effulgence.
The majestic space of the unborn embodiment of the Dharma
Stamps all samsara and nirvana with its seal.
The practice that has no true nature,
And the presence that has no attachment,
Do not go beyond the significance of reality,
So our contemplation is to abide in equanimity.

The majestic space of our unhindered embodiment of pleasure
Is not to be grasped as an object of the two extremes.
The Great Vehicle cuts through obscurations,
And is luminous without regard to what is external or internal.
It propagates virtues that have no outflows,
And teaches the paths for the four kinds of people,
So for those who are obstructed at the doorway of the path
And who are afflicted in the abodes of their origins and applications
Its characteristic is to be without obscurations.

The non-abiding manifest embodiment is indefinite.
It draws the six classes of living beings upwards,
And teaches them virtues that do have outflows.
It does good works for the sake of living things.
It knows the thoughts of its disciples.
It unites them with its methods and its compassion.
It is conscious of who has what,
So it is particularly noble.
It is majestic.

My effulgence is the mind-space of the three embodiments.
A remedy for what is disagreeable is not present in this.
I am alone and I am fit for thunder.
I am the embodiment of the Dharma.

So he spoke.

From the Royal Tantra on the Brilliant Diffusion of Majestic Space, this is chapter twenty-six: Revealing the Three Embodiments to Myself.

REFUTING CAUSE AND RESULT
AND RECOGNIZING THE THREE EMBODIMENTS

Then again the King of Teachers, the Blessed One, gave his entourage instruction on his profound intent:

The completely pure space of the dominion of the Dharma
Is a majestic spaciousness that liberates everyone,
But in the playfulness in which they do not know their own true natures
The six kinds of living beings are forced
By thoughts that are in reference to intellectual cravings
To encounter sorrow.

Where there is no birth or death,
They see birth and death.
The sorrows of their situations are inconceivable.
Where there is nothing,
They see something,
And are deluded.

Through descent into the core of the six collections of consciousness
They are thrust onto the narrow ledges of sorrow,
But when they stop up the doors to the four kinds of birth,
They are liberated into the space where there are no births or endings.
We have been liberated from the beginning,
So our continuum is not broken.

Those whose understandings expand on this greatly
Rely on non-conceptual meditation as a remedy.
They are forced onto the narrow ledges
Of clinging to a position about the path.
They earnestly seek an objective that does not exist.
They lay praise and blame on the significance of cause and result.
They are ensnared by the quests of their bodies, speech, and minds.
To seek from someone else is a mistaken pathway.

By descending to the core of philosophical conclusions,
They are stuck on the narrow ledges of clinging to positions.
They cut themselves off from the mistaken paths
At the door of which they have entered,
And are without any birth or ending,
So they are liberated into space.

We have been liberated from the beginning,
So our continuum is unbroken.
Reality has no birth or ending,
But we see dharmas that change and are destroyed.
We seek an objective which has no birth or death,
And we are forced onto the narrow ledge of the holy words of the Ati.
We lust and lust after the subtle meaning,
Then our understanding and comprehension of our experience
Rises up as our enemy.
We are ensnared by the knot of majestic self-liberation.

We descend upon the core of reality,
And are trapped on the narrow ledge of the instructions.
We close the door of making our good ideas be shared,
And we are liberated into a space where there is no birth or ending,
So our continuum is not broken.
There is no breaking the continuum of the three embodiments,
So our yearnings for extremes are liberated into their own place.

Uncontrived self-liberation is the dominion of the Dharma.
Even the innumerable Buddhas of the past
Truly became Buddhas in this inborn state.
Even the innumerable Buddhas of the future
Primordially become Buddhas in this unhindered state.
Even the innumerable Buddhas of the present
Are dwelling in this space that has no birth or ending.

The Royal Tantra on the Brilliant Diffusion of Majestic Space

Their virtues are inconceivable.
Positionless wisdom arises within us.
Positionless manifestations spread out from us.
We are self-originating from out of our dominion.
This is most astonishing.

Precious jewels and the things we want and need
Are like the space of the sky and miracles.
They are self-originating and self-pacifying.
They melt into space.

There is nothing that is beyond being thrown into our dominion.
The sentient beings that dwell in the three realms,
And even the Buddhas that dwell in the three times,
Are not beyond being lost in this state.
Without joining it or leaving it,
We dwell within in.

This has no augmentation or obscuration,
So all the sentient beings who dwell in the three realms,
In the measure of a mere instant,
In just a single moment,
Are Buddhas,
But there does not turn out to be more of them.
There does not turn out to be fewer sentient beings.

Their causes, conditions, and results are one.
They remain without diminishing, suppression,
Augmentation, or obstruction.
We attribute them to have causes, conditions, and results,
But there is no basis for any dharmas
That we would take up or put down.
There is no basis for anything.
There are no obstructions.
Habitual tendencies are not present in our dominion.
There is no basis on which we would put them,
So to worship the Victorious Sugata,
Or to kill the sentient beings in the three realms,
Are dharmas of virtue, evil, and the unpredictable,
But white and black karmas do not leave any traces.
They are like the pathways of the birds,
And are self-liberating.

Further,
The dharmas that are the true nature of our dominion
Do not have a final exhaustion in our dominion.
The five elements arise within our dominion.
All the outer and inner vessel and its contents,
The five good things we desire and the five poisons
Are the miracles of our dominion,
But they do not remain here as fixed entities.

It is like the ocean and its waves,
Or like the shining clouds in the dominion of the sky:
They fade into space without a trace.
This is the grave of all samsara and nirvana.
It is the majestic path where we leave our sorrows behind.

The Bodhicitta is the basis of all things.
This totally pure basis of all things is the dominion of the Dharma.
It is like the sky,
For it has no end.

There are no grounds for deviation that exist.
This is free from crevasses.
We designate things as being grounds for deviation
Or as being crevasses,
But in truth they do not exist.
They are merely taught as topics of interpretable significance
For the sake of the *Kriya*.

We may practice the karmas of virtue and non-virtue,
But no result will emerge.
We are finished with teaching about things that have causes and results.

If we say that causes and results are true,
Does a cause create a result or not create it?
If it creates it,
The result will turn out to be a cause.
There will be the problem that our understanding is backwards.

If it does not create the result,
Then the result that appears from it
Will not be able to be born after it,
So causes and results would be separated,
And results would not be realized.

The Royal Tantra on the Brilliant Diffusion of Majestic Space

There would be nothing to generate,
And no one who generates it,
So any truth in causes and result is simply not proven.

This being so,
Cause and result are adventitious dharmas.
The meaning of self-origination has no breaks in its continuum.
There are no breaks in the continuum of the three embodiments,
So it happens that there are no breaks in the continuum of their virtues.

Emotional problems and wisdom
Are not to be divided into separate things.
For those who do not understand,
They are the three realms.
For those who understand,
They are the space of the three embodiments.
They are there from the beginning,
So it is not necessary to seek them.

For those who do not understand,
There are three poisons.
For those who understand,
They are the ambrosia of wisdom.
They come from themselves,
So we do not need to reject them.

Self-liberation without rejecting anything
Is the embodiment of the Dharma.
It has been here from the beginning,
So we do not need to work on it.
It is spontaneously realized without our working on it.
It is the embodiment of the Dharma.

So he spoke.

From the Royal Tantra on the Brilliant Diffusion of Majestic Space, this is chapter twenty-seven: Refuting Cause and Result and Recognizing the Three Embodiments.

TEACHING THE WAY THAT WE ARE GATHERED INTO THIS DOMINION

Then again the Blessed One spoke once more:

The many things that arise within reality,
Which may appear to be anything,
Are the ornaments of our dominion.
The bounteous appearances within reality,
Which has no borders or limits,
Are our own ornaments.

The enumerations that appear within reality,
Which is unspeakable,
Are a great wonder.

The absence of any three times in reality,
Which has no birth or ending,
Is a great wonder.

The accomplishment of all our purposes in reality,
Which is not to be visualized,
Is our own grace.

The space of wisdom,
Which has no final exhaustion,
Is within reality,
Which has no basic root.

Within reality,
Which does not pass away or change,
There is our own effulgence,
Which has no obstructions.

What we see in reality,
We see as being naked.
It has no obstructions or coverings.
It is most amazing.

The reality of occurrences
Is primordial Buddhahood.
It is not definite that it is anything.
It is an effulgence of playfulness.

The miracle itself is our own ornament.
Great equanimity is the space of our dominion.
The thing that brings together the hundreds of spacious doors
To our samadhi
Is our own dominion.

The majestic space that expands
Is our own grace.
The agent of its arising
Is our own dominion.
The agency of its purity
Is the space of our own minds.

This space also brings down blessings like rain,
Through the miracle that is the sky.
Our virtues are covered over like clouds,
But their blessings appear to us
From out of an absence of demarcations.
They appear to us to be entities.

They appear to be objects that do not exist.
Our dominion and the apparent world are miraculous,
But because they are indefinite and they manifest in playfulness,
Emptiness is the sign that opens the door of secrets.

The vehicles that seek the correct meaning
Of what appears to be agreeable or disagreeable

The Royal Tantra on the Brilliant Diffusion of Majestic Space

Are one,
But it is divided into enumerations.
Form, sound, odor, taste, tangibles, and all the rest:
The five good things that we desire,
Are ornaments for the dominion of the unborn.
They emerge from out of the base,
And are not to be hindered.

When we cut through them,
Using the power of mindfulness,
Or are ignorant,
Due to the darkness of unmindfulness,
Or accept things,
Due to our understanding of them as objects,
Or make assumptions about them,
Based on their being remedies,
Or have a seeking mind
That would reject what is disagreeable,
Or desire some understanding
That is higher than our minds:
These obscure our objective of total freedom.

We may not possess any obscuration of our purpose,
But due to conditions,
We see things revertedly.
The inherent nature of the sky has no obscurations,
But adventitious miracles can obstruct the sky.

Reality may not obscure us,
But not knowing our own face
Is an obstruction and an obstacle.
When we practice a cause,
It is an obstacle for our cause.
When we practice a condition,
It is an obstacle for our condition.
When we yearn for results,
This becomes an obstacle to our results.

We do not obstruct the doors that appear
To realities that have no causes or conditions.
They may appear to be causes.
They may appear to be conditions.
When we do not yearn for them to appear as results,

We will be free from all yearnings for apparent objects.

The *Hoṃ* cavity of spacious emptiness
Is entirely free of words that may be spoken.
The objects that appear are also totally pure.
The force of our yearnings is also totally pure.
The paths that we reject are also totally pure.
The emotional problems that are the things we must abandon
Are also totally pure.
The results that we see are totally pure.
The conditions that we search for are also totally pure.
The causes we generate are also totally pure.

Majestic purity is the dominion of the Dharma.
The purifier is the dominion of the Dharma.
The expander is the dominion of the Dharma.
The contractor is the dominion of the Dharma.
The absence of expansion and contraction
Is the dominion of the Dharma.

The body of the Victorious One is methodically built
From out of our dominion.
It is made from forms that do not forget.
We have neither distractions nor mindfulness,
So majestic equanimity is the sky of our mother.

It is the space of the All Good Mother herself.
Each and every sentient being in the three realms
Refers to her as their mother.
She is the All Good Mother.
While she gives birth,
She gives birth.
While she nourishes,
She nourishes.

The one we refer to as our father
Is the All Good One.
While he gives birth,
He gives birth.
While he supports us,
He supports us.

In the space of the All Good there is no base or support.
In the unborn dominion there is no birth or withering.
There is no birth or ending,
So this is beyond any nurturing or killing.
Anything at all may appear from out of nothing.
The mind itself is the ornament of majestic space.

So he spoke.

From the Royal Tantra on the Brilliant Diffusion of Majestic Space, this is chapter twenty-eight: Teaching the Way That We Are Gathered into This Dominion.

The Royal Tantra on the Brilliant Diffusion of Majestic Space

THERE IS NO BREAK IN THE CONTINUUM

Then again the Blessed One gave instruction to Vajradhara and the rest of them on the correct meaning:

From the center of the space of the uncontrived mind,
Self-originating wisdom arises,
Without our seeking it.
It possesses most thoroughly the above, the below,
The directions, and their boundaries.

In the dominion of solitariness,
Everything is clear.
Our seeing, hearing, and remembering:
Anything that appears to the face of our senses,
Is self-apparent from out of a single absence of objects,
So except for our effortless essence of purpose,
Nothing appears and nothing is obstructed.

In the mirror of the luminescent mind
There is the moon that appears,
And there is the mind that grasps it.
It is like a reflection or an illusion.

From an absence, we see a presence,
And they appear to be different.
The object and the moment of its appearance
Are the dharmas of the generative forces.
Even the subtle and coarse appearances of the three realms

Are appearances that come from ourselves.

They are our space.
They manifest for us,
And are our own adornments.
The things we see as existent,
Which are all the well-known dharmas,
And even the things that appear to be non-existent,
Which are all of the dharmas that we attribute,
Are no different than ourselves.

From the beginning it is obvious that we are non-dual.
We do not depend on anything.
We are liberated in ourselves.
It is not the case that one thing depends on another,
So the grounds for deviation of our being extreme
Are simply absent.

Without rejecting any extremes,
We are self-liberated,
So in not hindering anything at all,
Our perfection is majestic.

This is expansive.
It is great:
This space of the mind.
It is neither to be joined nor parted from:
This ornament of our dominion.
We do not move to any other realm
Besides this one.
There is no place to live anywhere else.

From a single thing that has no support,
Everything emerges,
So the vastness of the mind is miraculous.
It is a great wonder.
It is self-originating and self-evident.
It is most amazing.
It does not refer to anything else.

Even the designation we call a "Buddha"
Was made famous through the intellects of his disciples.
In the correct meaning there is no Buddha.

The Royal Tantra on the Brilliant Diffusion of Majestic Space

As it is,
There is no one other than ourselves,
And this is just an attribution that we give ourselves,
While there is no basis for the designation,
So there is no Buddha.

The meaning does not abide in the name
That is the thing that we designate.
This being so,
Everything is ourselves.
We exemplify ourselves to ourselves,
And so we refer to ourselves.

By looking we do not see.
This is a great wonder.
The real thing that we do not see
Is the unborn embodiment of the Dharma.

We see the meaning,
An awareness that has no awareness,
Which is an awareness of the meaning of non-duality.
The rising that is without arising
Is the way of what it means to be self-originating.

In the space of self-awareness there is no ignorance.
Ignorance and wisdom are non-dual.
Majestic pristineness is the space of our view.
Wisdom and unknowing are non-dual.
Unknowing is a majestic wisdom.
It has been present from the beginning.
It is a non-dual space.

It arises equanimously,
So there is no defining of it.
In this reality that may resemble anything,
There is no outside or inside.
It is a pervasive bliss.

So what do we reject?
What do we work on?
Whom do we lust after?

There is no base that we may call an abode,
So where would there be a crevasse for us to fall into?
The reality in which we see crevasses
Has been present from the beginning,
So there are no low areas.

There is no above or below,
So there is no high or low.
There is no high or low,
So there are no directions or boundaries.

We are gathered into a unity in which there is no near and far.
It encompasses everything,
So it is totally pervasive.
The base has been present in this way from the beginning.
Our essence has not been born,
From the beginning,
So our purpose is beyond the limitations of any visualization.

The object and the mind are one,
And they appear as one,
So there is no other face for us to appear to,
Other than our own.
We are not anyone else.
This is obvious.

The embodiment of the Dharma
Is obviously within the space of self-appearance,
So through using conventionalities that would say:
"It does not exist,"
We will not get any meaning.

All the dharmas that appear and are well known
Arise from themselves.
The Dharmas that are subsumed
Within the paths of samsara and nirvana
Arise from themselves and are gathered into themselves.
They are liberated into their own place,
So they have no real basis.

There are no conventionalities for them,
So they are beyond self and other.
There is no object or mind,

The Royal Tantra on the Brilliant Diffusion of Majestic Space

So this is a space of equanimity.

The Buddha is a self.[14]
He is not some other,
So everyone is also a true self,
And is subsumed within the embodiment of the Dharma.

We are one in the circle that is beyond self and other.
The Buddha is called: "Buddha."
This is merely the adventitious attribution of a name.
Adventitious dharmas do not have any intellect,
So do not attribute Buddhahood to our thinking minds!

All designations are ideas.
They are the reality of our conceptualizations,
So just as the mandala of the sun has no darkness,
There is no ignorance within the space of wisdom.

In the space of the embodiment of the Dharma
There are no conceptualizations.
There are neither conceptualizations nor non-conceptualizations.
We do not move out of the state of equanimity,
So ignorance and wisdom are not two things.

Even the Dharmas which I have created
Do not have any creator on the side,
So without any deed or doer,
They appear by themselves.
They are self-created by themselves,
And are self-originating.
So we designate them to be:
"Without causes and conditions."

In the reality where there are no causes and conditions,
Our true self is called: "The Bodhicitta."
Arising as its playfulness,
There are what we call:
"The dharmas that I have created."

Everything is gathered into the self,
So our true self is called: "The Bodhicitta."

---

[14] Tibetan: bDag. Sanskrit: Ātman

There is no deed or doer to be grasped dualistically.
Everything is our own miracle,
So there is no break in the continuum of self-originating wisdom.

So he spoke.

From the Royal Tantra on the Brilliant Diffusion of Majestic Space, this is chapter twenty-nine: There Is No Break in the Continuum.

TEACHING DHYĀNA MEDITATION

Then our teacher spoke once again:

Through our true natures,
Which are like the sky,
There are rainbow colors and masses of clouds
On the surface.
They have no causes or conditions,
For they are the sky itself.

In the sky,
Which is an effortless reality,
The samsara and nirvana of our awareness
Are adventitious.
They have no causes or conditions,
So they are our own realities.

We ourselves arise from out of ourselves,
Then splinter off on our own.
We emerge from ourselves,
Then land on top.
No matter how we may rise up,
There is a landing on what we must know.

Nothing whatever comes out of this,
So all the dharmas that we see as existent,
That appear and are well known,
Are the miracles of the space of reality.

We play by ourselves, with ourselves.
We practice by ourselves, with ourselves.
We are happy by ourselves, with ourselves.
We suffer by ourselves, with ourselves.

These are the aspects of our playfulness,
So there is no good or evil.
Existence and non-existence arise in an equality,
So clinging to positions is a delusion of our purpose.

In the space of equality
We dwell on whatever is pleasant.
Without seeking anything,
We land in space.

There is no engagement in or reversal of this.
We settle into our own places.
There is no going or coming.
We are pure in our own dominions.

There is no deed or doer.
We are free from seeking.
There is no change.
We are free from limitations.
There is no bondage or liberation.
We are free from cravings.

We have no hope or fear.
We are equal to the sky.
We have no equanimity.
We do not fall into extremes.

What we call "space" is a dhyāna meditation.
If we attribute a name to it,
We will contrive an account of it.

This awareness,
The continuum of which is unbroken,
Has no previous or later,
No going or coming.
There is no account by which it may be counted.
We do not fall into the position of limiting its vastness,

The Royal Tantra on the Brilliant Diffusion of Majestic Space

So we do not account for it in any enumerations.

We have no extremes or middles,
No directions and no borders,
So we do not account for them by enumerating them.

We have no above or below,
No higher and no lower,
So we do not account for them by enumerating them.

We have neither an outside nor an inside.
Everything is subsumed into one,
So we do not account for it by enumerating it.

Awareness,
The continuum of which is not broken,
Is present in us happily and easily.
We are neither distracted nor not distracted.
We neither visualize nor do not visualize.
We are neither clear nor unclear.
We are neither visible nor invisible.
We neither search nor do not search.
We neither see nor do not see.
We neither meditate nor do not meditate.

In a single instant we are without joining or parting.
We are present within the bliss of a majestic dhyāna meditation.
We are diffused within the space of great bliss.
This is why this is the dhyāna meditation
Of the embodiment of the Dharma that diffuses into space.

Whatever may appear,
We do not move away from happiness.
This is the dhyāna meditation
In which appearance is stamped with a seal.
We do not seek a place to put our experiences.
This is the dhyāna meditation that has no preferences
For objects or for the mind.

We do not put our hopes on equanimity,
So this is a dhyāna meditation
In which there is nothing to accept or to reject.
This is beyond all sessions and breaks,

So it is a dhyāna meditation the continuum of which is not broken.

This is the exhaustion that exhausts our emotional problems,
So it is a dhyāna meditation that is a meaningful reaching of the end.
We melt into the space of great bliss,
So this is a dhyāna meditation that has no passing away or change.

So he spoke.

From the Royal Tantra on the Brilliant Diffusion of Majestic Space, this is chapter thirty: Teaching Dhyāna Meditation.

TEACHING THAT THE UNBORN CUTS THROUGH TO THE ONE

Then again our teacher gave instruction to his entourage:

The majestic Dharma that has no true nature
Is astounding beyond our thoughts!
It is like this:

Through the door of birth of the unborn,
The miracle of birth occurs.
This is birth through the karma of the unborn.
The miracle emerges from ourselves.
The unborn is ourselves.
It is no one else.

Through the door of birth of the unborn,
Miracles are born from ourselves,
And the miracle of birth occurs.
The unborn is ourselves.
It is no one else.

Through the secret door of the unborn,
The unborn is born through the four places of birth.[15]
In merely being born we are not born.
The unborn is ourselves.

---

[15] Birth through the womb, the egg, moisture, and miraculous birth.

It is no one else.

Through the door of birth of the unborn,
By the full ripening of the karma that manifests as our conditions,
We may be born in the three realms of samsara,
But in merely being born we are not born.
The unborn is ourselves.
It is no one else.

Through the secret door of the unborn,
By the purity of our prayers from of yore,
We may be born as Bodhisattvas,
But in merely being born we are not born.
The unborn is ourselves.
It is no one else.

Through the surely secret door of the unborn,
By our samadhi,
The grace and power of the teachings,
And chants and recitations that take us to the end of counting,
We may be born as Vision Keepers.
The unborn is ourselves.
It is no one else,
While in merely being born we are not born.

Through the surely secret door of the unborn,
By the power of our prayers and the power of our samadhi,
Our higher perception and our connections into pairs,
We may be born as children of the Victorious Ones
In a vast and bounteous pure realm,
But the unborn is ourselves.
It is no one else,
While in merely being born we are not born.

Through the secret door of the unborn,
By our philosophical conclusions,
And the expanded and summarized versions we have studied,
We may be born as seekers on the path,
But the unborn is ourselves.
We are not born as anyone else.
In merely being born we are not born.

The Royal Tantra on the Brilliant Diffusion of Majestic Space

To be born in samsara among the six classes of living beings,
To enjoy the pure lands,
And all the Dharmas of the pathways of samsara and nirvana,
Are the unborn itself giving birth to itself,
So the unborn Dharma is taught in various ways.

Everything is born from the unborn.
When we say things in words
We contradict their meanings.

There are no contradictions to the meaning of the unborn.
There are contradictions in words that are conventionalities.
There is no contradiction in the Bodhicitta.
There are contradictions in reverted minds.

When we proclaim things in uncontrived words,
And even proclaim their unerring significance to the fortunate,
They will be exhausted as they appear.

To have no meaning is a cause for delusion.
Reversion and enlightenment are also realities
That are equal from the beginning.

The meaning of reality has no duality.
The reality that is unborn
Simply arises as the five elements,
And this vessel and its contents,
But the unborn is ourselves.
No other is born,
Yet in merely being born we are not born.

This reality that is unborn
Is the cause for the birth of masculine, feminine, and neuter.
We may take on a body that is male, female, or neuter,
But the unborn is ourselves.
No other is born,
But in merely being born we are not born.

The reality that is unborn
Is a cause for the birth of the five poisons and the three poisons,
But they merely arise as being our five emotional problems.
The unborn is ourselves.
No one else is born.

In merely being born we are not born.

Self-originating wisdom is unborn.
It is beyond all causes and conditions,
So it is a reality that has been present from the beginning.
It manifests as being the true basis for everything
That exists or does not exist.

The dharmas that we demarcate are divided up by the sky.
The understanding of the subject
Is what divides up reality.
Our understanding of appearances
Uses their emptiness to divide them up.
Our understanding of samsara and nirvana
Uses our awareness to divide them up.

In our understanding of birth,
Everything that transpires
Is divided up by the dominion of the unborn.

This dominion of the Dharma that divides up our understandings,
This sky,
Pierces the vision of all samsara and nirvana.
The totality of everything arises in a single moment.
It arises,
But in the unborn it is one.

So he spoke.

From the Royal Tantra on the Brilliant Diffusion of Majestic Space, this is chapter thirty-one: Teaching that the Unborn Cuts Through to the One.

TEACHING THAT THE CHARACTERISTICS OF THE BODHICITTA HAVE NO BIRTH OR ENDING

Then again our teacher gave instruction to his entourage, which no one joins or leaves:

Do not look anywhere else but here!
Looking and looking:
What a great idea!
If we do not look anywhere else but here,
We will not need to meditate on any other non-conceptuality.

Do not practice anything else but this!
Practicing and practicing:
We give birth to reverted views.
If we do not practice anything other than this,
We will not need to work on any other ideas or practices.

Do not seek anything else but this!
Seeking and seeking:
Our taking in and holding on increases.
If we do not seek anything other than this,
All the doors that we would enter do not exist,
So we will not need to study the levels and paths.

Do not work on anything else but this!
Working and working:

There is no end to it.
If we do not work on anything other than this,
We will not need to attain the status of Buddhahood.

That which is called a "human"
Is a Buddha.
If we do not understand what it means to be inseparable
We may work on it for an eon,
But we will not succeed.

When we abide in the intent of inseparability,
We may wander through the world,
But we will not be lost or separated.

The unborn and unending is taught in various ways.
The practice of objectives and the non-practice of them
Both come from a practice that has no ending.
Non-practice comes from the unborn.

We may depend on a place or not depend on one.
These come from a dependence that has no end.
Independence comes from the unborn.

Our true natures may be contrived or uncontrived.
They arise from contrivance that has no ending.
The uncontrived comes from the unborn.

To go beyond the Dharma, or not to go beyond it?
Going beyond it arises from the unending.
Not going beyond it arises from the unborn.

To demonstrate miracles, or not to demonstrate them?
Demonstrating them arises from the unending.
Not demonstrating them arises from the unborn.

To use exemplifications to land on top, or not to land there?
Landing there arises from the unending.
Not landing there is the state of the unborn.

To be free or not to be free of the exaggerations of demarcations?
Not being free of them arises out of the unending.
Being free of them arises out of the unborn.

The Royal Tantra on the Brilliant Diffusion of Majestic Space

To go around or not to go around a single true nature?
Going around comes from the unending.
Not going around is the space of the unborn.

A single essence has both happiness and sorrow.
Sorrow comes from the unending.
Great bliss is the state of the unborn.

A single characteristic has both appearance and emptiness.
Appearance arises from the unending.
Emptiness is the dominion of our unborn mother.

These are the two:
The unbroken continuum,
And what is temporary.
The temporary is not sure to be unceasing.
An unbroken continuum is the dominion of the unborn.

The absence of joining and separation
Is both permanent and annihilated.
The absence of anything to yearn for
Is both exaggerated and depreciated.
The absence of anything to accept or reject
Is both negated and proven.
The absence of self and other
Is both good and evil.
The absence of an outside and an inside
Is both an object and our minds.
The absence of passing away and changing
Is both birth and death.

This being so,
Each and every thing that is subsumed into pairs,
Be it unborn or unending,
Comes from ourselves.

Everything is born from the unborn.
Everything is ended through the unending.
In merely being born we are not born.
In merely ending we are not ended.

Birth is also unborn.
We are born from out of space.

In the dominion of the unborn
There is no cause for our being born.
Our ending is also without end.

We end up in space.
In the dominion of the immortal
There is no cause for death.
Awareness,
Which has no birth or ending,
Is a miracle that may be anything.
It is not definite.
Self-originating wisdom is victorious over the extremes.

The body of the Victorious One has no birth or death.
It is totally victorious over samsara's wars.
The body of the Victorious One
Is primordial Buddhahood.
It is totally victorious over the enumerations of the vehicles.
The body of the Victorious One has no high or low.
It is totally victorious over the faults and virtues of samsara and nirvana.
The body of the Victorious One is true equanimity.
Equanimity without preference is the space of our minds.

It is unborn and unending.
It is taught in many ways.
It is invisible and unspeakable.
It may arise as anything.
Its arising is self-evident.
Its liberation is self-liberating.

For these reasons,
Awareness that has no object
Is truly alone.

So he spoke.

From the Royal Tantra on the Brilliant Diffusion of Majestic Space, this is chapter thirty-two: Teaching That the Characteristics of the Bodhicitta Have No Birth or Ending.

OUR OWN POWER OF AWARENESS

Then again the King of Teachers spoke unerringly on the meaning of the teachings:

In the dominion of the true nature of the Dharma
We are one.
Each of us takes hold of their own characteristics separately.
It is because we cling to characteristics that we make the attribution: "Dharmas."

In the correct meaning,
They do not exist.
This is certainly true,
However,
There is the wrong way,
And there is the way that is not wrong.

We are holding onto our own characteristics.
Moreover, it is by force of a single self-evidence
That we arise from out of a single quality.
The markers of a body, speech, and mind
Are our own characteristics
That we cling to by ourselves.
These too are self-evident,
By the power of their being one.

For some, anger is the Bodhicitta.
For some, stupidity is the Bodhicitta.

For some, pride is the Bodhicitta.
For some, lust is the Bodhicitta.
For some, jealousy is the Bodhicitta.
Without moving from a single self-origination,
We ourselves hold onto our own characteristics.

Further, by the force of a single self-evidence
We are freed from the objects of our demarcations.
Forms, feeling, perceptions, assumptions, and consciousness:
These are the five heaps.
We use their true natures to divide them into five karmas.
We ourselves hold onto our own characteristics.

Further, by the power of our own awareness
Appearances are pure in their own place.
So there are the earth, water, fire, wind,
The sky, and all the rest:
These are the five elements.
We ourselves hold onto our own characteristics.

Further, by the power of our own awareness
We are freed from all grasping at reality.
Forms, sounds, odors, tastes,
Tangibles, and all the rest:
These are the five good things we desire.
We ourselves hold onto our own characteristics.

Further, by the power of a single self-evidence
There arise from a single self-awareness
Our eyes, ears, noses, tongues,
Body, and all the rest:
These are the five good things we desire.
We ourselves hold onto our own characteristics.

Further, by the power of a single self-awareness
Of a reality that may change into anything at all
There are white, yellow, red, green,
Black, and all the rest:
These are the five colors.
We ourselves hold onto our own characteristics.

Further, by the power of a single self-evidence
In a reality that has no edges or limits

The Royal Tantra on the Brilliant Diffusion of Majestic Space

There are the ten:
The four directions, the eight borders, the above, and the below.
We ourselves hold onto our own characteristics.

Further, by the power of a single self-evidence
In a reality that is unchanging
There are summer, winter, autumn, and spring:
These are the four seasons.
We ourselves hold onto our own characteristics.

Further, by the power of a single self-evidence
In a reality where there is no birth or decay
There are birth, age, sickness, and death:
These are the four sorrows.
We ourselves hold onto our own characteristics.

Further, by the power of a single self-evidence
In a reality that has no true nature
There are samsara, nirvana, happiness, and sorrow:
There are both good and evil.
We ourselves hold onto our own characteristics.

Further by the power of awareness itself,
In a reality that has no causes or results
There is a definite division between the karmas of virtue and evil.
We ourselves hold onto our own characteristics.

By the power of an awareness of duality itself,
In a reality that has no near or far,
There are the nine stages of the high and low vehicles.
We ourselves hold onto our own characteristics.

By the power of an awareness of duality itself,
In a reality that has no bondage or liberation,
There are both disagreements and remedies.
We ourselves hold onto our own characteristics.

By the power of our own awareness of duality,
In a reality where there is no is or is not,
There is an intellect that understands
And a mind that does not understand.
We ourselves hold onto our own characteristics.

By the power of our own awareness of duality,
In a reality where there is one basic root,
There are vast hundreds and thousands of enumerations,
But we ourselves are holding onto our own characteristics.

All appearances are self-evident.
Everything that arises arises by itself.
By the power of our awareness of all things
There is nothing whatever that is not immediately true.
In the space of our dominion there are no truths or lies.
Temporary results are also true,
So there is not a single thing that does not turn out to be true.
It is because we are thrown into an effortless dominion
That there is not even a single thing
That does not turn out to be a lie.

The majestic space of the reality in which there are no truths or lies
Is the abode of all the Buddhas of the past.
It is the support for all the Buddhas of the future.
It is the base for all those who dwell in the present.
This measureless palace that has no beginning or end
Is a path for all the sentient beings of the three realms.
It is the majestic pathway which brings forth
The six classes of living beings.
There is nowhere to transit to other than this dominion,
So it is a majestic land of bounteous abodes.

There is no transformation other than this space.
It is the majestic grave which brings us all together.
The mind itself is a charnel ground,
A space for pleasant experiences.

So he spoke.

From the Royal Tantra on the Brilliant Diffusion of Majestic Space, this is chapter thirty-three: Our Own Power of Awareness.

THE OCCURRENCE OF MIRACLES

Then again I spoke to my entourage:

The way it is is the supreme vehicle.
The way it is accounted for is the object of our views.
The way it seems is the abode of our meditations.
The way it appears is as our friend in practice.
The way it is possible is as the treasure of our rewards.

If we understand the meaning of the way it is,
We will be propelled into the land of the Buddhas,
So this is the supreme vehicle of the unsurpassed king.

The enumerations for the way it is accounted for
Perceive the unconfused in complete perfection.
The sight of naked reality is unsurpassed.

The meaning of the way it seems
Is to rest in our natural state without contrivance.
The king of samadhis is unsurpassed.

Whether we are moving, sleeping, eating, or walking
We use our three doors for any of the Dharmas,
Just as they appear.
We do not look for any good or evil,
Or anything to accept or reject.
This king of practices is unsurpassed.

The Royal Tantra on the Brilliant Diffusion of Majestic Space

The way that the Dharmas are possible,
And all the Dharmas that are impossible,
Is that they manifest as our own jewelry.
The majestic treasure of our rewards is unsurpassed.

Regarding the majestic treasure of an uncontrived mind,
Some see it as the king of views.
Some see it as an object for visualization in samadhi.
Some see it as a door of practice.
Some see it as something to work on.
Some see it as something not to work on.
Some see it as the king of vehicles.
Some see it as a knot of taking things in and holding onto them.
Some see it as a distraction of samsara.
Some see it as a cause for rejection.
Some see it as a study and a motion.
Some see it as the level of Buddhahood.
Some see it as the abode of samsara.
Some see it as an obstruction to their path.
Some see it as a guide for the forks in the road.
Some see it as a poisonous emotional problem.
Some see it as the ambrosia of wisdom.

Whatever we see,
Whatever appears,
And whatever is clear:
This is a majestic treasure.
It transforms into all the things that we desire.
It is like an assortment of jewels.

Due to conditions,
It may arise as anything.
It is, therefore, a precious jewel that brings us everything we desire.
Our minds dwell on this precious jewel.
Our objects are the conditions that it brings forward.
They are non-dual,
So this is the space of our rewards.

There is no object.
Do not conceptualize an object!
It is not that it absolutely does not exist,
But there is no object other than our minds.

The Royal Tantra on the Brilliant Diffusion of Majestic Space

There is no mind.
Do not grasp at a mind!
It is not that it absolutely does not exist.
Self-awareness does not grasp.
It is beyond conceptualizations.
In this, there is nothing to apprehend as an object.
In this, there is nothing to apprehend as a mind.

When we investigate,
We are subsumed within both objects and mind.
This majestic space does not grasp and is self-evident.
It also has no object.
This is the dominion of the Dharma.
It also has no mind.
This is the embodiment of the Dharma.

The majestic object that we organize
Is a space of pleasant delight.
The embodiment of the Dharma of great bliss
Is the fortress of a happy mind.
Self-originating wisdom is its master.
The one mind of the Buddha is its entourage.
Each and every one of us is imparted the empowerment.

Our own minds have nothing to do.
We are the kings of this dominion.
Complete perfection that is unconfused is our servant.
The totality of everything is gathered into this,
So the one that compiles it is the space of our dominion.

All things break off from this,
So the one that does the scattering
Is the dominion of space.
Miracles come forth from this dominion,
So it is that all things emerge from it,
And all things are gathered into it.
It is the great gatherer of all things.

The objects that it gathers
Are the grounds of practice for every yoga.
The dominion of the Dharma
Is the sky of the All Good Mother.
It is clear,

And has no outside or inside,
So we see the vessel and its contents as being one,
And our awareness descends into a golden vase.

Earth, water, fire, and wind:
The four elements,
Are an undammed river of compassion.
We may enjoy the five good things we desire,
But we will not be stained by their problems,
So no matter how subtle or coarse entities appear to be,
They are the miracles of the sky.

The sky is invisible,
And its miracles have no final exhaustion.
The sky encompasses all things.
Entities do not possess any emptiness.
They appear to have colors and shapes.

Insiders use the inside for their views.
We practice with our own force.
We move, sleep, eat, and walk.
Males and females lust after one another.
We do work and deeds.
We may be changed by conditions.
Our rewards may come forth in their time.
These are the virtues of the dominion of the ordinary.

The effulgence of the majestic space of the Bodhicitta,
The turning of the wheel of the Dharma,
To listen to it and to contemplate it,
To apply ourselves to the karmas of the ten virtues,
To quest for this and to work on it,
To dwell in an equanimity that does not search,
To cut through the distractions of our bodies,
To cut through the complications of our speech,
To remove the bustle of our minds,
To live separately by ourselves,
To go wherever we please without direction,
To have nowhere definite that we live,
To practice alone and to sit with many,
To depend on the distractions of entertainment,
To follow after objects and be changed by conditions:
All of these are the virtues of our dominion.

The mind itself is a majestic space.
By its grace wisdom is born in our spirits.
We see the exhaustion of the full ripening of karma.
We hold to the way and we mark out the way.
Our experience has no birth or ageing.
The damage of the elements does not afflict us.
The elements do not make obstacles for us.
We do not worry for our livelihoods.
We arrive at the teaching of transmissions,
And at explanations of the Dharma.
We have supernatural cognition and we let loose miracles.
We see those who are dwelling on the levels.
We give blessings and reveal miracles.
We are not under the control of others,
And we are in our own dominions.
We do not hinder the ordinary.
It is just like the miracles of the sky:
From out of an absence of entities,
A heart-essence arises.

Cause and result are not present in our spirits,
So our minds are a majestic space,
And we are powerful because of this.

So he spoke.

From the Royal Tantra on the Brilliant Diffusion of Majestic Space, this is chapter thirty-four: The Occurrence of Miracles.

DECISIVE CONTEMPLATION

Then again I discussed this clearly with my entourage:

When we see this heart of enlightenment,
We see all the Buddhas at the same time.
We do not see them because our prayers are pure.
We see them because our minds are pure.

Our own minds are pure and stainless.
They are not pure because we have washed them.
They are pure because we do not cling to positions.
Clinging to positions is a spontaneously realized majesty.

We do not succeed by seeking this or by working on it.
We succeed by dwelling with it from the beginning.
Primordially established reality does not change.
It does not come forth from either causes or conditions.

The things we must know abide in our own dwelling.
Self-originating wisdom is the ancestor of the Victorious Ones.
It is the father of all the sentient beings of the three realms.
It is the mother of the Victorious Ones of the three times.
It is the treasure that is revealed on the supreme path of yoga.
It is the field we travel over on the level of the Mahayana.
It is the weapon that cuts off the noose that ensnares us.
It is the knife that cuts through the neck-rope of emotional problems.
It is the sky where we flee from the enemy of collective destruction.
It is the person who protects us from the four Maras at our borders.

It is the war that overcomes the cities of the six classes of living beings.
It is the knife that kills our three secret enemies.
It is the effortless All Good One of our own minds.
It is the overall ancestor of us all.
It does not pass away or change.

The sentient beings of the three realms are born from this.
The unborn is the dominion of our All Good Mother.
The Victorious Ones of the three times come from her.
Even the contemplations of the five kinds of yoga
In their unity have arisen from her space.
The Mahayana has no separations,
So from the beginning we have surmounted it,
Without any travelling.

We use the weapon of self-originating wisdom
To cut through the two kinds of bondage.
The outsiders will not be destroyed with grammar and logic.
This is a vajra fortress.
It has no birth or death.
Self-originating people overwhelm the four Maras.
We use a contemplation that does not pass away or change
To systematically overcome the cities of the six classes of living beings.
We use the reality that is of a single true nature
To mix together the triad of outsiders, insiders, and those in-between.
Then we cut through the darkness of the extremes at the roots.

To have or not to have doubts
Is a mind with a dualistic vision.
The meaning of effortlessness
Is not a dualistic vision.
In a state of indivisibility,
Our intellects dwell in happiness.

To have or not to have a quest and a practice
Is a mind of hope and fear.
In the dominion of particularities,
There are no hopes or fears.
In a state of equanimity,
Our intellects dwell in happiness.

To have or not to have any bondage or liberation
Is a mind that negates or proves things.

The Royal Tantra on the Brilliant Diffusion of Majestic Space

The mind of great bliss has nothing to negate or to prove.
In the significance of equanimity
Our intellects dwell in happiness.

To have or not to have any samsara or nirvana
Is a mind that takes things in and holds onto them.
In the one circle there are no divisions.
In the significance of being uncontrived
Our intellects dwell in happiness.

To have or not to have anything to work on
Is a mind of conceptualizations.
By working on things we will not find the welfare of others.
In a state of effortlessness,
Our intellects dwell in happiness.

To have or not to have anything to exemplify
Is a mind of the external and the internal.
We are beyond all talking and speaking,
So in freedom from conventionalities
Our intellects dwell in happiness.

No matter where we seek,
There is only reality.
No matter what we attribute through the door of names,
There will be no certitude in the name,
So reality is attributed on ourselves by ourselves.

No matter what we say through the door of enumerations,
We will not touch upon anything by numbering,
So reality counts itself by itself.

As things are,
The Dharmas that appear and are of this world
Are self-evident,
So we look for others.
In the state of decisiveness,
Our intellects dwell in happiness.

Do we take our bodies for ourselves?
Do we give birth to ourselves?
Do we die for ourselves?
Do we bring any benefit upon ourselves?

Do we inflict harm on ourselves?

Who is the creator of both birth and death?
Where do both benefits and damages come from?
When we have decided that there is a single self-evidence,
There is a state of effortlessness,
Our intellects dwell in happiness.

So he spoke.

From the Royal Tantra on the Brilliant Diffusion of Majestic Space, this is chapter thirty-five: Decisive Contemplation.

TEACHING THAT WE HAVE RECEIVED THE EMPOWERMENT FROM THE BEGINNING

Then again the Blessed One gave instruction to those who were in his entourage:

It is due to the way in which we settle into our own places
That our awareness, which is like the sky,
Dawns on us to be a thing that does not pass away or change.
It has no distraction or non-distraction.
No matter what we create,
It is the space of this.

This supreme dominion that is not to be joined or parted from
Is limitless and is brilliantly diffused,
So it is not a field of practice that we may exemplify with words.
It is a field of practice for the fortunate,
Those who have emerged from the space of knowledge,
And on whom awareness has dawned.

This is a field of practice for yogins
Who have much study,
Who do not change their minds,
Who have melted into unspeakable space:
Intelligent ones whose ideas are most brilliant,
Those who are determined from the beginning,
Whether or not they have been shown this.

Through the use of any meditation or any thing to be meditated on
We do not find any object or one who has an object,
So it is not necessary to kill any enemy
That would be our conceptualizations about depression and wildness,
Or seeking and non-seeking.

From the beginning,
Within this majestic golden vase,
The reality which is present is generally pervasive,
So we do not harbor any ideas about selves or others.
The three realms are a field of the equality of ourselves and others.
The Sugatas of the three times are self-appearing.
There is not even an atom of any object
That we must hear about from others,
And that we do not understand from ourselves.

In the majestic space of the reality of our own minds,
A variety of demarcations will all become clear,
But we do not move away from the intent of equanimity.
Those who work to see something other than themselves
Have deluded minds that envision a duality.
They desire to meditate and have seeking attitudes.

The delusion is not in anyone else,
So a majestic settling into ourselves
Is the space of equanimity.

The majestic space of equanimity has no preferences,
So we dwell in it without any settling or non-settling.
The majestic settling into the base
Is not something to seek.

Look again.
Look again.
Look at your mind!
There is nothing to see.
We see the view of our own minds.
We are beyond the limitations of visualizations.
Awareness is the view of the golden vase.
The view of self-awareness is the empowerment of effulgence.
Without being trampled on by emotional problems and karma,
We have achieved it from the beginning,

So it need not be imparted.
Our view is that we empower ourselves.

Meditate again.
Meditate again.
Meditate on your mind!
See the meditator whose mind has no mediation.
To be free from the object that we would demarcate
Is the meditation of the golden vase of awareness.
The empowerment of effulgence is the meditation of self-awareness.
Without being trampled by emotional problems or karma,
We have acquired it from the beginning,
So it need not be imparted.
Our meditation is that we empower ourselves.

Practice again.
Practice again.
Practice on your mind!
See the practice of the mind that has no practice.
To be liberated from the extremes
Of taking things on and rejecting them
Is the practice of the golden vase of awareness.
The practice of self-awareness is an empowerment of effulgence.
Without being trampled by emotional problems and karma
We have acquired it from the beginning,
So it need not be imparted.
Our practice is that we empower ourselves.

Work on it again.
Work on it again.
Work on your mind!
See the reward that is a mind that has nothing to work on.
To be liberated from the extremes of hopes and fears
There is the reward of the golden vase of awareness.
The reward of self-awareness is an empowerment of effulgence.
Without being trampled by emotional problems and karma
We have acquired it from the beginning,
So it need not be imparted.
Our reward is that we empower ourselves.

This being so,
The equanimity of reality
Has no object,

Nor any keeper of an object,
So it does not hold to any self or other.

Awareness turns out to be self-empowering.
It is inherently present in the state of equanimity.
The way that awareness dawns in this
Is that it is self-evident in everything,
Both external and internal.

We acquire self-empowerment by ourselves,
So we do not move from the state of equanimity.
We do not dwell on the objects that we demarcate.
Objectless awareness is present in the golden vase.
From the beginning it is non-dual,
So we do not partition the state of the circle into divisions.

The golden vase of the Buddha's wisdom
Abides in the demarcations of the conceptualizations of sentient beings.
Our own effulgence is a non-dual awareness.
Samsara and nirvana are not to be divided,
So there is no transgression of what it means to be equanimous.

The awareness of samaya is our own effulgence.
Entities and non-entities arise in an equality
Within the positionless contemplation of equanimity.

An awareness of understanding is our own effulgence.
Buddhas and sentient beings are equal within our dominion.
The relative and the ultimate are equal within our dominion.
Faults and virtues are equal within our dominion.
The high and the low,
The directions and the borders,
Are equal within our dominion.
The meaning of equality does not move.

An awareness of experience is our own effulgence.
We have acquired it from the beginning,
So it need not be imparted.
When it arises,
It arises into equality.
When the effulgence of awareness that has no good or evil
Is present,
It is present in equality.

When the effulgence of awareness that has no good or evil
Is liberated,
It is liberated into equality.

The effulgence of awareness that has no good or evil
Is not trampled on by our emotional problems or karma.
From the beginning we have acquired
The empowerment into the self-effulgence
Of the awareness of good works,
So it need not be imparted.

Even though inequalities may appear,
There is a dominion of equality.
It manifests as our absence of both equality and inequality.

Inequalities may be present,
But there is a dominion of equality.
It is present in the absence of both equality and inequality.

Inequalities may be liberated,
But there is a dominion of equality.
We are liberated in the absence of both equality and inequality.

Self-arising and self-liberation
Are the effulgence of awareness itself.
The self-effulgence of the awareness of good works
Is an empowerment of purity.
We have acquired it from the beginning,
So it need not be imparted.

Arising and non-arising are absent in our dominion.
Abiding and non-abiding are absent in our dominion.
Liberation and non-liberation are absent in our dominion.

At the time of their arising, they arise within us.
Self-arising is to take our own place by ourselves.
At the time of their abiding, they abide within us.
Self-abiding is to take our own place by ourselves.
At the time of their liberation, they are liberated within us.
Self-liberation is to take our own place by ourselves.

In arising we abide.
In abiding we are liberated.

In being liberated we arise.
There is no break in the continuum.

Because there is no break in the continuum,
There is no cause and result.
Because there is no cause and result,
There are no obstacles.

In the reality where there are no obstacles
We are not cut off by the crevasses of samsara.
Because we are free from crevasses,
We do not take on bodies.
Without bodies,
What grounds for deviation will we fall into?

We do not pass away or change through the three times.
From the beginning,
This is the space of the All Good One.
From the beginning,
We have no birth or death.

This is the state of Vajrasattva himself.
Awareness is self-empowering.
This is called: "A real empowerment."
We see our own face by ourselves,
And we conclude by calling it: "Buddhahood."

So he spoke.

From the Royal Tantra on the Brilliant Diffusion of Majestic Space, this is chapter thirty-six: Teaching that We Have Received the Empowerment from the Beginning.

TEACHING THE SPECIFICS ON EMPOWERMENT

Then again our teacher gave instruction to the entourage who were none other than his own true nature:

The Bodhicitta has no good or evil.
All dharmas are Tathagatas.
We do not move from a state of equality,
But in the way of the three:
Outer,
Inner,
And secret,
We rely on the material in a mandala
To impart the empowerment of the implements for the empowerment,
Then we generate the Bodhicitta of great bliss.
We do not turn away from the objectives of the Secret Mantra.
This is well-known as "the external empowerment."

To teach about the inner empowerment:
From our ordinary body we transform into a god.
Our self acquires the empowerment of the god in our own body.
Through meditation we become clear as being gods.
When this happens,
The body that is holding onto a self does not remain.
When our body has been empowered into being a god,
We let out our intentions
Into the grounds where the empowerment is happening,
And the Master imparts the empowerment.

The teachings on knowledge and taking this into our experience
Are explained to one who is called a "recipient."

The actual event that is called an "empowerment"
Is not something that anyone else does.
The wisdom of awareness is present in ourselves.
It does not change due to the power of our emotional problems.
It is because we have it in ourselves
That it is called an "empowerment."
We are not empowered by anyone else,
So it is called an "empowerment."
We empower ourselves,
So we are empowered.

There is something that is famous
That is called a "secret empowerment,"
But we acquire it by its natural force.
It is just when our own body is clear as being a god
That we inherently do not abide in any grasping at a self.
The self-empowerment of wisdom is a perfect mandala.
Self-aware wisdom enables self-empowerment.
This is a jewel treasure of inexhaustible wonders.

The empowerment makes a transformation
In the wheels of our bodies, speech, and minds.
That is why it is called an "empowerment."
The reason that it is kept secret
Is that by the grace of the power of an invisible substance
All of the Tathagatas appear from themselves,
And act to give birth.

If we teach this topic to those of small intellects,
Who are of the mean vehicles,
They will be afraid,
And there is the risk that we will become slothful.
If we keep it secret, we will succeed.
This is why it is presented as a "secret empowerment."

So he spoke.

From the Royal Tantra on the Brilliant Diffusion of Majestic Space, this is chapter thirty-seven: Teaching the Specifics on Empowerment.

SAMAYA ARE NOT TO BE NUMBERED OR PROTECTED

Then again our teacher, the Blessed One, gave instruction to his entourage, who were none other than himself:

The Bodhicitta is free from faults.
It teaches all the Dharmas:
The teachings that are not to be taught,
And the teachings that are to be taught.

The Bodhicitta has no faults,
But by force of the work to train,
There are a variety of methods.
These have been proclaimed by the Buddhas of the three times.

This is the majestic treasure of the meaning of the upadeśa instructions:

Samaya is called "samaya."
This is not something that is kept in reserve.
Our own view is our samaya.
All the dharmas that appear and are well known in the world
Are subsumed within our own minds,
So by not transgressing them,
We acquire self-empowerment.
We know that they have no transgression or failing,
So things will appear just as we visualize them.

This also turns out to be the base or cause
For the totality of everything,
Nothing excluded,
So it is our own Bodhicitta.
It turns out to be the true basis of all samsara and nirvana,
Their source of origin.

At the moment we acquire self-empowerment by ourselves
Everything, with no exceptions, is the Bodhicitta.
This is our own miracle,
So we have no anxiety about samsara and nirvana.

Not to transgress this is our samaya.
When we are dwelling on the meaning of this,
However we may see and however we may be known,
However we are designated and however we may be attached,
However we meditate and however we practice,
However we abide and are present,
We do not transgress the meaning of this.
That is what is called "samaya."

To be absent,
To be plain,
To be alone,
And to be spontaneously realized.

This is what is called "the samaya of absence:"
When an object and one who keeps an object are both absent,
There is nothing to protect and no borders of protection.

The samaya of plainness has the true nature
Of having no borders to protect.
We do not conceptualize virtue and non-virtue.
We have no problems about failure,
And no virtues in not failing.
It is because we have no faults or virtues
That we are plain.

The samaya of being alone
Is that we have no experience or non-experience,
So we have neither faults nor virtues.
Everything is at one within us,
So even the objects that we would protect are alone.

The self that is protecting them is simply alone.
The problems in our experience are also alone.
The wonders that we do not experience are simply alone.
Nothing goes beyond ourselves,
So this is called "the samaya of being alone."

The samaya that are spontaneously realized
Are that when everything is simply present within us
We have no other objects,
So we do not visualize any extremes.
The reality that is beyond extremes has no position,
So even the things we have to protect are gathered within this.
Even the things we do not have to protect are gathered within this.
Even the faults and virtues of our experience and non-experience
Are gathered into this,
So it is spontaneously realized.

Not to transgress this is the supreme samaya.
The three times are not separate from this,
So we do not give any name to our vows.
We have no preferences on the faults and virtues of the Dharma.

People will experience a clinging to their intellects.
This is why a variety of trainings have been proclaimed
As remedies for our taking things in and holding onto them.

As for what we must protect with our bodies,
We must not be contemptuous
Toward the guru who teaches us the upadeśa instructions,
Or toward our vajra kindred.

As for what we must protect with our speech,
We must not say unpleasant things, even in private,
And we should also give up on idle chatter.

As for what we must protect with our minds,
We must not have cause to be desirous, hateful, evil minded, or jealous,
Even for an instant.
We use an assortment of pleasing things
To make offerings that are brilliantly delightful.

The root and branch samaya
That are held in common in the scriptures of the Secret Mantra,

Being the proclamations of the Victorious Ones,
Are clear.

This Ati is primordially protected,
So even if we protect it there will be no fault.
It is our adornment.
If we do not protect it there is no fault.
It cannot be transgressed.
As it has no transgression or failure,
It is beyond any borders of protection.
It has no borders or limits,
So it diffuses into bliss.
This is the samaya of the diffusion into the space of great bliss.

So he spoke.

From the Royal Tantra on the Brilliant Diffusion of Majestic Space, this is chapter thirty-eight: Samaya Are Not to Be Numbered or Protected.

TEACHINGS ON TOUCHING AND MEETING WITH THE THREE EMBODIMENTS

Then again the Blessed One spoke on his own purpose to his entourage, which was none other than himself:

Because it lacks the extremes of birth and destruction,
The majestic space of effortlessness is the state of the sky.
Because it lacks any divisions or clarifications,
Anything to take up or to remove,
It is an expansive space that is like an island of gold.
Because it dawns on us without having any outside or inside,
The Bodhicitta lacks the extreme of failure.
Because it clears away the darkness of the extremes,
The lamp of wisdom shines within our dominion.

The Bodhicitta does not reject the four extremes,
So it not touched by the problems there are with the extremes.
By its force, we cut through all the grounds for deviation.
In the mind itself,
Which has no crevasses,
The three bodies are spontaneously perfected,
Without any search,
But we give them the names of samsara and nirvana,
And use their having causes and results
To cling to differences.

The Royal Tantra on the Brilliant Diffusion of Majestic Space

The six classes of living beings,
Through the four abodes of birth,
Are the miracles
Of the brilliant diffusion of the dominion of the Dharma.

We are born from this dominion,
And we hold onto this dominion.
What we take in and what we hold onto,
The object and the mind,
Are different,
But in being the miracles
Of the brilliant diffusion of the dominion of the Dharma,
We are born from this dominion,
And we hold onto this dominion,
While in the state of this dominion
There is nothing to take in
And nothing to hold onto.

The inspirations of the Buddhas of the three times
And the extent of the knowledge of the Sugatas
Arise from this dominion,
And are known within this dominion.

Unhindered knowing is the dominion of the Dharma.
Unhindered things to be known are the effulgence of awareness.
An encounter with our body, speech, and mind occurs,
And our space is a self-liberation that has no duality.

The circle is the Bodhicitta itself.
It is the true basis for the totality of everything.
Its unhindered characteristics may appear to be anything.
In the varieties of the Dharma, nothing is definite.
When we see our own senses nakedly,
Their reality is clear.

The relaxation of appearances is the river of the awareness.
We dwell in a space of blissful self-understanding.
The pristine six bodies[16] dawn on us.
Our wisdom is self-evident.

This is the space of our reality.

---

[16] sKu drug

The Royal Tantra on the Brilliant Diffusion of Majestic Space

It is not to be obstructed.
It is clear without having any outside or inside.
In the mirror of the self-aware mind,
The appearance of a self-evident dominion arises.
We do not transgress ourselves,
So from the beginning we are neither distracted nor not distracted.

Sitting in our uncontrived natural state,
Our own way is clear.
With an inner relaxation of our bodies and minds,
We settle into whatever we like.

Our knowledge is fearless.
We do not search.
We live like the people who have no work.
In a reality that is neither rigid nor relaxed,
We settle our bodies and minds on whatever we like,
And we are happy.

No matter how we sit,
That is our state.
No matter how we move,
That is our state.
In all our paths of behavior:
Moving, sitting, eating, and walking,
We do not move away from self-evident space.

This self-evident Bodhicitta
Is inherently lacking in any going or coming.
The body of the Victorious One does not go or come.

No matter what I say,
I am saying it to myself.
No matter what I speak on,
I am speaking to myself.
No matter how I am perfect,
I am perfect for myself.
I talk and speak to myself by myself.

In the Bodhicitta there is no talking or speaking.
The unspeakable is the speech of the Victorious One.

No matter what I think about,

The Royal Tantra on the Brilliant Diffusion of Majestic Space

It is my own state.
No matter what I investigate,
It is my own understanding.
In the Bodhicitta there is no thought or understanding.
Freedom from thoughts and understandings
Is the mind of the Victorious One.

Anything at all may appear from nothing.
This is well-known as the "manifest embodiment."
I make myself feel pleasure by myself.
This is called the "embodiment of perfect pleasure."
It has no real basis,
So it is called the "embodiment of the Dharma."
The three embodiments that are our rewards
Are spontaneously realized,
So they are taught to be a single indivisible space.

Everything comes forth from the space of spontaneous realization.
All the forms of the external, the internal,
And of birth and motion,
Are embodied without position.
We play in our bodies.
They are wheels of inexhaustible adornments.

Grammar and logic are well-known
To be excellent, average, or poor.
Our speech has no position.
We play in our speech.
It is a wheel of inexhaustible adornments.

In the indivisible ultimate truth
We are one in essence.
Our minds have no position.
We play in our minds.
They are wheels of inexhaustible adornments.

Our virtues, good works, and all the rest
Have no position.
They are self-originating for everyone.

It accomplishes everything that we desire,
So the dominion of the Dharma is a precious jewel.
From the base,

We do not search for this,
So everything is self-originating and self-evident.

It transforms into anything we desire.
It is the glory of compassion.
It subsumes everything,
With no exceptions,
So it is the root of every Dharma,
The Bodhicitta.

It is neither to be joined with nor parted from,
So it is the embodiment of the Dharma.
It is non-dual,
So it is the Bodhicitta.
We have no self or other,
So it is equanimity.

The dominion of the Dharma has no position or preference.
It works equally for everyone.
It is the glory of compassion.
Everything is encompassed by the Bodhicitta.
It carries the welfare of living beings to the end.
Our good works are perfected in the Bodhicitta.
It has no passing on or change.
It is the embodiment of the Dharma.
The unborn shines within the dominion of the Dharma.

In the dominion of the Dharma there is no high or low.
No matter what it appears to be,
It is a space of equality.
In the Bodhicitta there is no above or below.
It has no mouth or bottom.
It is the dominion of the Dharma.

This dominion may arise as anything,
Whether external or internal,
But in the space of effortlessness,
There is no outside or inside.
This pristine indivisibility is a space of unity.

In this space of unity we may practice anything.
We see ourselves,
And we meet and touch.

We practice ourselves,
And we meet and touch.
It is like the teeth on a razor and like an elephant.
We ourselves cut through our cravings by ourselves.

So he spoke.

From the Royal Tantra on the Brilliant Diffusion of Majestic Space, this is chapter thirty-nine: Teachings on Touching and Meeting with the Three Embodiments.

THERE ARE NO APPLICATIONS FOR THE SIX COLLECTIONS

Then the Blessed One once again gave instruction:

The three times have no birth or ending,
So there are no breaks in the continuum
Of the dominion of the Dharma.
It is an unchanging and uncompounded space.
It overcomes all the extremes.
It is a blazing and majestic vajra hammer.
It bedazzles every position.
It is the king of all the upadeśa instructions.
It brings forth the Buddhas of the three times,
So the wisdom of our awareness is the dominion of the Dharma.

It bedazzles our taking things in and holding onto them,
So the self-awareness of emptiness
Is the space of enlightenment.
All the enumerations of the wonders of its greatness,
However many there may be,
And with no exception,
Are our own dominion emerging from our own dominion.
This is the supreme method.

Unhindered self-evidence is the ornament of our playfulness.
It is the unborn dominion of all things.
It is the majestic and spontaneously perfected

Embodiment of the Dharma.
It bedazzles entities,
So emptiness is a space for the Bodhicitta.

The dominion of emptiness has no obstructions.
It is the measure of the knowledge
Of the Victorious Ones of the three times.
To crave for an absence is the extreme of emptiness.
Bedazzling self-awareness is the space of enlightenment.

In the true nature of the Bodhicitta
Appearance and emptiness are non-dual from the beginning.
We do not see any two extremes.
This is beyond conceptualizations.
We are liberated from the extremes that may be visualized,
So a non-dual lack of craving is the Bodhicitta.

Compassion brings forth inconceivable miracles.
Without hindering the four extremes,
It bedazzles them.

It is equal to the great,
And it is equal to the small.
It is the Bodhicitta.
Because it is equal,
Its greatness is equal to the great.

The embodiment of the Dharma is neither great nor small.
It is not to be visualized,
So it is like the sky.
It may reveal its works and practices to be anything.
The manifestations of unhindered compassion
Are embodiments that are not defined.
They may appear as anything.
They are my own playfulness.

I practice playfulness
As an embodiment of perfect pleasure.
I am served by myself.
No matter what I do,
It is a space for my three embodiments.

The Royal Tantra on the Brilliant Diffusion of Majestic Space

The uncompounded is the dominion of the Dharma.
The three embodiments arise from this dominion by themselves.
Samsara and nirvana also arise within us.
We do not move from this state.

Reality that is self-evident and self-liberating
Bedazzles all our demarcations.
The unchanging majestic space of the mind itself
Encompasses us in totality,
Like the space of the sky.

Our playfulness is undefined.
It may arise as anything.
The inexhaustible space of the miracle of compassion
Appears as an ornament for the dominion of totality.

There are no dharmas other than this dominion,
So we are beyond any objects that are negated
In their being anything else.
Our six sensory collections are liberated into their own place,
So we bedazzle any ideas there may be about demarcations.

Appearances are not restricted,
So their condensation and expansion
Is the effulgence of the Bodhicitta.
The reality that is not anything at all
May appear to be any of the many things,
So the effortless Dharma is amazing and astounding.

Everyone has been empowered with all the vehicles
Of samsara and nirvana.
The effortless Dharma uses our own power
To effortlessly be one,
And to bedazzle all the extremes.

In this, there are no extremes or other objects.
We do not move anywhere other than the space of effortlessness.
Freedom from all the extremes is total freedom.
The indivisibility of samsara and nirvana is All Good.

In the space of the All Good
There is no samsara or nirvana.
The indivisibility of birth and death is All Good.

In the space of the All Good
There is no birth or death.
The indivisibility of happiness and sorrow is All Good.

In the space of the All Good
There is no happiness or sorrow.
Self, other, permanence, annihilation,
And all the rest:
They are indivisible.
They are All Good.

In the space of the All Good
There is no self or other.
In the space of the unborn
There is no permanence or annihilation.
To grasp at something that is non-existent
As being existent
Is a delusional designation.

Everything is All Good,
And is spontaneously realized.
We arise from a unity.
This is great bliss.

All the extremes,
With no exceptions,
Are liberated into their own place.
The demarcations of taking things in and holding onto them
Are bedazzled.
All the extremes,
None excepted,
Are one in this dominion.

We are alone and have no rivals.
We are supreme and are brilliantly majestic.
We are the embodiment of the Dharma,
The greatest of the great.
We are naturally present.

The spaciousness of the All Good
Is the dominion of the Dharma.
It is like a king.

The Royal Tantra on the Brilliant Diffusion of Majestic Space

It does not move.
It bedazzles all our demarcations.

It has taken all samsara and nirvana under its control,
But it does not move from the intent of equality.
All things are one within the All Good.
What is not good as well as what is good are one.
The All Good has no good or evil.

Even disunity is unity in their being one.
All things are gathered into this spontaneous realization.
Even those that are unrealized are gathered into this realization.

In spontaneously realized equanimity
There is no realization or non-realization.
We are one.

From the one,
The many arise.
Everything arises without preference.
This is the dominion of the Dharma.

In the dominion of the Dharma there is nothing to do.
The dominion is itself a unity.
It is not to be sought after.
Searching and working on things arise up out of our own dominion.
They are not to be sought anywhere else,
So what do we seek?
On what do we work?

Working on things and seeking for them
Are our own minds.
There are no objects to seek for.
They appear to us ourselves.

Through meditation we do not see anything else.
There is no basis for working on things.
There is no abode for it.
There is nothing whatever that comes from somewhere else.

The embodiment of the Dharma does not go or come.
There is no falling away from the meaning of equality.
We are beyond extremes,

So there is no self or other.

So he spoke.

From the Royal Tantra on the Brilliant Diffusion of Majestic Space, this is chapter forty: There Are No Applications for the Six Collections.

THE SUPREME PRACTICE

Then again our teacher gave instruction to his entourage:

Miracles are called "miracles."
They occur out of our concern for what we are working on.
If we are working on something definite,
There is only one.

Buddhas arise from themselves.
We work on our own rewards.
Through working on them,
We do not acquire them from anyone else.
We succeed at our own rewards.

There is no duality of a self and an other.
We work on our own results by ourselves.
Our virtues are perfected in ourselves,
So we work on our own rewards by ourselves.
Our remedies are not with anyone else,
So we work on our own rewards by ourselves.

For the methods by which we must work on things
There are what are called "retreats," "close retreats,"
"Practices," and "great practices."
That which is called the "rite of a retreat"
Is the Bodhicitta of the Atiyoga.

Samsara and nirvana are not a duality,
So on the level of Buddhahood,
We are primordially in retreat.

Self-originating wisdom dawns on us,
So in a state of our understanding,
We are primordially in retreat.

The three embodiments turn out to be real,
So in our supreme status,
We are primordially in retreat.

We do not take up or put down any dharmas,
So in our equanimity,
We are primordially in retreat.

We do not cling to any preference between appearance and emptiness,
So in our indivisibility,
We are primordially in retreat.

In our definite understanding
There are no others,
So in our supreme contemplations,
We are primordially in retreat.

The Ati is a self-originating retreat.
This is called a "close retreat:"

We use chants that are not spoken
For a close retreat into the space of not speaking.

We use a samadhi that is not to be visualized
For a close retreat on non-abiding.

We use a mudra that may transform into anything at all
For a close retreat on being without grasping and attachment.

We use the blessings of our own majestic way
For a close retreat on being without breaks in our continuum.

We use the miracle of majestic playfulness
For a close retreat on seeing what is real.

The Royal Tantra on the Brilliant Diffusion of Majestic Space

We use an understanding of warmth that is not to be experienced
For a close retreat on being without desire.

The Ati is a self-originating close retreat.

As for the thing that is called a "practice:"

In the mandala of self-originating wisdom
We set up gods who are our own self-evident playfulness,
Then we get together implements that have no causes or conditions,
And use understandings that have no basic root
To do a practice on effortless majestic space.

In the mandala of the expansive space of reality
We set up gods that are our own unhindered playfulness,
Then we get together the implements for both samsara and nirvana,
And we do a practice on the meaning of indivisibility.

In the mandala of our spontaneously realized true nature,
We set up gods for the dominion of the unborn,
Then we get together the implements of a multitude of appearances,
And we do a practice that is not to be visualized.

In the mandala of the Bodhicitta
We set up gods who are the great bliss
Of the embodiment of the Dharma,
Then we get together the implements for uncompounded deities,
And do a practice on the absence of birth and death.

The apparent world is a dharma for the five elements.
The majestic element is the Blessed One.
He brings forth everything we wish for.
He is a precious one.
It is through the compassion of the five elements
That a multitude of harvests of juicy fruits ripens.
The reward for our practice is the five good things we desire.
This is the virtue of ordinary practice.

The rewards for special practices
Are a space in which our three embodiments have no birth or death.
They have been present from the beginning,
So it is not necessary to practice for them.

The Royal Tantra on the Brilliant Diffusion of Majestic Space

For a spontaneously realized reward without any practice
There is what is called a "great practice."

We enter through the doors of the Bodhisattvas,
And purify ourselves for ten million eons,
And we may even succeed at reaching Total Light.
We do not harbor any external or internal obscurations or coverings,
And the virtue there is in this is a Total Light.
Without working on it,
We abide in a spontaneously realized reward.

We enter through the doors of the Kriya Tantra,
And practice for seven human lifetimes,
But we do not succeed at even becoming a Vajradhāra.
We have nothing to join to or to separate from,
And we are indestructible.
The virtue there is in this is that we are Vajradhāras.
Without working on it,
We abide in a spontaneously realized reward.

We enter through the doors of the Both Tantra,[17]
And by being connected to higher and lower views and practices
We work on a vajra samadhi,
But we have no connection
To an immersion that retains what is not empty.
The virtue there is in this is that we are Vajradhāras.
Without working on it,
We abide in a spontaneously realized reward.

We enter through the doors of the Yoga Tantra,
Then we practice for five human lifetimes,
And in this we succeed at reaching Dense Array,
But by an unpolluted complete perfection,
We already have the wonder of Dense Array.

We enter through the doors of the Mahā Yoga,
Then we practice for three or two human lifetimes,
And we succeed at reaching Lotus Keeper in them.
We see an unerring wisdom that has no position.
The virtue there is in this is Lotus Eyes.
Without working on it,

---

[17] Also known as the Upa Yoga.

We abide in a spontaneously realized reward.

We enter through the door of the Comprehensive Yoga,[18]
Then we practice for one human lifetime,
And there is the Great Mass of Letter Wheels.
We succeed at self-originating wisdom.
The unborn wheel of the Dharma
And its turning without any break in its continuum
Have the virtues of the two accumulations,
While they are a Great Mass of Letter Wheels.
Without our working on it,
We abide in a spontaneously realized reward.

All of these are indivisible.
They are one within the All Good One,
So there is also the level of indivisibility.

From the beginning,
It has been present within us,
And we surmount it here in the present,
So the majestic practice is that of the All Good.
It is the practice of a self-originating objective.
Its good works are free from efforts and searches.

Our emotional problems are pacified into their own place,
So the Bodhicitta is famous for its peace.
Its works are growing into excellence,
So the Bodhicitta is famous for its growth.
Our awareness achieves self-empowerment,
So the Bodhicitta is famous for its power.
We cut through our delusions at the root,
So our Bodhicitta is a wrathful one.

So he spoke.

From the Royal Tantra on the Brilliant Diffusion of Majestic Space, this is chapter forty-one: The Supreme Practice.

---

[18] Also known as the Anu Yoga

TEACHING THE TRANSMISSION THAN WHICH THERE IS NO HIGHER

Then again the Blessed One gave instruction:

Do not sit.
Look at the space of your mind.
The mind itself is a measureless palace of majestic space.
We do not see it by looking at it.
When we settle,
It is clear.
Any place that we settle is a natural bliss.

Do not sit.
Meditate on the space of your mind.
We do not get clear by meditating.
We get clear by settling.
Any place that we settle we are happy with ourselves.

Do not sit.
Practice on the space of your mind.
Through practice we do not finish.
Through settling we finish.
Any place that we settle we are happy with ourselves.

Do not sit.
Work on the space of your mind.
We do not find this by working on it.

The Royal Tantra on the Brilliant Diffusion of Majestic Space

We lose it by seeking for it.
In a space that is not to be visualized
We are happy.

No matter how we look at it,
It is a space of great bliss.
The space of great bliss has no wide or narrow.

However we may meditate,
It is a state of great bliss.
The state of great bliss has no break in its continuum.

No matter how we practice,
It is the dominion of great bliss.
The dominion of great bliss has no deeds or searches.

No matter how we work on it,
It is a space of great bliss.
The space of great bliss has no passing away or changing.

Our view is a majestic space,
A most spacious space.
Our meditation is a majestic space,
Profound and most deep.
Our practice is a majestic space,
Forceful and most fierce.
Our result is a majestic space,
Transforming into everything we desire.

The majestic space of our ideas
Is a most happy intellect.
We have no place to put our experiences,
So do not take positions or preferences for your views!

The mind has no base or support,
So do not tie down your samadhi with a referent for visualization!
Self and others are not a duality,
So do not practice taking things up and putting them down!
Samsara and nirvana have no division or clarification,
So do not seek hopes and fears in your rewards!

In the inside of the sky,
Nothing emerges.

The Royal Tantra on the Brilliant Diffusion of Majestic Space

In the inside of our own minds,
There is no Buddha.
The things that emerge are the miracles of the sky.
Buddhas are the miracles of the mind.
Even the totality of sentient beings
Are our own minds.

In the inside of the sky,
Nothing emerges.
In the inside of our minds,
There is no view.
The things that emerge are the miracles of the sky.
Views are the miracles of the mind.
There is nothing to see.
This is our own mind.

In the inside of the sky,
Nothing emerges.
In the inside of our minds,
There is no samadhi.
Samadhi is a miracle of our minds.
Non-meditation is also our own minds.

In the inside of the sky,
Nothing emerges.
In the inside of our minds,
There is no practice.
Practice is a miracle of the mind.
Non-practice is also our own minds.

In the inside of the sky,
Nothing emerges.
What emerges is the miracle of the sky.
In the inside of our own minds
There are no rewards.
Our rewards are the miracles of our minds.

Our not working on things is also our own minds.
The five elements are also the dominion of the sky.
The outer and inner vessel and contents are the dominion of the sky.
The five kinds of good things that we desire
Are the dominion of the sky.
The dominion of the sky is also the space of our minds.

The Royal Tantra on the Brilliant Diffusion of Majestic Space

Buddhas and sentient beings are the space of our minds.
Samsara and nirvana are the space of our minds.
The outer and inner vessel and contents are the space of our minds.
Happiness and sorrow are the space of our minds.
Birth and death, self and other, are the space of our minds.
View, meditation, practice, and result are the space of our minds.

In the space of our minds there is no birth or death.
Because there is no birth or death,
It is like the sky.

The space of our minds does not pass away or change.
Because it does not pass away or change,
It is like a vajra.
The mountain of the vajra is not destroyed or broken.

On the trunk of spontaneously realized positionlessness
The leaves of both samsara and nirvana grow.
In the sky that is effortless and is not to be seized,
The sun and moon of the heart-essence of the three embodiments rise.
The city of the delusions of the six classes of living beings
Is a Buddha field of great bliss.
In the sprouts of our designations of what we take in
And what we hold onto,
The fruit, which is the embodiment of the Dharma of great bliss, ripens.

The six classes of living beings and their four abodes of birth
Are manifest Buddhas,
So their Bodhicitta is not to be stopped.

The earth, water, fire, and wind:
The four elements,
Are for the sake of the welfare of living beings.
The Blessed Ones actually do appear as the perfection of pleasure.
Their Bodhicitta is not to be stopped.

Markings are not present in the space of the sky.
It is not to be visualized,
So the embodiment of the Dharma is something that actually appears.
This is the true nature of the Bodhicitta.

The Royal Tantra on the Brilliant Diffusion of Majestic Space

Lust, hatred, stupidity, pride, jealousy,
And all the rest:
The five poisons and the three poisons of our emotional problems
Are the actual appearance of self-originating wisdom.
The space of enlightenment is not to be stopped.

The dharmas of the apparent world:
Samsara and nirvana, cause and result,
Are our awareness coming forth as something real,
So the space of enlightenment is not to be stopped.

To put this significance into order,
There are interpretable meanings and definitive meanings.
The Anu on down
May use self-awareness
To say anything about their validations for the truth,
But they do not put it into order.
They are ensnared by heavy grasping,
And they have lost their hold on reality.
They view things in terms of positions,
So their intellects are deluded.
Playfulness arises without any position,
But they cling to extremes.
This is the Mara that ensnares them.

When we crave for existence,
We get the extreme of permanence.
When we crave for non-existence,
We get the extreme of annihilation.
When our intellects crave
For the duality of permanence and annihilation,
This is grounds for deviation from the heart-essence of enlightenment.

I have put this into order definitively.
All the dharmas of the apparent world:
Samsara and nirvana,
Are spontaneously realized without rejecting their basis,
So positionlessness is put in order as being pure.

Our essence is not definite,
So self-originating wisdom puts it into order.
In its significance it is unborn,
So it is put into order as being without any clinging to dualities.

Our true selves are beyond beginnings and endings,
So there are no beginnings or endings,
No previous or later,
And in the absence of birth, death, and transfer,
We have put them into order.
For this reason we are victorious over all the lesser vehicles.

The Ati is the validation of primordial liberation.
The teaching of the validation of what this means
Will depend on the instructions of the Victorious Ones.
Through their blessings there is a lineage.
The profound aural lineage is a definitive transmission.
It is a description of the meaning of the Atiyoga.

So he spoke.

From the Royal Tantra on the Brilliant Diffusion of Majestic Space, this is chapter forty-two: Teaching the Transmission than Which There Is No Higher.

RECOGNITION OF THE FIVE EMBODIMENTS AND THE FIVE GREATNESSES

Then again the Blessed One gave instruction to the entourage that was none other than himself:

O Mother,
The spacious Dharma of the Mahayana
Has arisen for everyone.
It liberates everyone.
It is most amazing.

When appearances arise,
We see reality.
I see what I did not see before.

When sorrows arise,
We see great bliss.
Happiness and sorrow are non-dual,
And unchanging reality arises as an appearance.
I see what I did not see before.

When sentient beings arise,
We see Buddhas.
Buddhas and sentient beings are non-dual,
And unchanging reality arises as an appearance.

When samsara arises,
We see nirvana.
Samsara and nirvana are non-dual,
And unchanging reality arises as appearance.
I see what I did not see before.

When the holder of a dharma arises,
I see reality.
When emotional problems arise,
I see wisdom.
Emotional problems and wisdom are non-dual,
And unchanging reality arises as appearance.

There are these and all the rest.
Everything that is gathered into dualities
Is entirely unhindered.
Reality arises as appearances.

When we open up our understanding of the bodies of sentient beings
We will pierce through to a vision of the bodies of Buddhas.
Buddhas and sentient beings are non-dual.

When we open up our understanding of the entities that appear,
We will pierce through to a vision of the dominion of emptiness.
Appearance and emptiness are non-dual.

When we open up our understanding of the demarcations of suffering,
We will pierce through to a vision of the finest great bliss.
Happiness and suffering are non-dual.

When we open up our understanding
Of the demarcation of being a subject,
We will pierce through to a vision of positionless reality.
Subjects and reality are non-dual.

When we open up our understanding
Of the demarcations of emotional problems,
We will pierce through to a vision of self-originating wisdom.
Emotional problems and wisdom are non-dual.

These and the rest of all the dharmas
Are non-dual and are unchanging.
They are the arising of the appearance of me.

The Royal Tantra on the Brilliant Diffusion of Majestic Space

Reality is non-dual.
These and the rest of all the dharmas are indivisible.
We are liberated into our own place.

Both cause and result are unhindered,
But this is beyond both cause and result.
Samsara and nirvana are unhindered,
But we are liberated from both samsara and nirvana.

Further,
You may ask how we are liberated from them.

Sentient beings appear to be substantial,
But they are placed in order as being insubstantial Buddhas.

Sentient beings are more important than Buddhas.
When we have made a determination in the space of non-duality,
We will also believe that we are liberated into our own place.

Appearance is more important than emptiness.
Indefinite appearances are self-evident,
So emptiness is put into order as not to be grasped.
When we have made a determination in the space of non-duality
We will also believe that we are liberated into our own place.

Sorrow is more important than happiness.
It is through the demarcations of sorrow, craving, and attachment
That we put into order great bliss and non-attachment.
When we have received the instructions, we will believe them.
When we have made a determination in non-duality,
We will also believe that we are liberated into our own place.

Subjects are more important than reality.
Our demarcations for a subject are our own continuum,
So we put unborn reality into order.
Subjects and realities are indivisible,
So when we have made a determination in the space of non-duality
We will also believe that we are liberated into our own place.

Emotional problems are more important than wisdom.
It is by the nooses that ensnare us in emotional problems
That self-originating wisdom is put into order.

The Royal Tantra on the Brilliant Diffusion of Majestic Space

Emotional problems and wisdom are inseparable,
So when we have made a determination in the space of non-duality,
We will also believe that we are liberated into our own place.

These and all the rest of the dharmas:
Throughout all time they are indivisible.
When we have made a determination in the space of non-duality
We will believe that we are liberated into our own place,
And when we have made a determination about these beliefs
Our experience of understanding will be a happy intellect.

There is no liberation from this dominion,
So when we throw off our heaps,
We will be liberated in this dominion.
There is no changing away from space.

The dharmas that we demarcate are only names.
Everything is liberated into the space of totality.

Sentient beings are liberated into the space of Buddhas.
There is no break in our continuum,
So we are manifest embodiments.

Appearances are liberated into the space of emptiness.
There is no break in our continuum.
We are perfect enjoyment.

Subjects are liberated into the dominion of reality.
There is no break in our continuum.
We are embodiments of the Dharma.

Sorrow is liberated into the dominion of great bliss.
There is no break in our continuum.
We are embodiments of the vajra.

Emotional problems are liberated into the space of wisdom.
There is no break in our continuum.
This is described to be truly
The embodiment of enlightenment.

Further,
The manifest embodiment is not to be defined
According to any characteristics.

The embodiment of pleasure abides in the state of great bliss.
The embodiment of the Dharma has no demarcations.
The embodiment of the vajra is beyond destruction or violation.
The embodiment of the Bodhicitta has no birth or death.

Further,
They are designated through what they mean.
Because there is no form,
There is the space of enlightenment.
It has no color or shape to be apprehended.
It has no characteristics,
So it is like the sky.

In the dominion of the Dharma,
We are primordially Buddhas.
We bring forth miracles,
So we are like the sky.

In the Great Spirit,[19]
We are primordial Buddhas.
We are non-dual,
So we are like the sky.

In being this,
We are primordial Buddhas.
We do not stay anywhere,
So we are like the sky.

In actuality,
We are primordial Buddhas.
We do not depend on anything at all.
We do not help or harm anything at all.
Everything is equal,
So we are like the sky.

Everything comes from everything,
So the Buddha has no Buddhahood.
In the expansive and majestic space of the mind itself
Where there are all the dharmas,
With no exceptions:
Samsara and nirvana,

---

[19] bDag nyid chen po. Sanskrit: Mahātman

In our five greatnesses
We are actually Buddhas.

So he spoke.

From the Royal Tantra on the Brilliant Diffusion of Majestic Space, this is chapter forty-three: Recognition of the Five Embodiments and the Five Greatnesses.

EVERYTHING IS PERFECTION WITHOUT END

Then again I gave instruction to my entourage:

In this spacious door of the Secret Mantra
There are no imperfect Dharmas at all.
The Dharmas of samsara and nirvana
Are from the beginning non-dual and perfect.

The Dharmas of cause and the Dharmas of result
Are from the beginning indivisible and perfect.

The Dharmas that we teach and the Dharmas that we work on
Are from the beginning without a system,
And are perfect.

Ultimate Dharmas are not to be worked on,
From the beginning we have not worked on them,
And are perfect.

Happiness and sorrow have a similar cause, and are perfect.
Compounded dharmas and the uncompounded
Are from the beginning neither good nor evil,
And are perfect.

Dharmas that are white and Dharmas that are black
From the beginning are not to be taken up or rejected,
And are perfect.

The Royal Tantra on the Brilliant Diffusion of Majestic Space

Subjects and realities,
The relative and the ultimate Dharmas,
From the beginning are not to be hindered or worked on,
And are perfect.

Emotional problems and wisdom,
Those that are born into and shiver within the apparent world,
And all the Dharmas,
In which nothing is impossible:
In the center of the space of self-originating wisdom
There is nothing that is not perfect.

The great perfection is spontaneously realized.
It is unsurpassed.
When we have made a determination in equanimity,
All things are, in fact, self-originating wisdom.

In time,
There is no previous or later.
The Ati cuts the three times into one.
The Anu on down are the lower ones.
They count for an eon,
And they count for a human lifetime.
They believe that results come from causes,
But we do not reject them.
We bring them together into one.
So there are no differences in the three times.
They have a single true nature,
So we are liberated into space.

In this state our continuums are unbroken.
In the true nature in which our continuums are unbroken,
Samsara and nirvana are equal.
We have no preferences,
So we do not look for anything else.

This is the reality of primordial Buddhahood.
In this we enjoy ourselves.
This is the reward of a positionless majestic treasure.

There are various kinds of sorrow in samsara,
But they are trifling realities.
A reward of great bliss dawns on us.

With the exception of this,
We have no rewards.

The thing that we call "most pure"
Is also called "the mandala of the Victorious One."
It is nowhere other than the space of equanimity.

Our field of practice is indivisible.
This itself manifests as the field of the Victorious Ones,
So do not seek your rewards anywhere else!

Have no hope.
Have no fear.
Be completely liberated!

The mind itself is a self-originating wisdom.
Its self-evidence arises without a position.
When we do not understand that it has a single true nature,
For some it is there.
For some it is not.

The division of good and evil
Interferes with our equanimity.
We use our minds to understand that the Buddha is good,
And so we understand that sentient beings are evil,
But in essence there is no good or evil.
This is certainly true,
But in the intellects of people good and evil do appear.
Good and evil are conceptualizations of the mind.

Conceptualizations and emotional problems
Are the Dharmas of samsara.
If we understand them,
There is nothing to reject,
So they are like the sky.
They are like miracles.

In the space of equanimity there are no differences.
The continuum of indivisible playfulness is not broken.

There are the playfulness of our natural dominion,
The playfulness of the force of compassion,
And self-originating self-evident playfulness.

The playfulness of our natural dominion
Is that we have appeared from the beginning
To be both samsara and nirvana.

The playfulness of the force of compassion
Is that we are unhindered in our concern for our disciples,
We work without position toward the welfare of living beings:
For sentient beings who are made from their own karma,
There are Buddhas who are made from the karma of their compassion.
They appear in the essence of their three manifestations.

Self-originating self-evident playfulness
Is that in reality,
The continuum of which is not broken,
There is no emptiness or decay.
It is like the space of the sky,
Or like a miracle.

There is no: "It is this,"
Or any: "It is not this."
We arise in purity, without any position.
We are self-originating and self-pacifying.
We are not definite.
We appear without having any cause or conditions.
We arise as if we were both causes and conditions.
We are liberated as if we were both a cause and a condition.
We arise as if we were both permanent and annihilated.
We are liberated as if we were both permanent and annihilated.
We arise as if we were both samsara and nirvana,
As if both samsara and nirvana had no liberation,
As if everything arose from itself,
And everything was liberated from itself.
We arise as being different,
And as being non-dual.
This is self-originating self-evident compassion.

We do not move from our dominion.
This is certainly true,
But we have been empowered into all of the Dharmas.
We have been empowered into all of the nations.
We have been empowered through all time.
We have been empowered over all events.

The Royal Tantra on the Brilliant Diffusion of Majestic Space

We have been empowered over all the vessels and their contents.
We have been empowered over all agglomerations.
This is also the playfulness of our compassion.

We have been empowered into the peace of the Buddha,
To turn the wheel of the Dharma,
To abide in the Dharma of peace,
And in the nirvana that has no outflows.
This is the playfulness of the dominion of compassion.

Great miracles are neither difficult nor easy.
Without hesitation they come forth from us.
They come forth without regard
To whether we are looking or are not looking.
They come forth without regard
To whether we are meditating or not meditating.
They come forth without regard
To whether we seek them or do not seek them.
They come forth without regard
To whether we work on them or do not work on them.

The field of the practice of self-originating wisdom
Is a positionless awareness,
So however it may appear,
We do not look for problems.

It has no outside or inside,
So it is beyond being an entity.
It is not hindered by anything at all.
It is not to be apprehended.
It dawns on us without any cause or conditions.

There is nothing to ask about.
This is difficult to investigate.
We do not hinder or work on anything.
It dawns on us as an equality,
So there is no good or evil.

The Dharmas are subsumed within the mind,
So Buddhas and sentient beings are a space of unity.
We arise in equality.
We are liberated in equality.
We have no good or evil.

The mind itself turns out to be the basis of all things.
The true nature of everything that happens is the mind.
The mind and the sky are indivisible.
This is presented as an analogy,
But in meaning, they are one.

We are perfect.
We are perfect.
We are perfect in the sky!
The five elements are perfected in the state of the sky.

We are perfected.
We are perfected.
We are perfected in our dominion!
The Dharmas are perfected in the dominion of the mind.

We are clear.
We are clear.
We are clear in the sky!
Entities are clear in the state of the sky.

We are clear.
We are clear.
We are clear in our dominion!
The Dharmas are clear in the dominion of enlightenment.

We are liberated.
We are liberated.
We are liberated into our dominion!
Our demarcations are liberated into the dominion of the Dharma.

Even the dharmas of the outer and inner vessel and contents
Are liberated into the space of the uncontrived mind.

Wisdom is not created.
It is self-originating.
It is clear.

We are liberated into the space of the unchanging circle.
Our mandala encompasses everything,
Both external and internal.
Even the dharmas of the outer and inner vessel and contents

The Royal Tantra on the Brilliant Diffusion of Majestic Space

That were not gathered together,
Are gathered into thusness.
Without being expanded upon,
This dawns on all samsara and nirvana.
Even the dharmas of samsara and nirvana,
The external and the internal
Are unborn and are totally pure from the primordial.

Unhindered awareness is clear to us.
Self-luminous awareness has no position.
We do not crave the duality of samsara and nirvana.
We do not crave the duality of cause and result,
So we are beyond the understanding of both former and later.
We do not crave the duality of faults and virtues,
So we are beyond the understanding of both help and harm.
We do not crave the duality of virtue and evil,
So we are beyond the understanding of both acceptance and rejection.

To be without conceptualizations and be without a position
Is the basis of all things.
The base is not present in the extreme of a base.
It is not present,
But it dawns on us.
It is the substance of all things.

Our own essence is not present in any extremes.
Non-duality is beyond births and endings,
So in our purpose we do not dwell on any extremes of purpose.

Unborn awareness has no object.
It has no previous or later,
No beginning or end,
So it does not abide in any true self.
We are free from beginnings and ends.
We also do not dwell on the extreme of being separate.
We are beyond the Dharmas of causes, conditions, and results.

This is a reality that is beyond any Dharma.
It arises in a space that has no causes or conditions.
Uncontrived great bliss
Is the embodiment of the Dharma.

So he spoke.

From the Royal Tantra on the Brilliant Diffusion of Majestic Space, this is chapter forty-four: Everything is Perfection Without End.

TEACHING THAT THERE IS ONE CHARACTERISTIC

Then again the Blessed One gave instruction to his entourage:

We do not move away from the dominion of our purpose.
We are naturally pure.
We are perfect Buddhas.

We are spontaneously realized,
So we cut through the levels of status.
We have no definition,
So we put things into order.
Our true nature is completely pure,
So we do not reject anything.
We are spontaneously realized.
We do not hinder anything at all.

We have no definition.
We do not dwell anywhere.
We are completely pure.
A single purity creates all things.

All dharmas are a dominion of total purity.
Our nature is spontaneously realized.
We do not hinder anything at all.
We have no definition.
Without dwelling anywhere we are completely pure.

Without rejecting anything we are spontaneously perfected.

A single spontaneous realization creates all things,
So the Dharmas are a dominion of spontaneous realization.
In our true natures we have no definition,
So without rejecting anything we are spontaneously realized.

We do not dwell anywhere.
We are completely pure.
We may arise as anything at all.
We have no definition.
A single indefinite thing creates all things,
So in the dominion in which all things have no definition
We appear from out of a single true dominion.

We are alike.
We are alike.
This is a majestic equality.
There is no heart-essence that reaches the end
Of all the teachings of the Buddha,
Other than this one.

All the Victorious Ones of the three times
Absolutely do not harbor any inspiration that is other than this one.

There are multitudes who desire to attain a final result,
And enter through the doors of the Secret Mantra,
But they are exhausted in teachings
That are for those who interpret the rules,
Whose with perverted desires,
And those who have lusts and cravings.

We are all brought together in thusness.
In this uncontrived thusness
The practice of the Dharma and its rejection are Solid Cuts.[20]

We cannot turn them away.
They are directly indirect.
They are brethren who do not hold to the level.
They have no virtue.
They have no evil.

---

[20] Khreg chod. This is also a name for a kind of meditation.

The Royal Tantra on the Brilliant Diffusion of Majestic Space

They diffuse into the darkness.
We do not hinder the nature of anyone.
Spontaneous realization has no position.

With the exception of this one,
There will appear many manuals on the beliefs of the views.
They do not blend the intellect with the Dharma,
And they crave for the extreme of equanimity to be a position.
They do not give birth to an understanding of Total Awareness,[21]
So they cut the unity that has no object into preferences.
The self-originating does not arise without a position,
So they meet with riddles in a space of darkness.

Everything is brought together here.
Do not work on it!
This is the spontaneously realized dominion of the Dharma.
It is insubstantial.
Its essence is not to be apprehended.
We are all liberated into a single circle,
So we are beyond the conventionalities
That make us into two.

We are all perfected in a single effortlessness.
This is beyond the extremes of hope and fear.
It is not necessary to seek it.
There are no problems that we must be rid of,
So where would there be any virtues for us to take up?

This is primordially viewed,
Primordially meditated,
And primordially practiced,
So what entity would we achieve as a reward?

It is viewed from the primordial,
So it is beyond any objects.
It is primordially meditated,
So it is without any visualizations.
It primordially cuts through,
So it is not to be sought after.
It is primordially realized,
So there is nothing to work on.

---

[21] Kun rig

The Royal Tantra on the Brilliant Diffusion of Majestic Space

Majestic primordial liberation is the dominion of the Dharma.
It is naturally removed from all entities.
It is the progenitor of all entities.
It is the true nature of all things.
It appears in an equality with each and every thing.

In the definitive intent,
There is one circle.
When we cling to characteristics,
It manifests as being different.
It arises this way,
But we are brought together within it.
We appear within it.

The true nature of all things
Is the dominion of the Dharma.
When we understand
That this is the root of the dominion of the Dharma,
We are liberated within its space.

This is the place of liberation for all samsara and nirvana.
It is like the clouds in the sky,
And like a rainbow.
It arises without a definition,
In the way of an illusion.

We have no clinging or attachment,
So we are free from problems.
The dominion of the sky has no real basis.
There is no eternity in the space of reality.
There is no other space
For this dominion that is beyond entities and is insubstantial
Other than the space of reality,
So even though we arise without position,
We are our own true selves.

The Dharmas of the path and the result
Also appear from us,
Without our seeking them,
So our precious wish-fulfilling jewel,
That has no birth or ending,
Is our embodiment as the Dharma.

It is the basis for the directionless arising of wonders.

Our manifest embodiment may be anything.
It is not definite.
We are unhindered in our concern for our disciples.

To dwell in the state of equality is perfect enjoyment.
We appear on the level of the Mahayana,
But we emerge from a dominion that does not appear at all.
We arise from the dominion of the Great Spirit.

The contemplations of all the Victorious Ones
Do not move away from the space of our three embodiments.
The true meaning of secrecy emerges from ourselves.

So he spoke.

From the Royal Tantra on the Brilliant Diffusion of Majestic Space, this is chapter forth-five: Teaching that There Is One Characteristic.

THE MISUNDERSTANDING OF THE GREAT PERFECTION

Then again our teacher gave instruction to his retinue, which was none other than himself:

Because it is the highest summit of the vehicles,
The Atiyoga is the great perfection.

Like the king of the mountains,
Its altitude is high.
It is the summit of all the vehicles.
It is the greatest of the great.
We are naturally present.

The spacious heart of the All Good One
Is present by its own power,
So it bedazzles all the subsidiary vehicles.

So it is that our own awareness,
By its own power,
Turns our understanding away from the space of equality.
In the single majestic space,
To understand and not to understand,
To be liberated and not to be liberated
Are non-dual and equal.

We arise from out of a unified equality,
So we are great.

As an analogy,
The majestic garuda bird,
Even while it dwells in the womb,
Bedazzles all the nagas.
Its feathered wings reach their measure in the egg.
It removes the covering of the egg by itself,
And it plays in equality through the waves of the vast expance.
This is impossible for the other birds,
But it is possible for the majestic garuda alone.
On the paths of all the dominions of the atmosphere
It is happy.

Those who understand and those who do not understand are liberated.
There is no now or later.
The liberated and the unliberated are equal.
Our equanimity has no break in its continuum.
Once we have gradually travelled over the stages of the nine vehicles,
We will desire to be liberated from the Tantras.
We will study them intensively,
And reject them.
In believing that our Buddhahood must come from a cause,
Anything we understand will be misunderstood.
To understand that the Mahayana is in ourselves
Is to be happy.

In any case,
Everything,
With no exceptions,
Is a space of great bliss.
It is the embodiment of the Dharma itself.
In the majestic space of the natural embodiment of the Dharma
There are not even a few who are not liberated.
We pull ourselves out from the dominion of the Dharma,
And so we are embodiments of a true vajra heart.

In that my body is full blown with habitual tendencies,
I have perfected the effulgence of my true heart.
I have crossed over the narrow passage of birth and death.
I have thrown off my body, without any bardo,
And I do not depend on awareness alone,

The Royal Tantra on the Brilliant Diffusion of Majestic Space

For I am inseparable from all of samsara and nirvana,
So without limiting my vastness or falling into a position
I have brought forth manifestations that have no positions,
And without being hindered by anything,
I engage in all things,
None excepted.

I have understood the meaning of riding the wind of effortlessness.
This is a field of practice for every yogin.
It is not fit for all those people who have small intellects,
And whose knowledge is of the inferior vehicles.
This is for teachers who are fit for the Ati,
Those who dwell in the majesty of a primordially realized reward,
While they continue to come forth through the miracle of birth.

Those who hold to the demarcations of cause and result
Have erroneous intellects due to the power of their delusions.
The reality of the Ati has no causes or conditions.
I teach that it encompasses all things.
This is not fitting for the lower ones.

The Atiyoga is the core of correctness.
Buddhas and sentient beings are the same,
So there is no difference in their contemplations or their practices.
To designate samsara and nirvana as being a duality
Is a delusion.

Those who have intellects
That practice on the duality of subjects and objects
Are the lower ones for whom this teaching of the non-dual Ati
Is not suitable.
The Atiyoga is the core of suitability.
In the absence of any conceptualization or non-conceptualization,
To believe that we will be liberated after we understand
That we are liberated into the dominion of the unborn,
Is to be an enemy of equanimity.

With the Ati we are taught an equality.
This is not acceptable to those who are below this.
The Atiyoga is the core of acceptability.
Through the special qualities of the method by which we exemplify it,
We do not reject anything that must be spoken,
While the unspeakable Solid Cut[22]

Is the word of a fool.

This teaching is indivisible from its meaning,
But it is not fitting for the lowly.
The Atiyoga is the core of fittingness.
The view of the great perfection
Has no limits to its depth.

In the reality of primordial majestic pervasion
To impute a fault, saying: "It does not make contact"
Is to have a darkened intellect that does not understand limitlessness.

The teaching that has no borders and that cuts through words
Is not acceptable to the winds from the below.
The great perfection is the core of acceptability.
In the essence of the single circle
Our understanding of the ways and reasons things arise
Is turned around.
We cut through the hopes and fears there are
In wanting a reward.

We have no hope.
We have no fear.
We are equal to the sky!

We are spacious.
We are majestic.
Reality is majestic!

The heart of a Victorious One is equal to the sky.
We have nothing to reject or to acquire.
We are a majestic circle.
We are self-arising from out of the space of reality.
We are liberated into our own place.
We are liberated into our own dominion.
We are liberated into an absence
Of both understanding and non-conceptualization.

In this reality that is non-dual,
We are liberated into an absence of good and evil.
This is impossible for those who are below us.

---

[22] Khreg chod

The Atiyoga is a Dharma of possibility.

As an analogy,
When baby blue sheep are climbing on the rocks
They are happy and at ease,
Unlike any others.
This is impossible for the other animals.
By the power of their responsiveness it is possible for them.

In the majestic space of effortless awareness,
Everyone, with no exceptions, is liberated,
But this is not possible for those who have quests and practices,
Who are committed to be people of the inferior vehicles.
The inspiration of extreme yoga[23]
Is equal to the sky.

We are happy to be on a path that is spacious, effortless,
And that has no limits.
All Dharmas are Buddhas,
So our awareness has no objects,
And has nothing to depend on.
It is not possible that it wander in samsara.

Things that are possible are topics that we must understand.
A view of objects and subjects
In which we believe in material things
Is a space for the inferior.

We are liberated in the sky.
We are liberated into our own place.
Without anything to depend on,
We are liberated into our own place:
Into space.

The one circle has no angels or corners.
In the reality of majestic pervasiveness
It is not possible to appear as a duality.
Things that are possible are topics that we must understand.
The division of unity and separateness
Is a practice for deluded minds.

---

[23] Shin tu rnal 'byor, the Tibetan translation of "Atiyoga."

We are liberated into the one.
We are liberated into our own place.
We are liberated into our own place:
Into the space of reality.

Self-originating wisdom in its significance
Has no causes or conditions.
It is not possible that the five poisons arise,
According to the presentations on what is possible,
But the five poisons do arise,
And are believed by the lowly to be the pathways of samsara.
They do not attain enlightenment,
But turn into obstructers.

We are liberated in self-origination.
We are liberated into our own place.
We are liberated into the space of self-originating wisdom.
We are spontaneously realized.
We have no position,
We are beyond any extremes,
So it is impossible for us to fall into a position.

Clinging to positions is a topic for the worldly.
Through their cravings for limits on the views of their positions
They do not understand equality,
And they turn into demons.

We are liberated without position.
We are liberated into our own place.
We are liberated into a positionless space of spontaneous realization.
This is a reality that has no real demarcations.
We dwell in unhindered emptiness.
It is impossible that we arise as appearances.
To be self-evident without being definite is a topic for the worldly.

We are liberated into our own place,
Where appearances are indefinite.
We are liberated into our own place:
Into the space of emptiness.

We have no divisions or clarifications.
We are liberated into our own place.
We are liberated into our own place:

The Royal Tantra on the Brilliant Diffusion of Majestic Space

Into the space of spontaneous realization.

We have no joining or parting.
We are liberated into our own place.
We are liberated into our own place:
Into the space of the circle.

Anything may arise.
We are liberated into our own place.
We are liberated into our own place:
A space that has no definition.

We appear within form.
We are liberated into our own place.
We are liberated into the space
Of self-liberating appearances.

We echo forth in sound.
We are liberated into our own place.
We are liberated into the space where what we hear is self-liberating.

The dharmas that appear and that echo forth,
And anything that arises through the five doors
Of our seeing and hearing,
Is such that we see our own face by ourselves,
So we have no other object to see as being a duality.

There is no duality.
There is a majestic equality.
Objects and our minds are liberated into a space of equality.

There is a single equality that may arise as anything.
There is a single true dominion that may arise as anything.
It makes all good things to be born.
It is the basis for the appearance of every siddhi.
It is the unsought precious jewel.
It is the unstained, unopened supreme treasure.
Everything is present within this state.
Everyone is liberated without any work or effort.

So he spoke.

From the Royal Tantra on the Brilliant Diffusion of Majestic Space, this

The Royal Tantra on the Brilliant Diffusion of Majestic Space is chapter forty-six: The Misunderstanding of the Great Perfection.

PRESENTING THE ENTOURAGE WITH ADVICE

Then again the Blessed One advised his entourage on this Tantra:

All of my Dharmas are one in the space of reality. This is the holy palace of the dominion of the Dharma. It is the space of the All Good One, and is neither wide nor narrow. It is the unborn dominion of the All Good Mother. It is an unborn and unending treasure that brings forth miracles. It is the place where the three embodiments of the Buddha work for the welfare of living beings. It is the path that brings the sentient beings of the three realms to liberation. It is the majestic path of total purity, a cave for the contemplation of total liberation. It is like the light of the sun and the moon, it is luminous and totally pervasive. If we investigate it, we do not find anything. If we let it be, it arises in various ways.

Buddhas, sentient beings, samsara, nirvana, the vessel, and its contents: The meanings of all these Dharmas that are well known are gathered here in this. Without this, it is impossible that a Buddha appear. This is the effortless heart-essence of the Dharma that even the Victorious Ones of the three times have difficulty in understanding.

Understand that this is the spacious path of the Dharma that has been marked out!

So he spoke.

From the Royal Tantra on the Brilliant Diffusion of Majestic Space, this is chapter forty-seven: Presenting the Entourage with Advice.

THE ENTOURAGE REJOICES IN THE TEACHER

Then Vajrasattva and the rest of the entourage began to rejoice, and they addressed him with these words:

O Great Leader!
Blessed One!
We rejoice that you are a supreme protector and refuge
Who serves to benefit your disciples:
Those who have reverted views,
And all the rest.

You use reality,
Which is like the sky,
To be totally pervasive
In your work for the welfare of living beings.

You do not move away
From the dominion of your contemplation.
You have no motion or shaking.
We praise you and bow to you.

You use the sun of self-originating wisdom
To clear away the darkness of ignorance,
And to open up the star-port of wisdom.
We rejoice in your shining lamp.

The Dharma and the anti-Dharma are indivisible.
You work to teach them to be truly equal.

You are neither close to or distant from anyone,
While you work for the welfare of living beings.
We praise you and bow to you.

There are inconceivable numbers of paths and doors of entry,
But you work to teach them to be surely one.
We rejoice in you,
O Supreme Teacher.

You are a treasure of equanimity.
We praise you and bow to you.

So they spoke.

From the Royal Tantra on the Brilliant Diffusion of Majestic Space, this is chapter forty-eight: The Entourage Rejoices in the Teacher.

The father of all the Buddhas of the three times,
The mother of every yogin,
The life-force that does not split samsara and nirvana,
The unfailing royal insignia,
The shining lamp that is like a butter lamp of wisdom
Shining into space,
The so-called Royal Tantra on the Brilliant Diffusion of Majestic Space,

Is finished.

THE TIBETAN TEXT

Images from the rNying ma rgyud 'bum mTshams brag dgon kyi bri ma, National Library, Royal Government of Bhutan, Thimpu, 1982. 46 Vols. Volume 9, pp. 446-617.

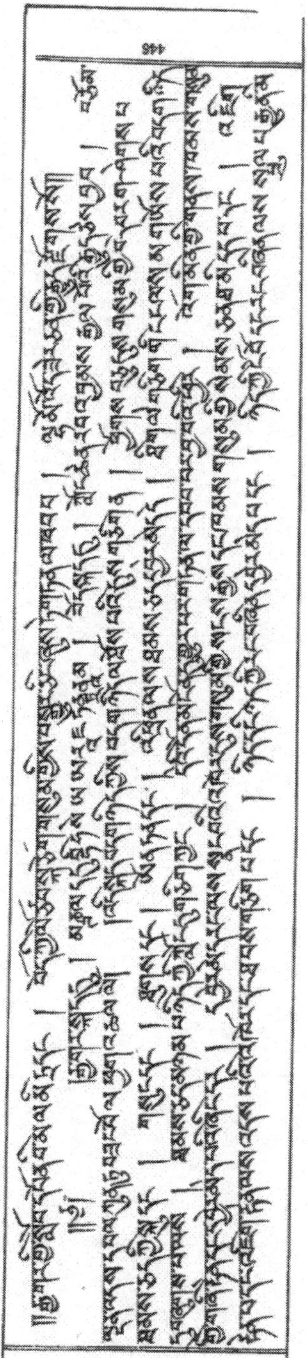

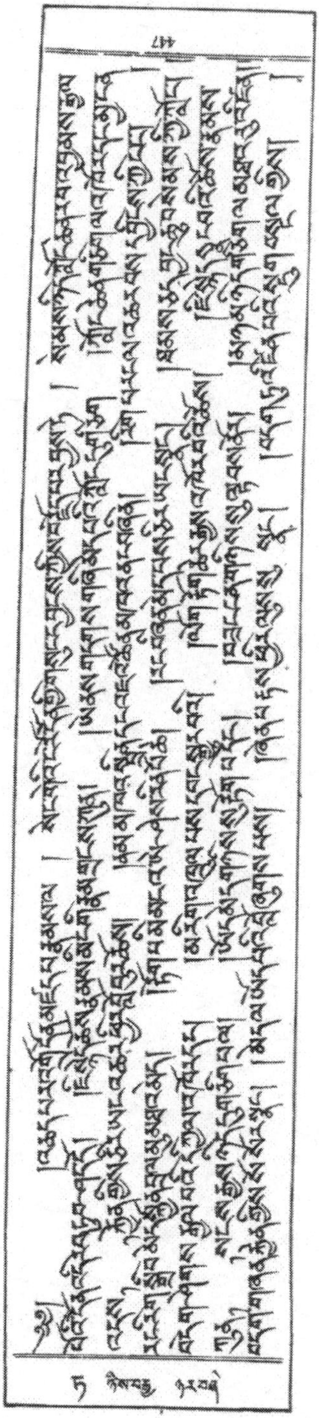

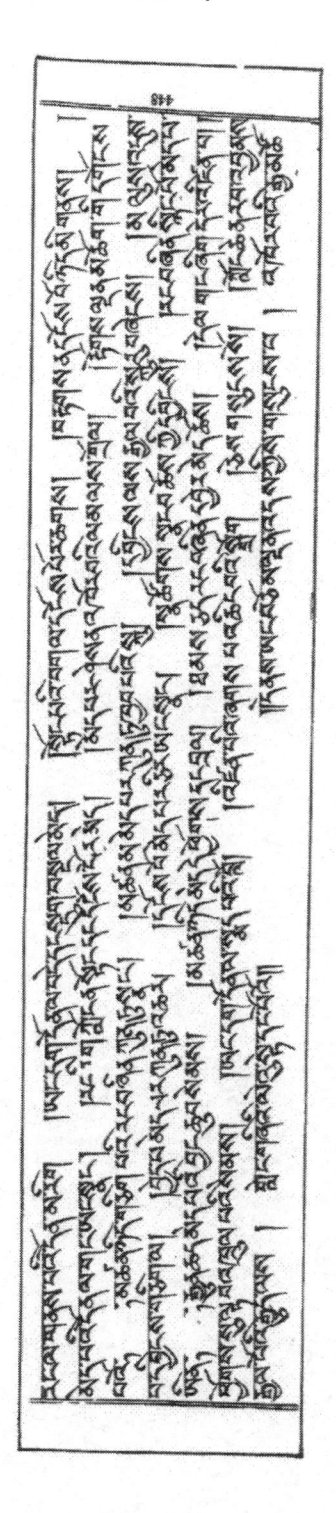

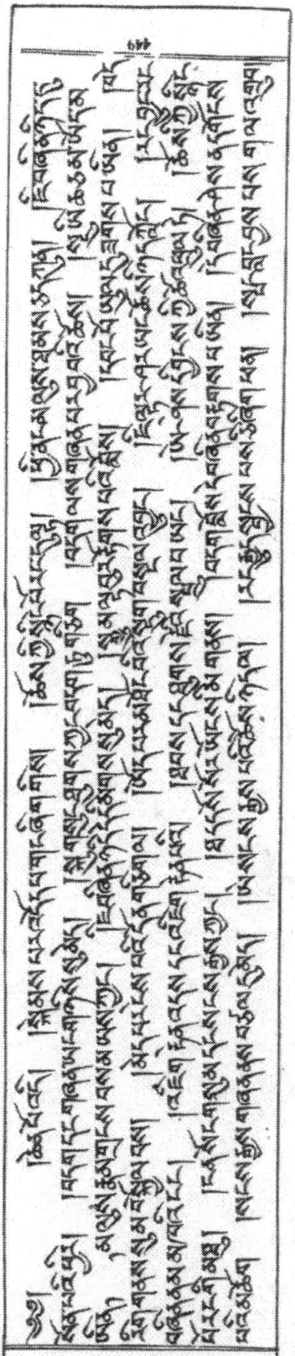

The Royal Tantra on the Brilliant Diffusion of Majestic Space

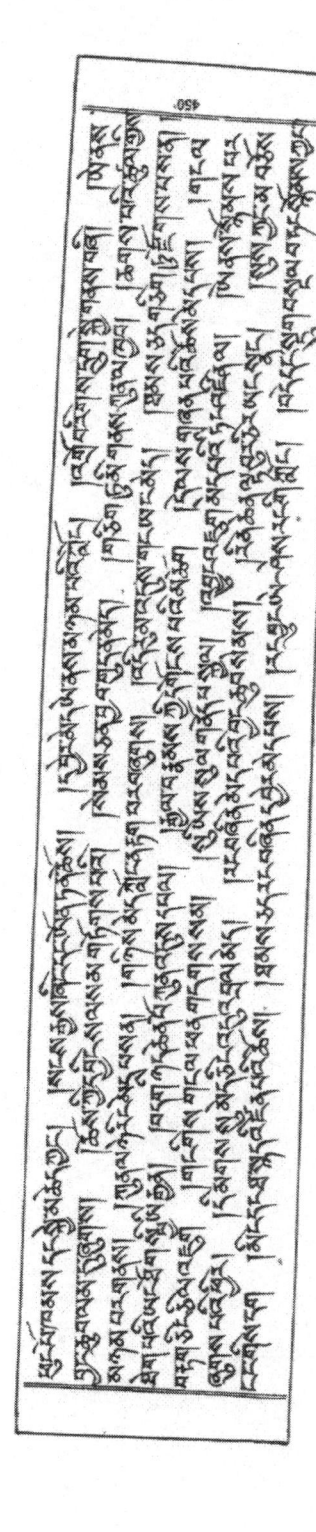

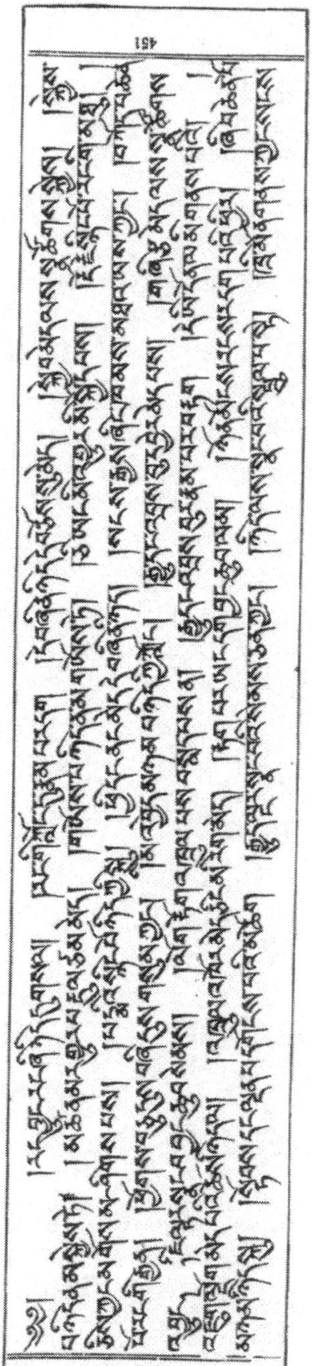

The Royal Tantra on the Brilliant Diffusion of Majestic Space

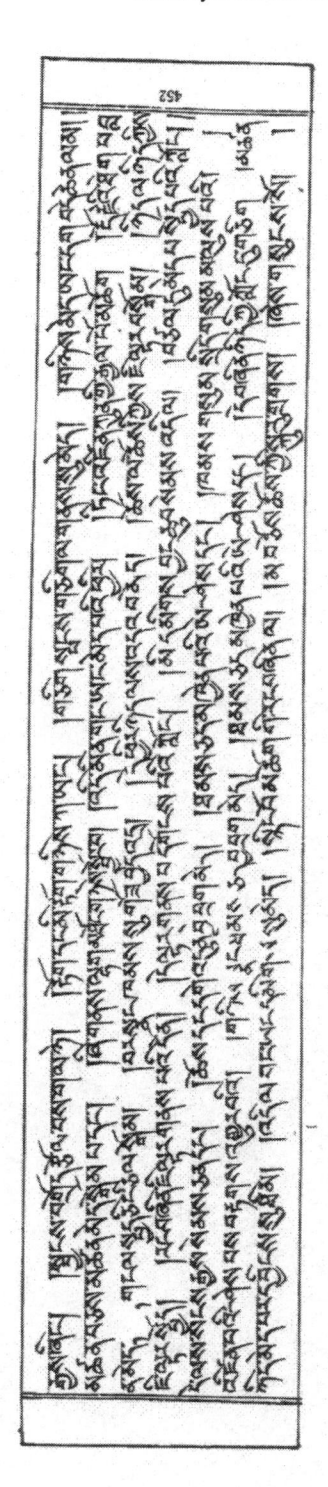

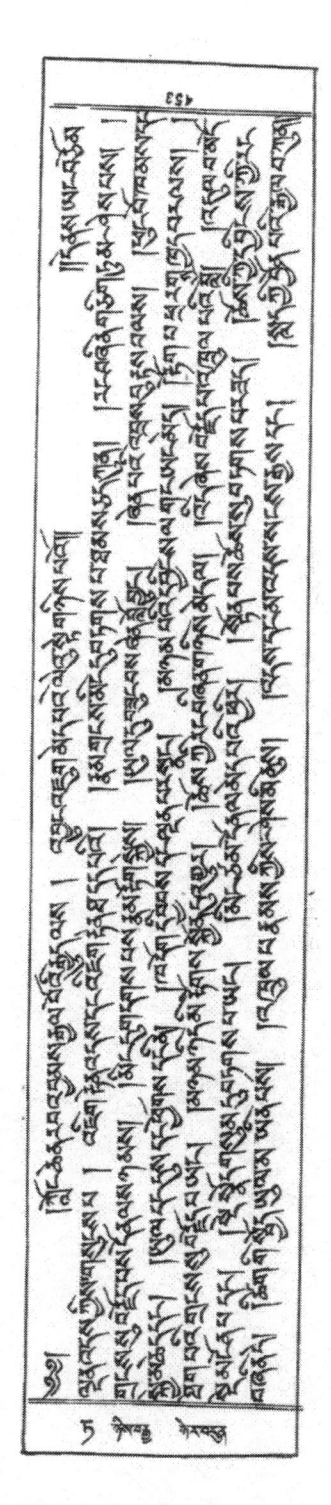

The Royal Tantra on the Brilliant Diffusion of Majestic Space

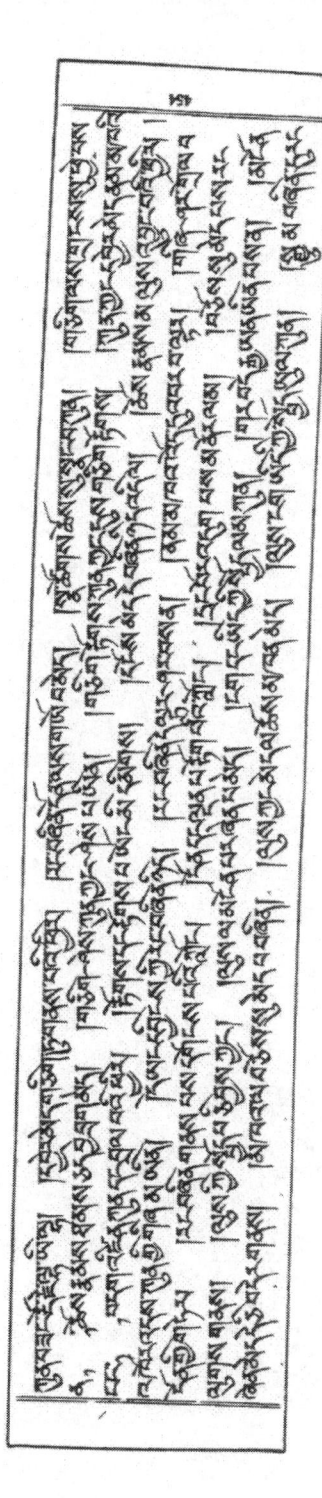

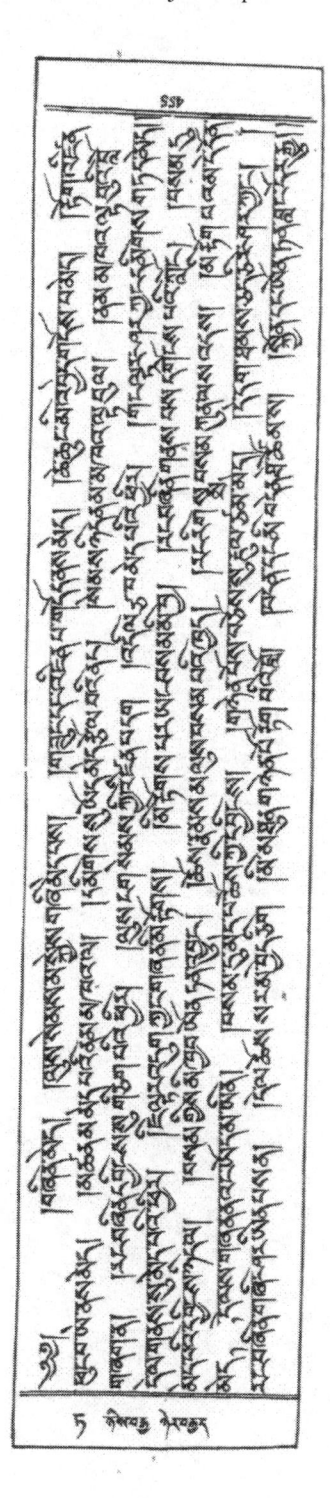

The Royal Tantra on the Brilliant Diffusion of Majestic Space

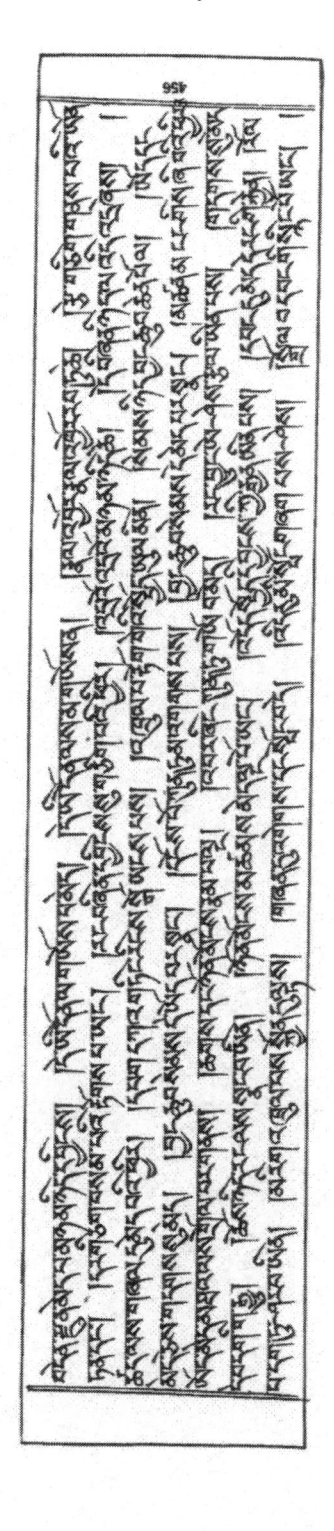

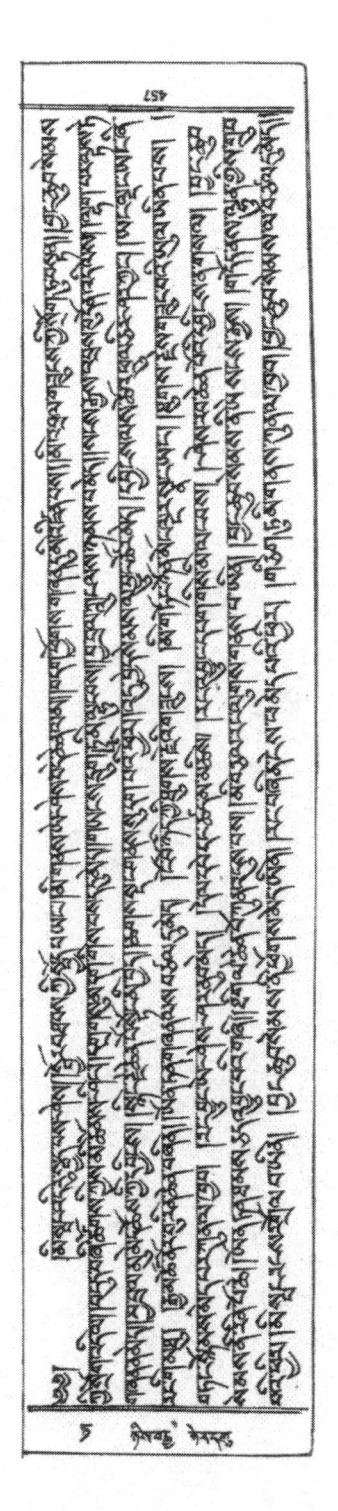

The Royal Tantra on the Brilliant Diffusion of Majestic Space

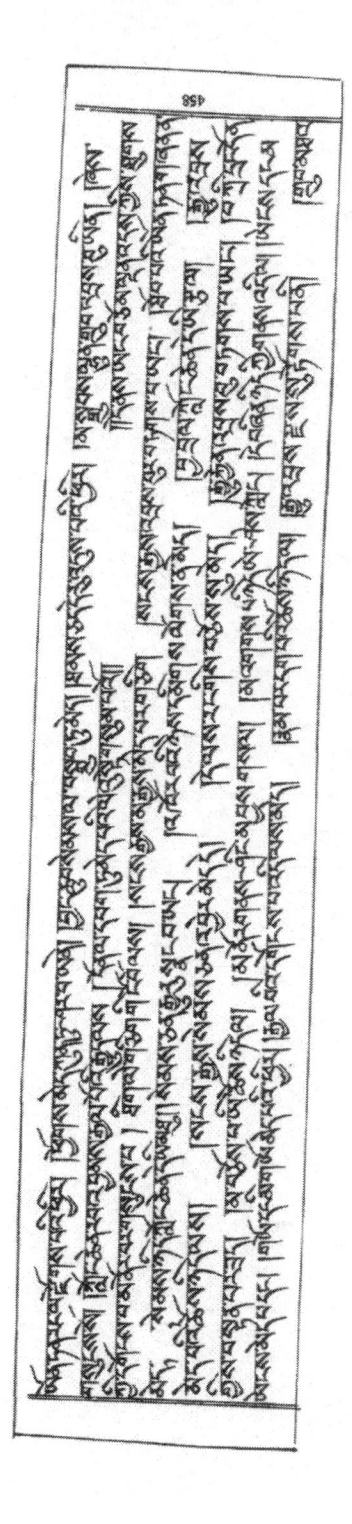

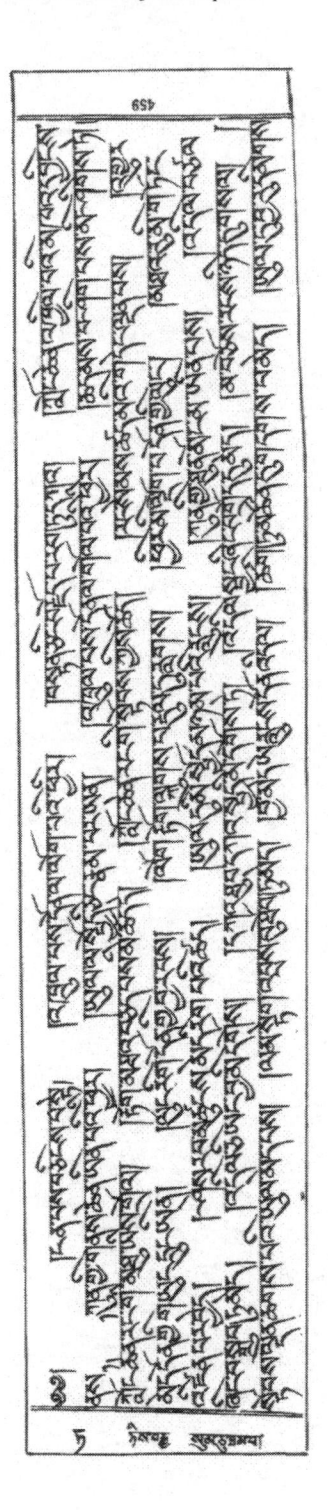

The Royal Tantra on the Brilliant Diffusion of Majestic Space

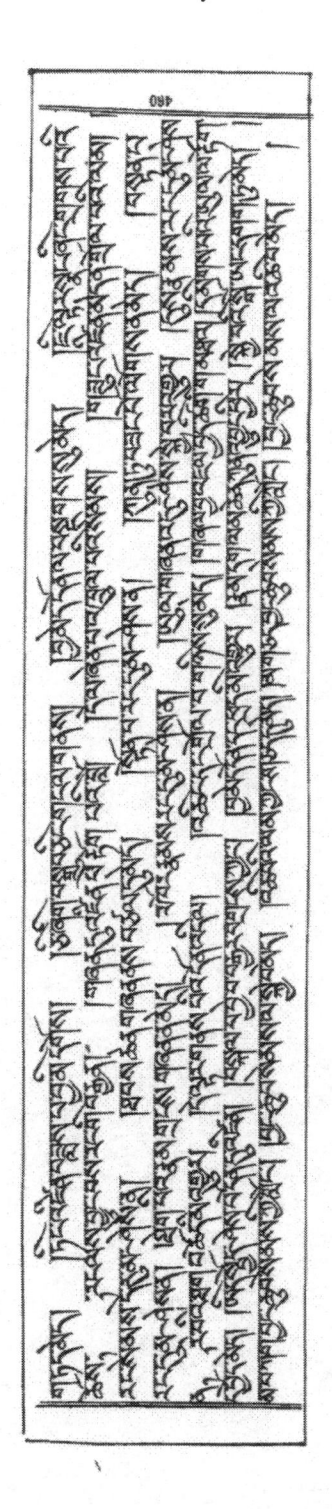

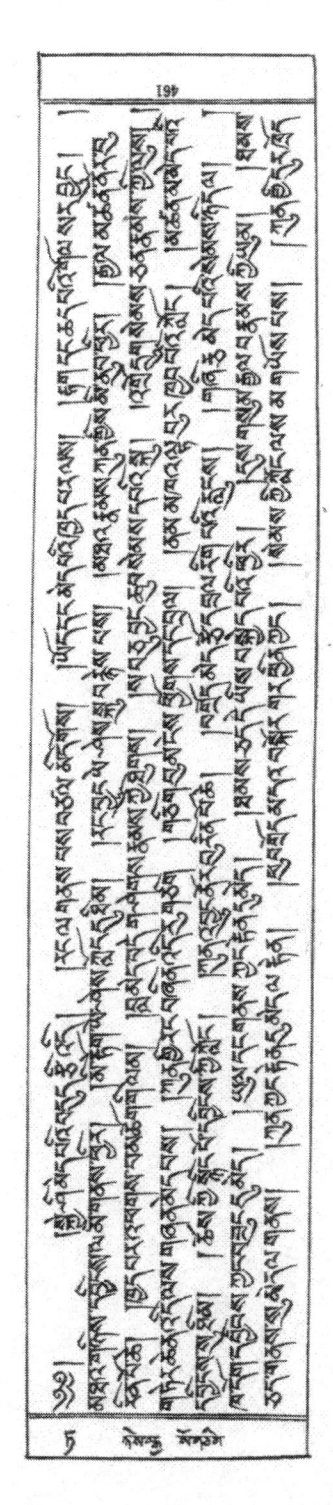

The Royal Tantra on the Brilliant Diffusion of Majestic Space

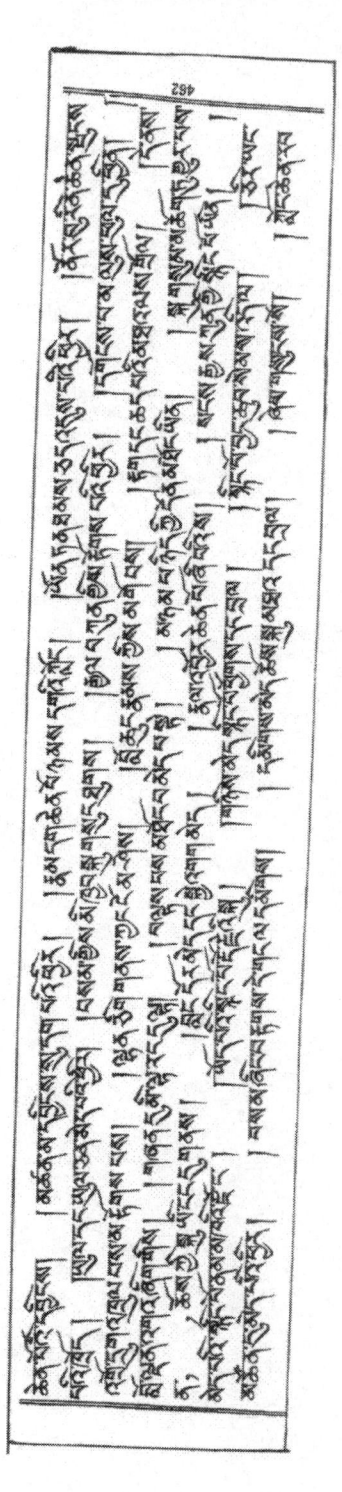

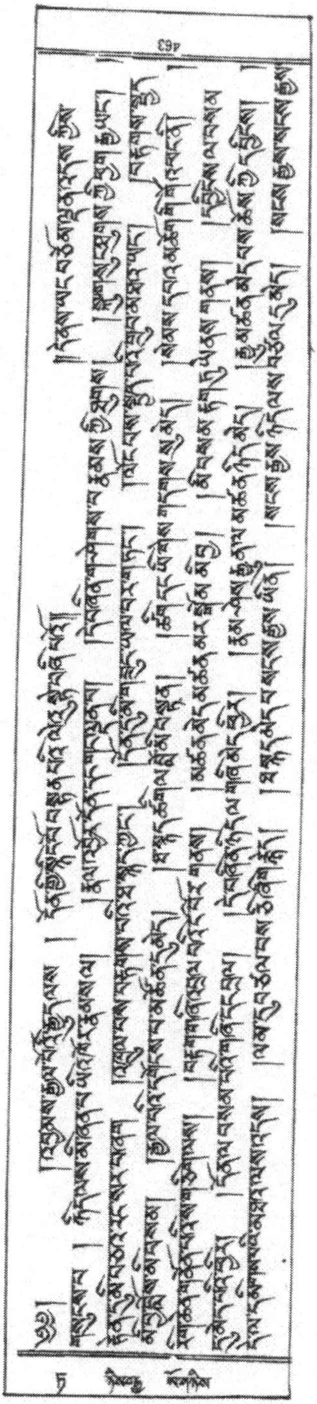

The Royal Tantra on the Brilliant Diffusion of Majestic Space

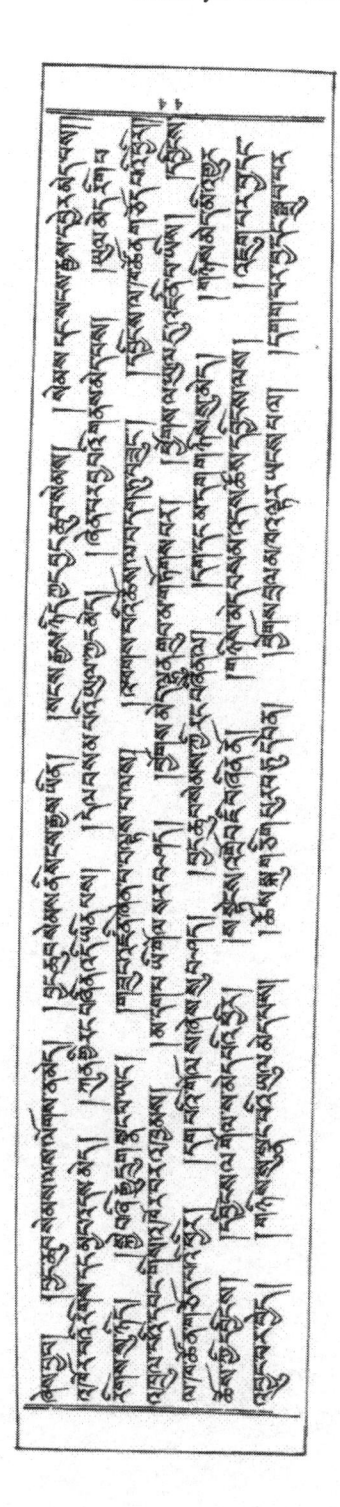

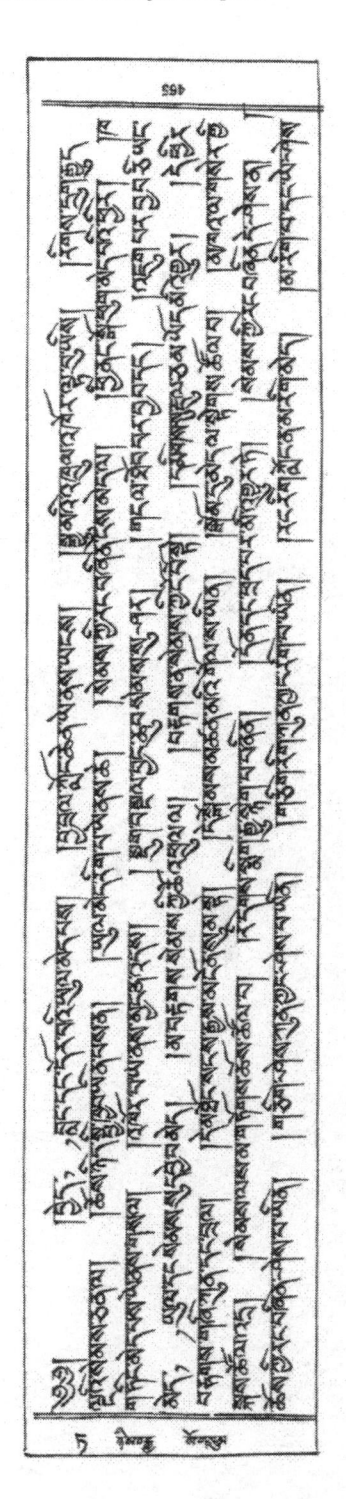

The Royal Tantra on the Brilliant Diffusion of Majestic Space

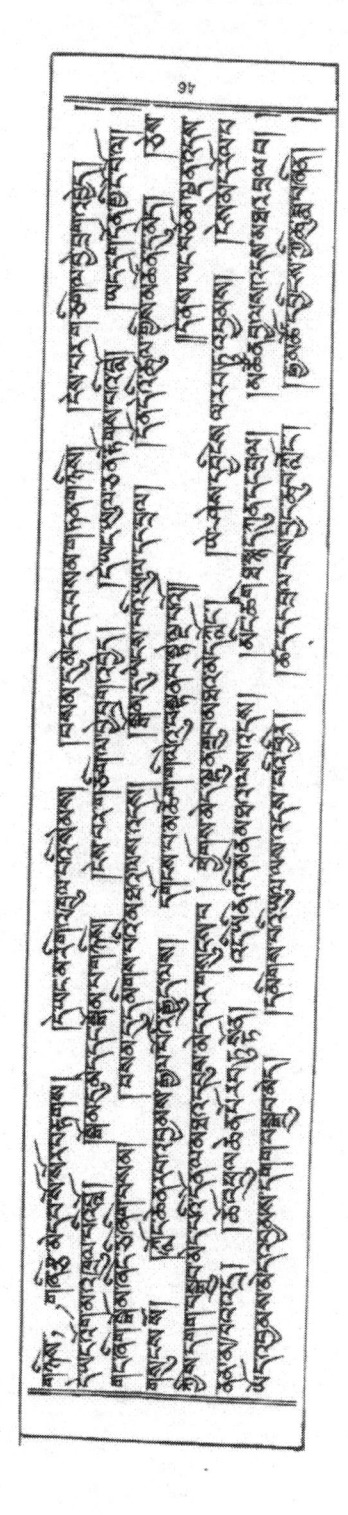

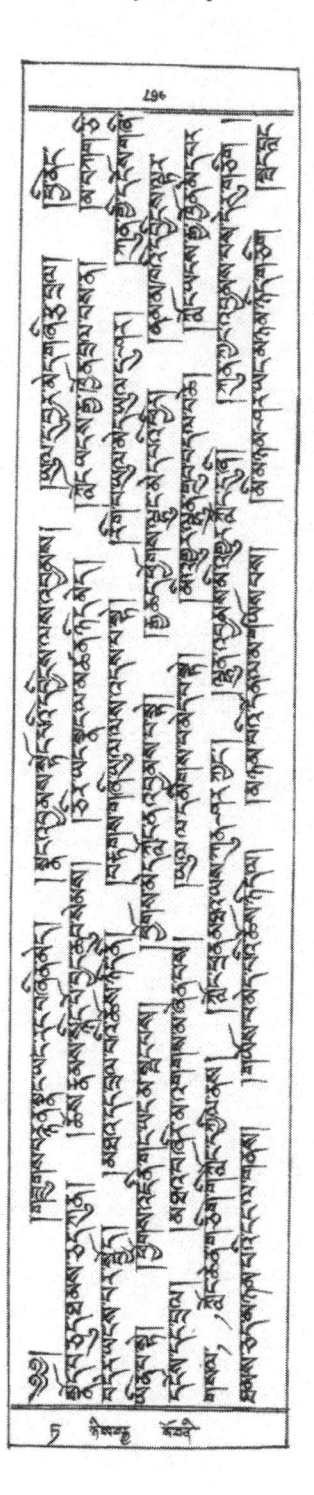

The Royal Tantra on the Brilliant Diffusion of Majestic Space

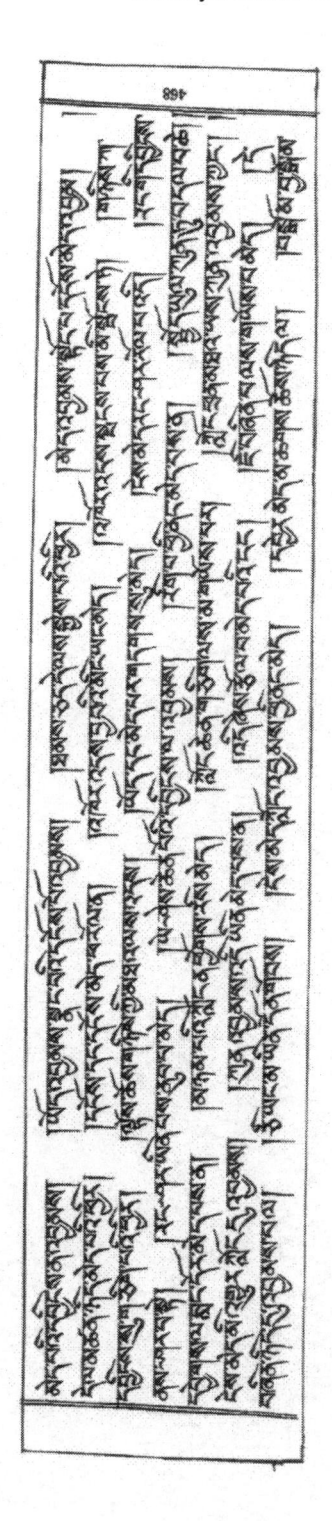

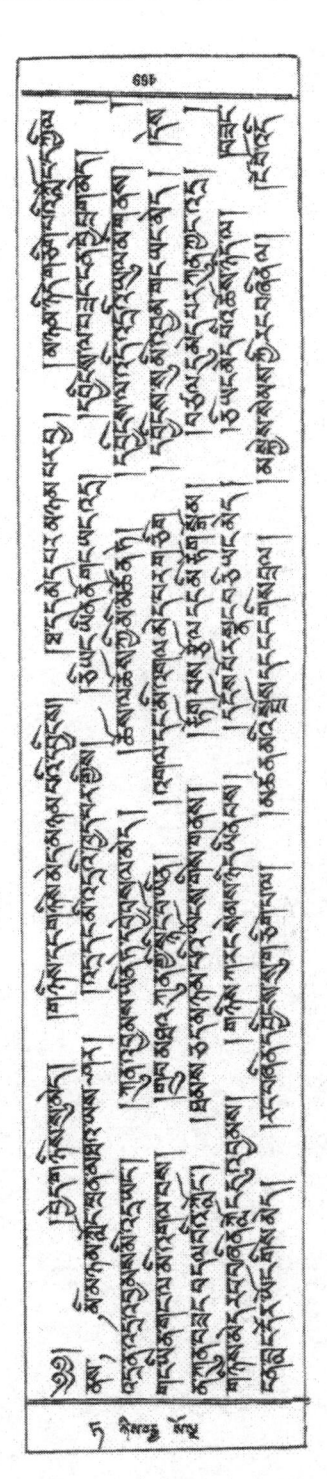

The Royal Tantra on the Brilliant Diffusion of Majestic Space

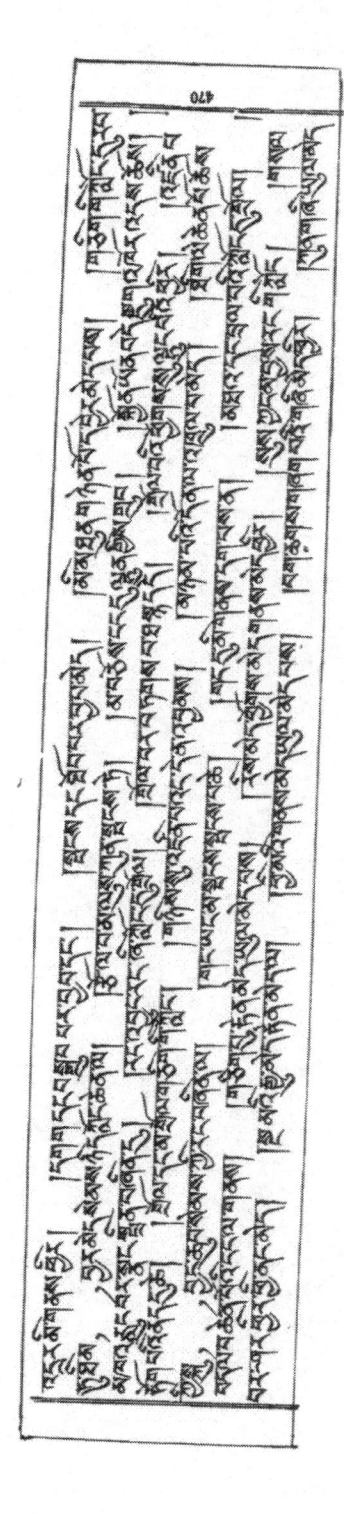

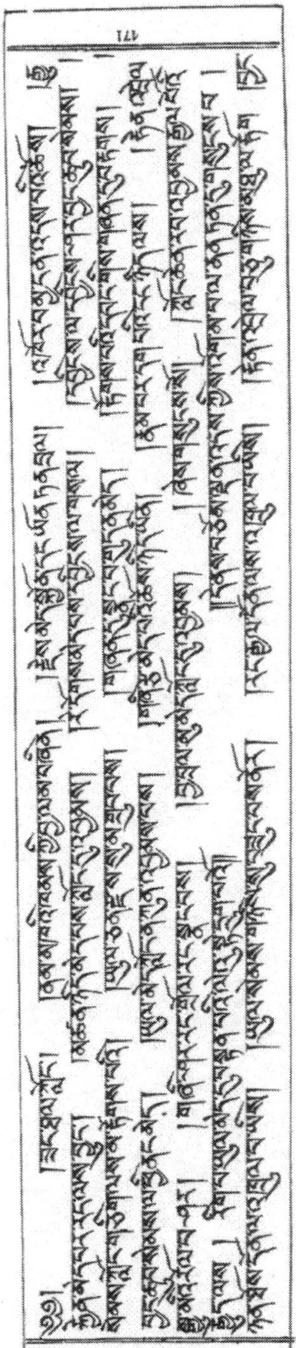

The Royal Tantra on the Brilliant Diffusion of Majestic Space

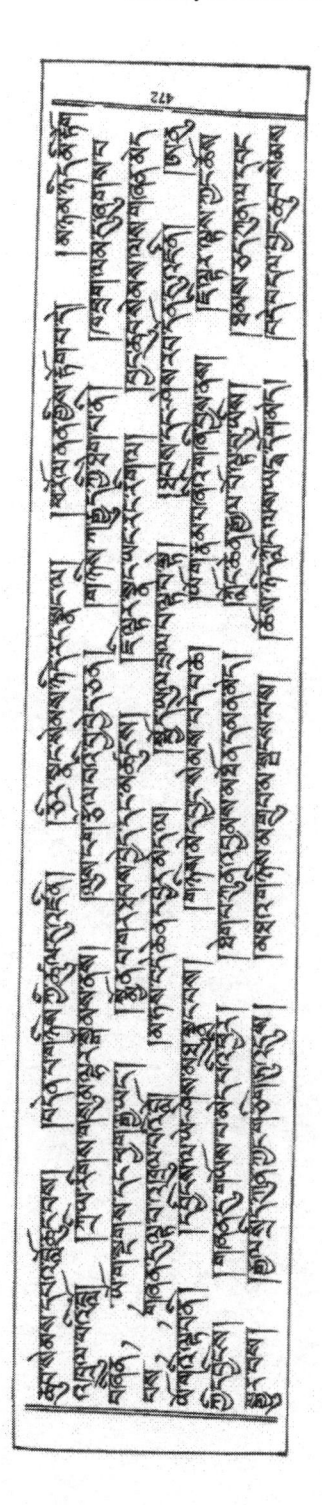

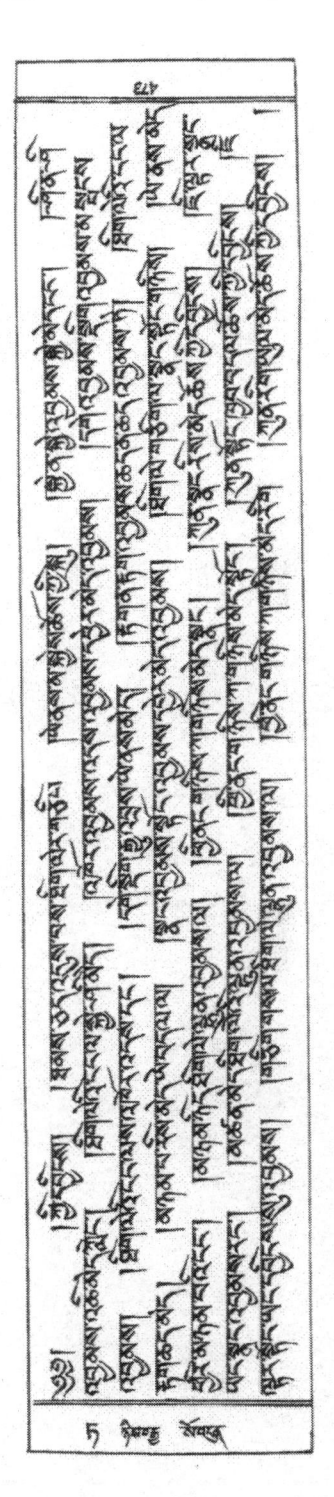

The Royal Tantra on the Brilliant Diffusion of Majestic Space

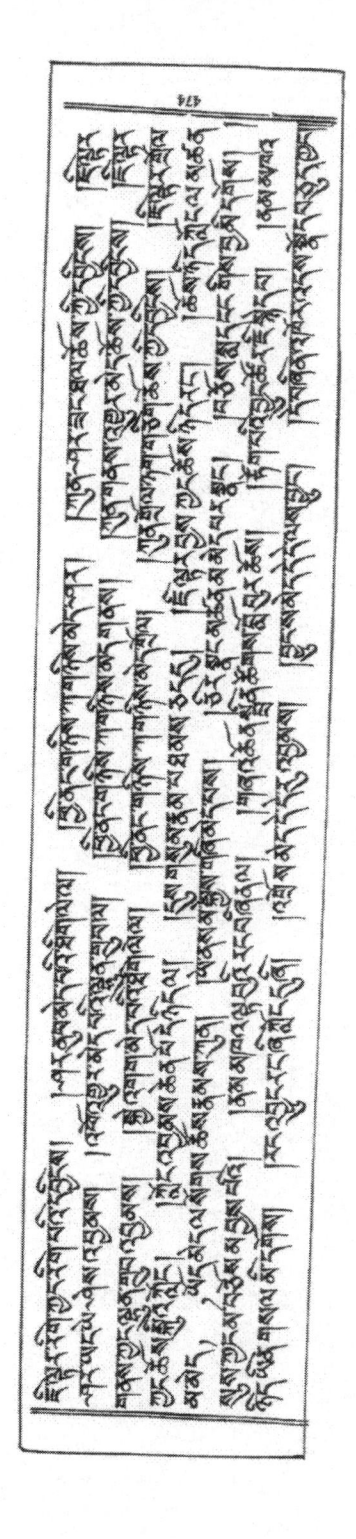

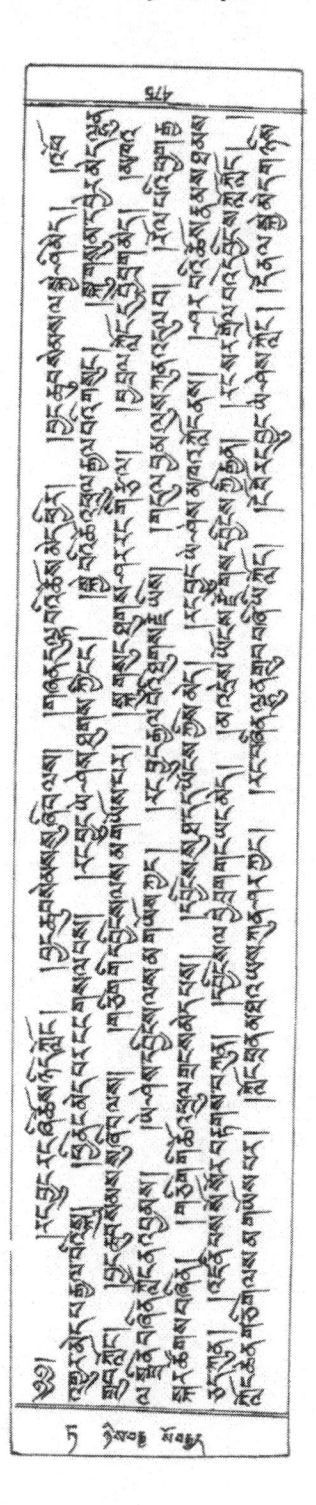

The Royal Tantra on the Brilliant Diffusion of Majestic Space

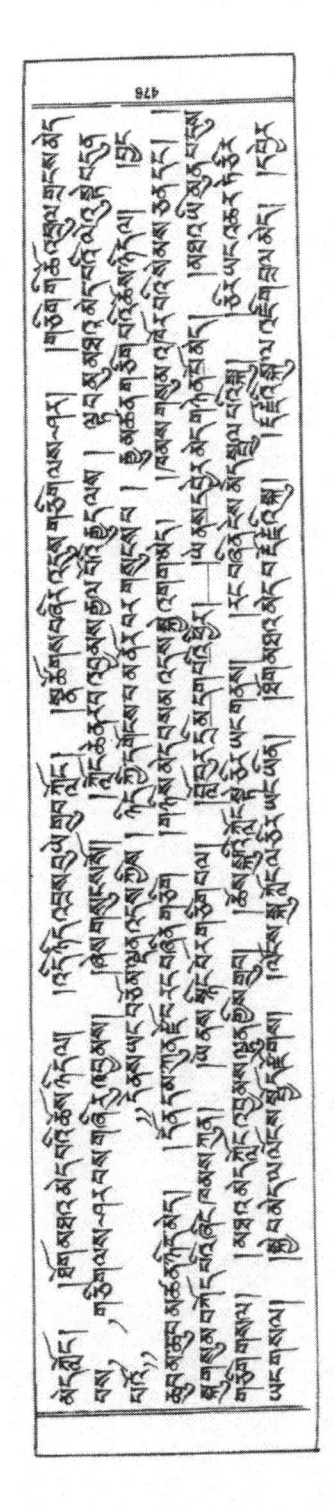

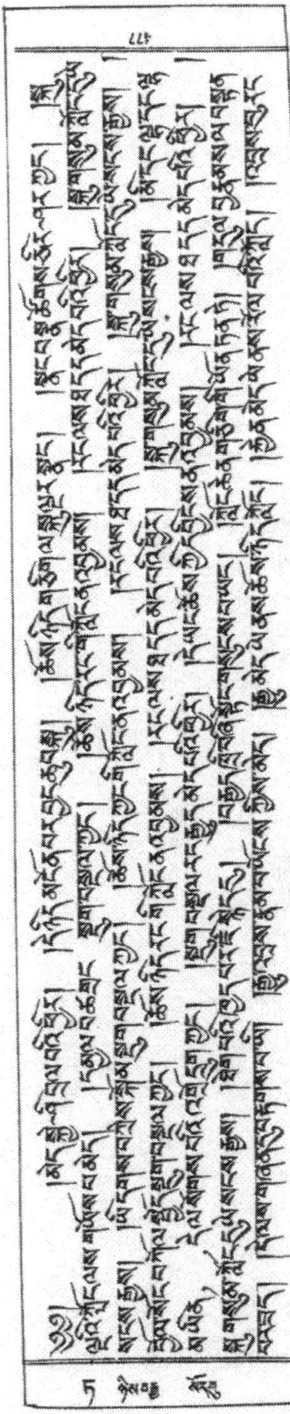

The Royal Tantra on the Brilliant Diffusion of Majestic Space

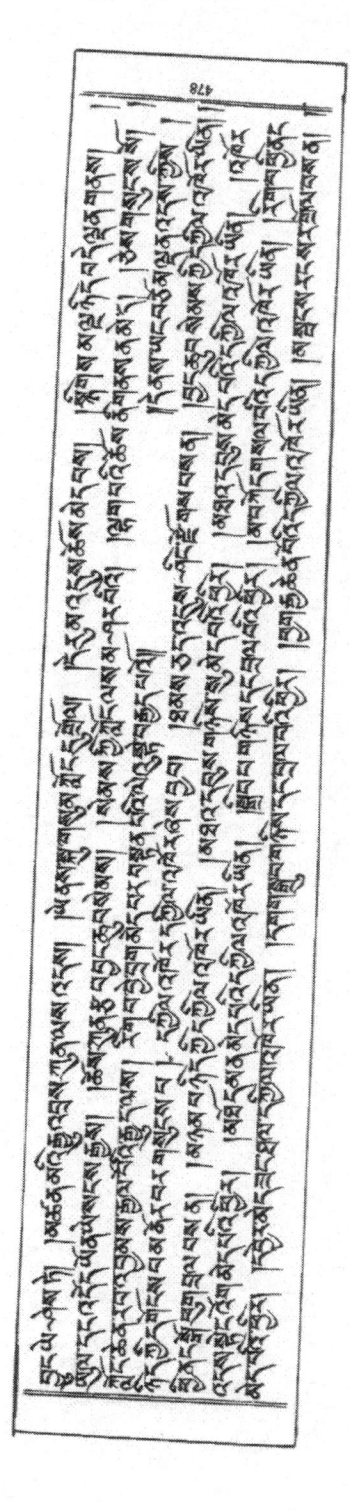

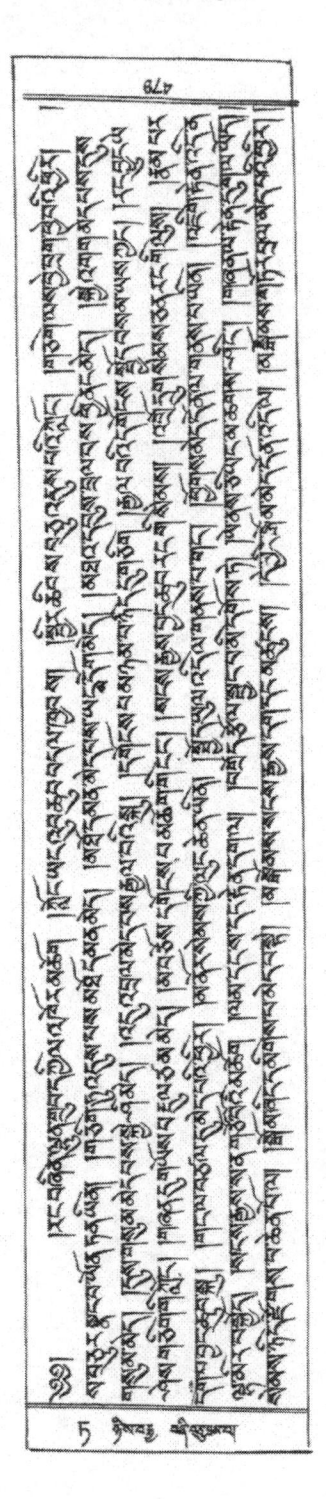

The Royal Tantra on the Brilliant Diffusion of Majestic Space

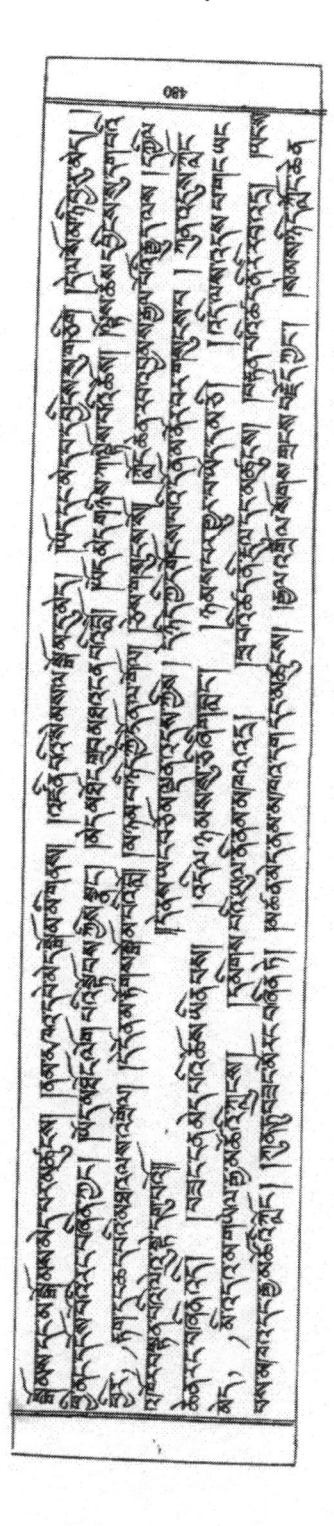

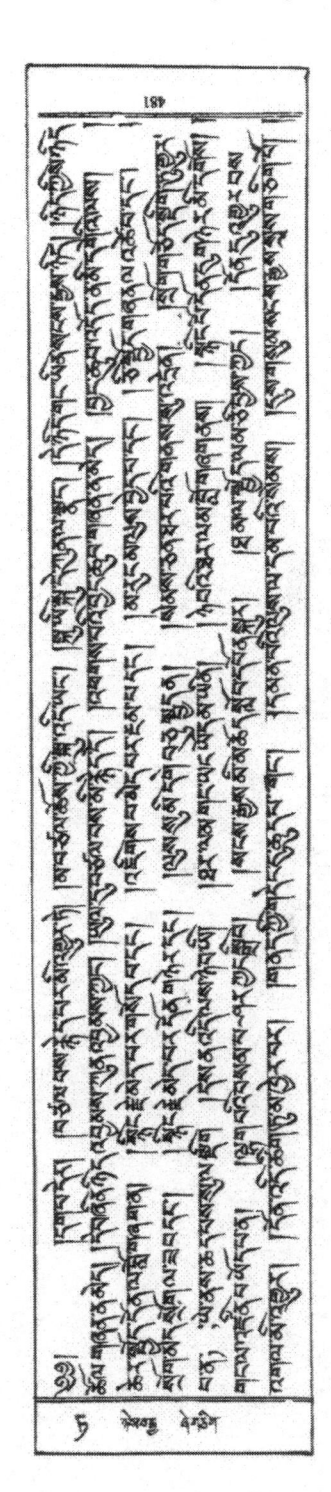

The Royal Tantra on the Brilliant Diffusion of Majestic Space

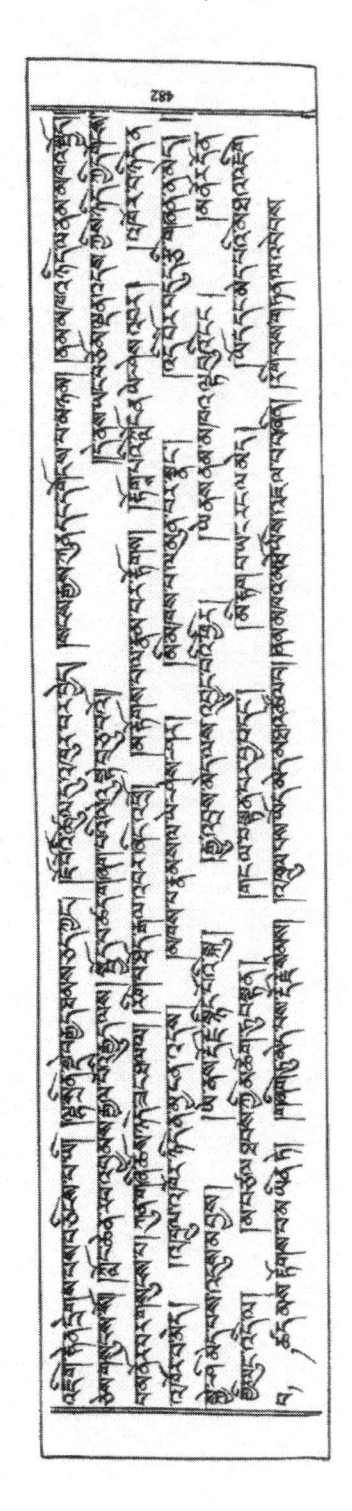

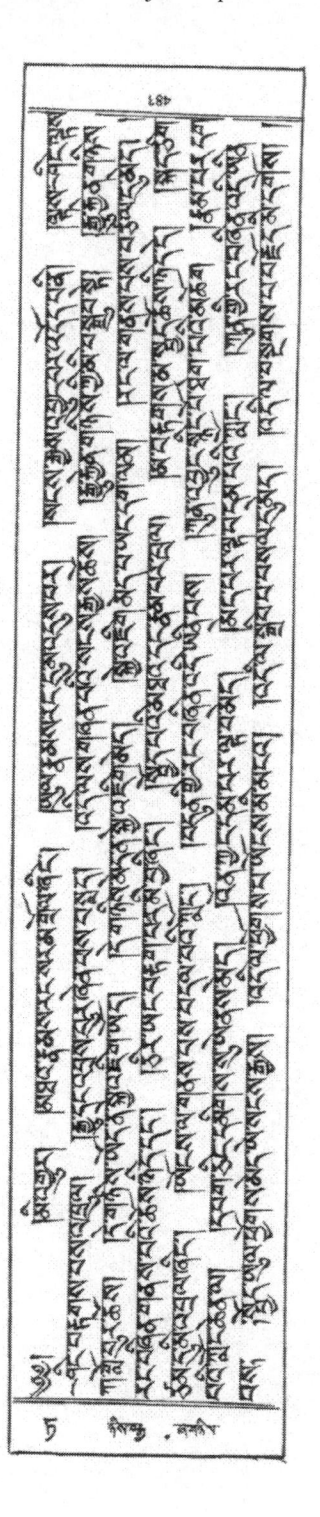

The Royal Tantra on the Brilliant Diffusion of Majestic Space

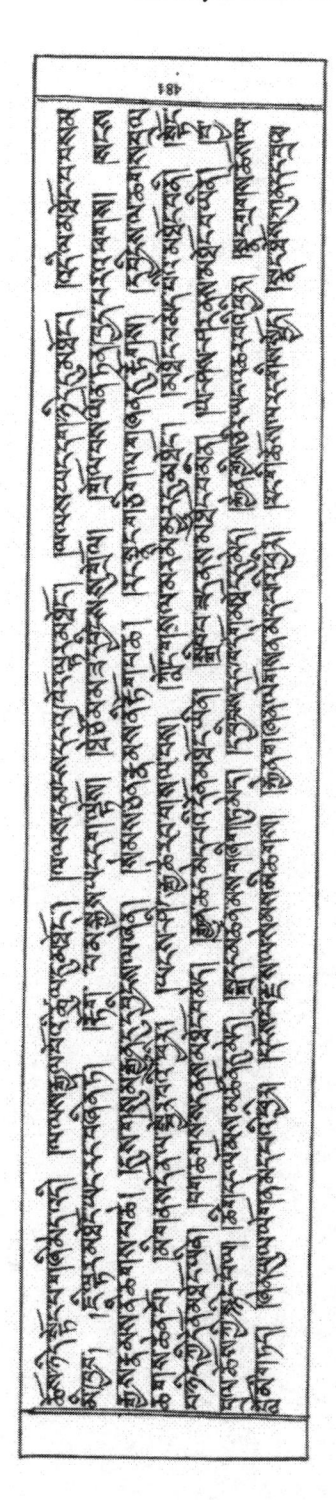

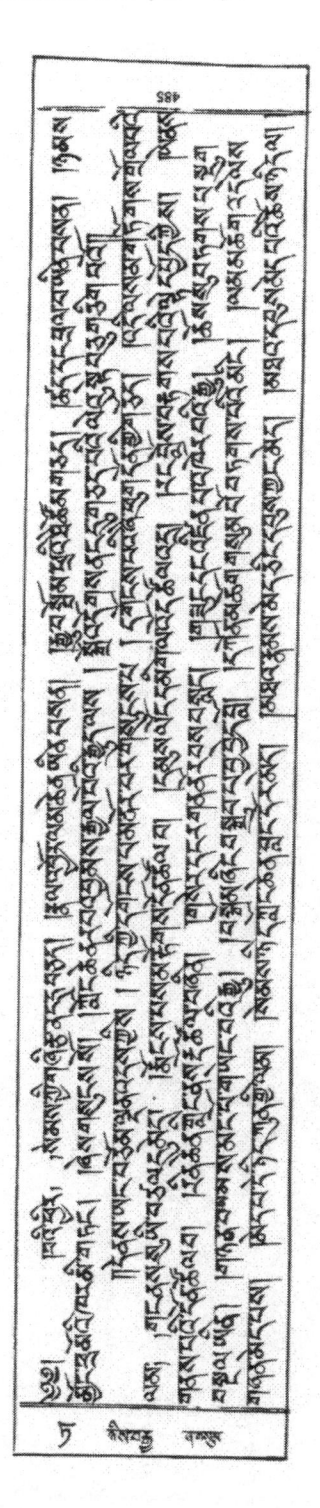

The Royal Tantra on the Brilliant Diffusion of Majestic Space

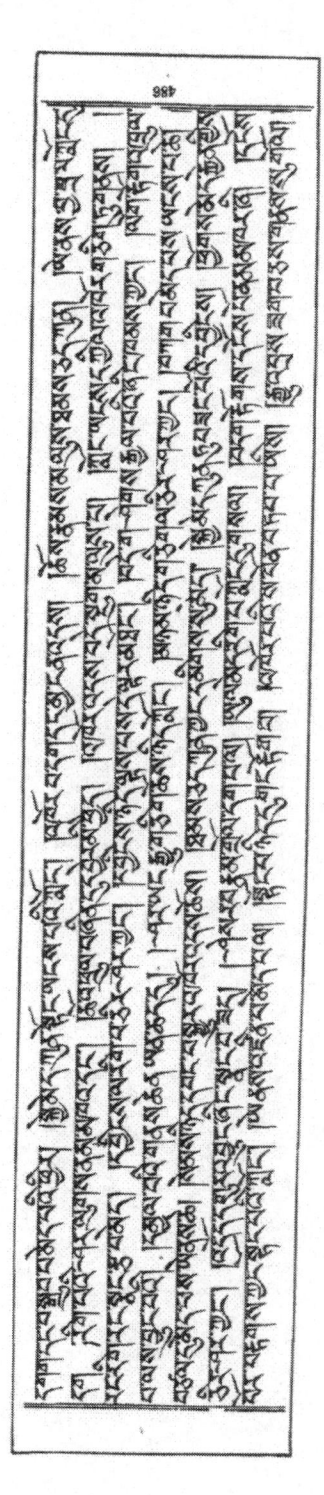

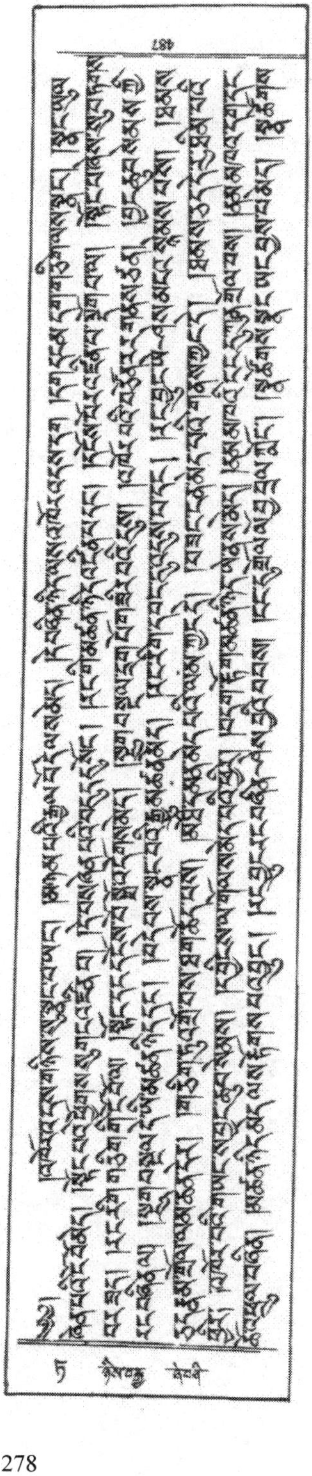

The Royal Tantra on the Brilliant Diffusion of Majestic Space

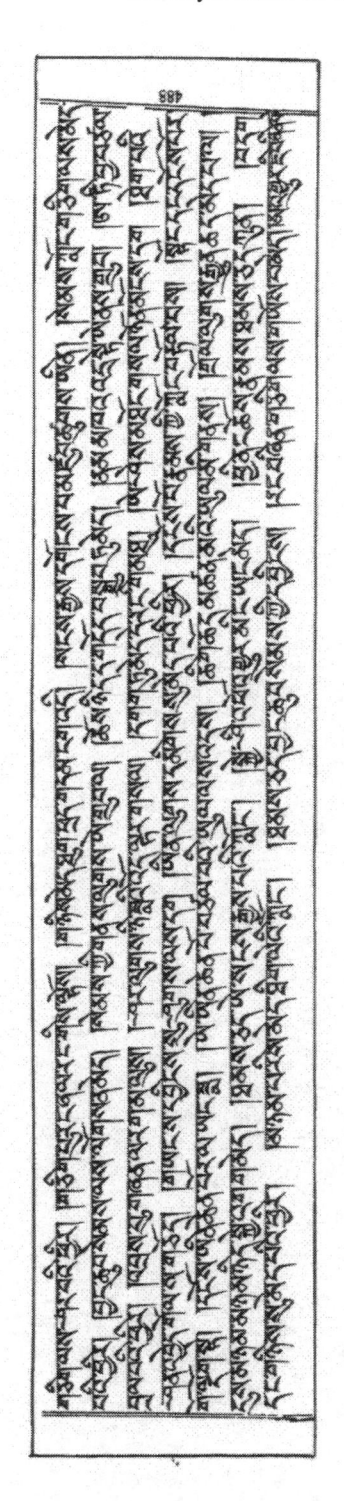

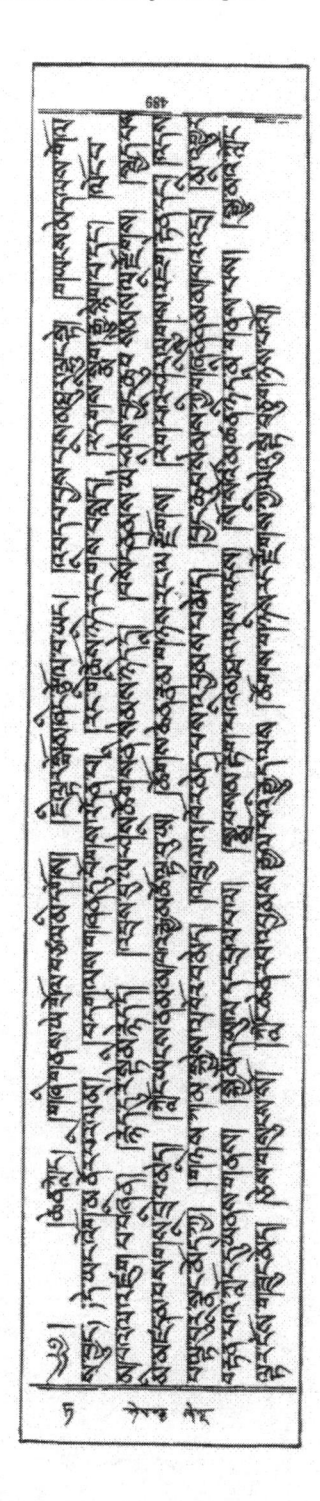

The Royal Tantra on the Brilliant Diffusion of Majestic Space

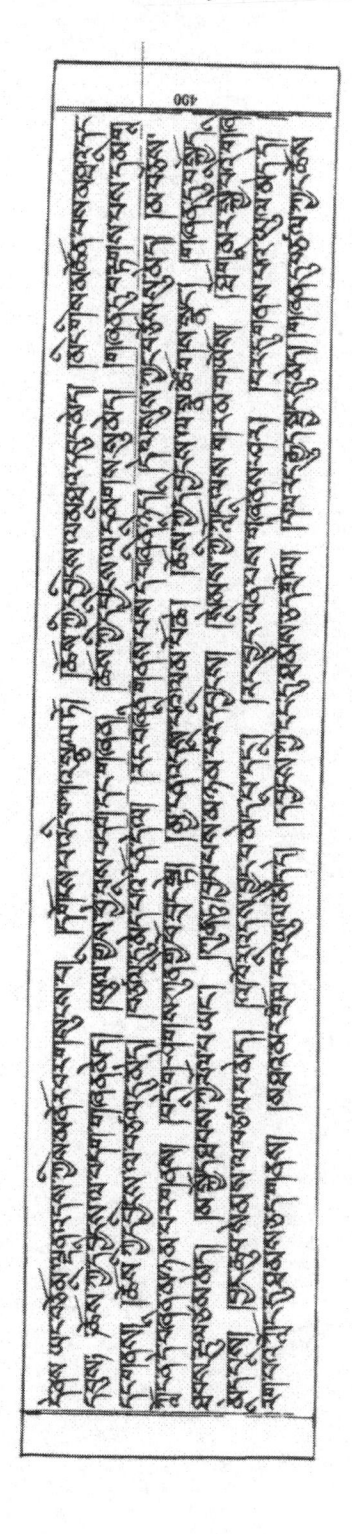

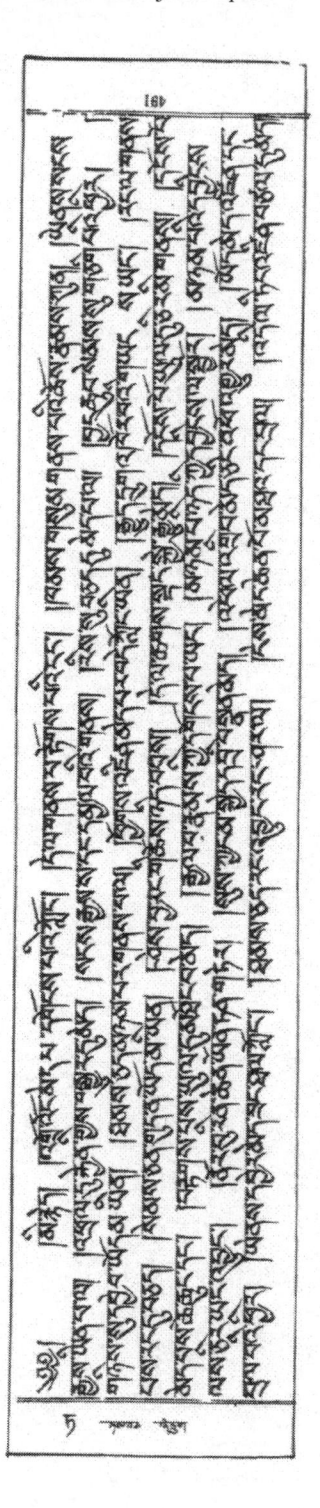

The Royal Tantra on the Brilliant Diffusion of Majestic Space

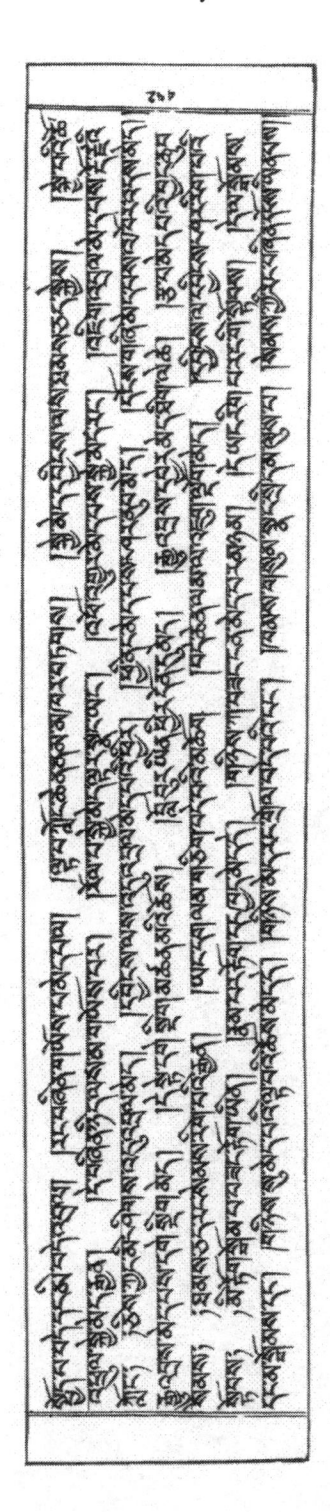

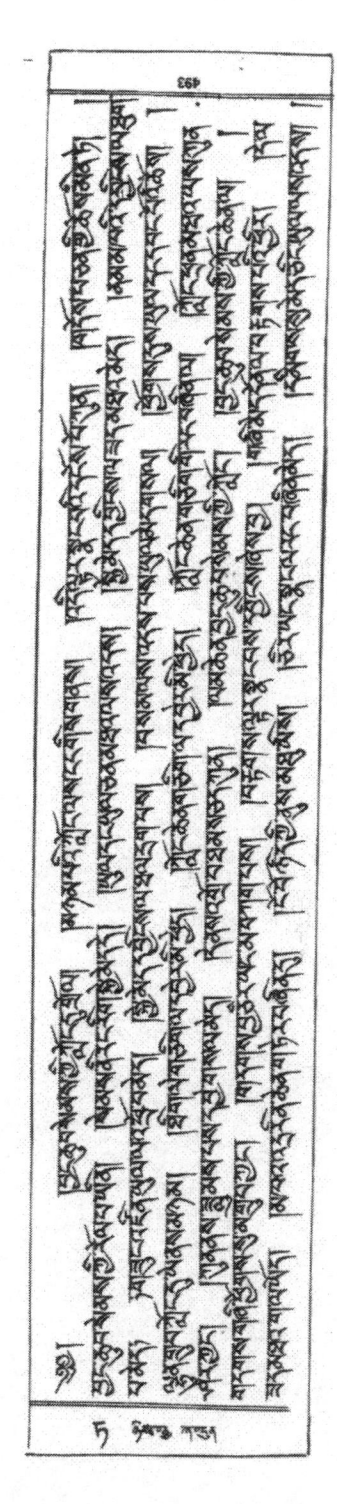

The Royal Tantra on the Brilliant Diffusion of Majestic Space

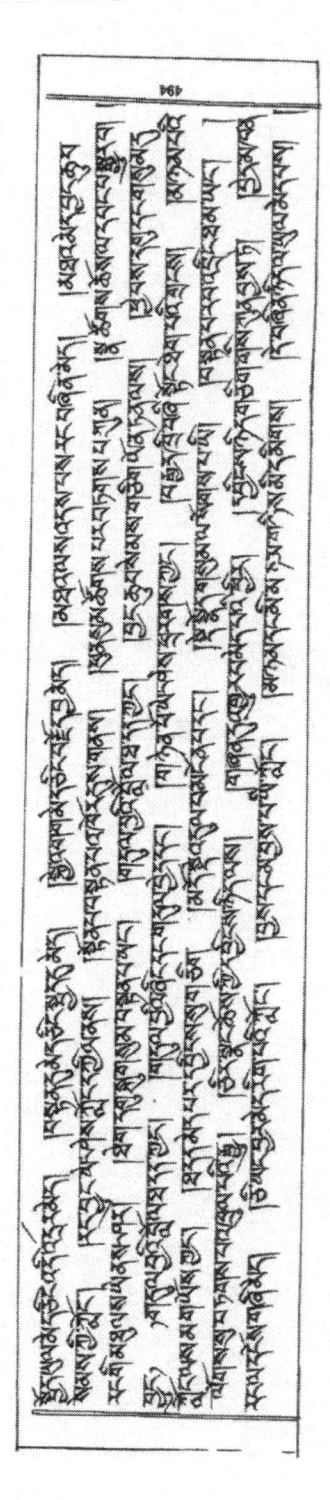

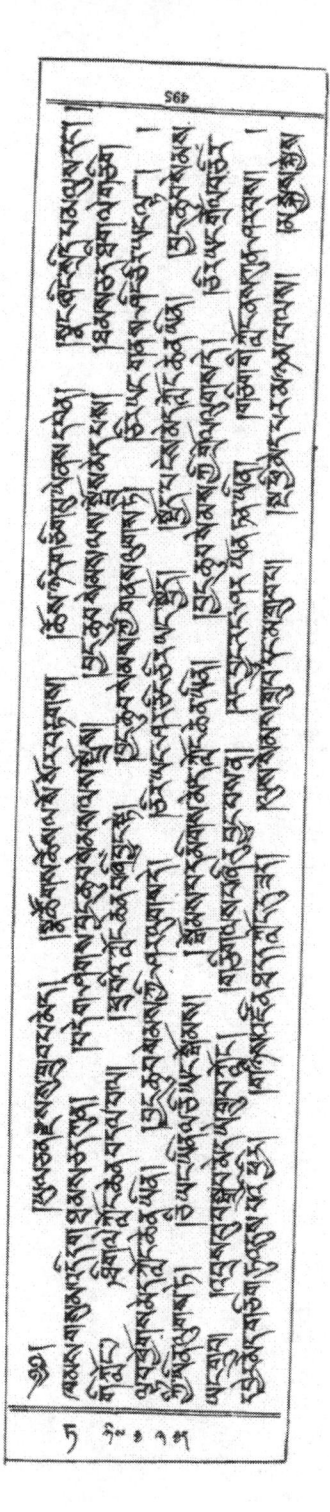

The Royal Tantra on the Brilliant Diffusion of Majestic Space

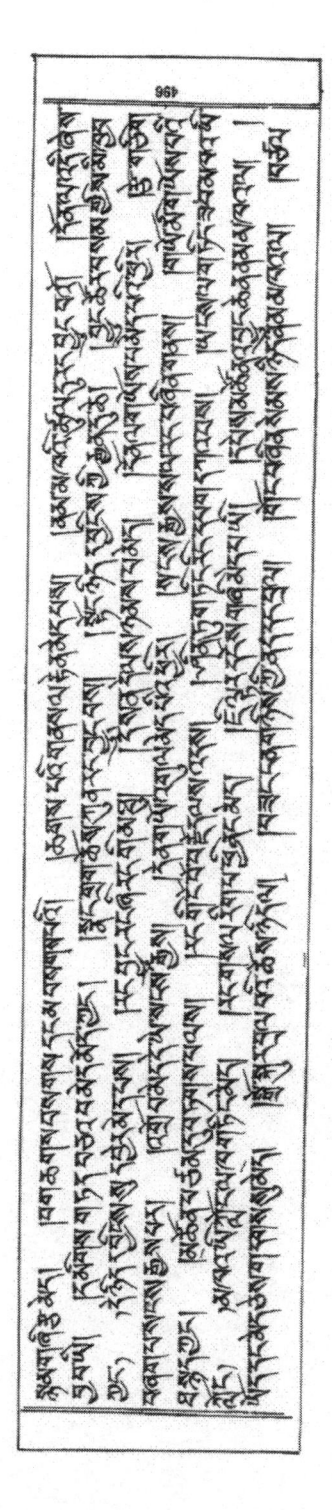

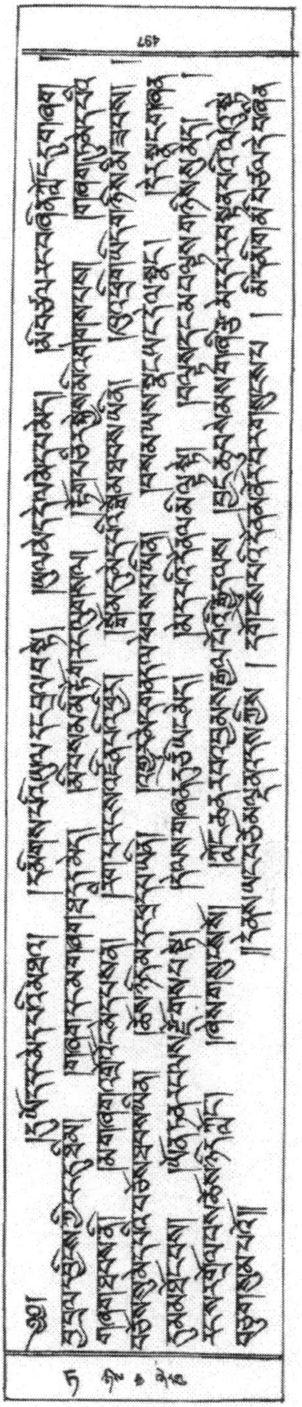

The Royal Tantra on the Brilliant Diffusion of Majestic Space

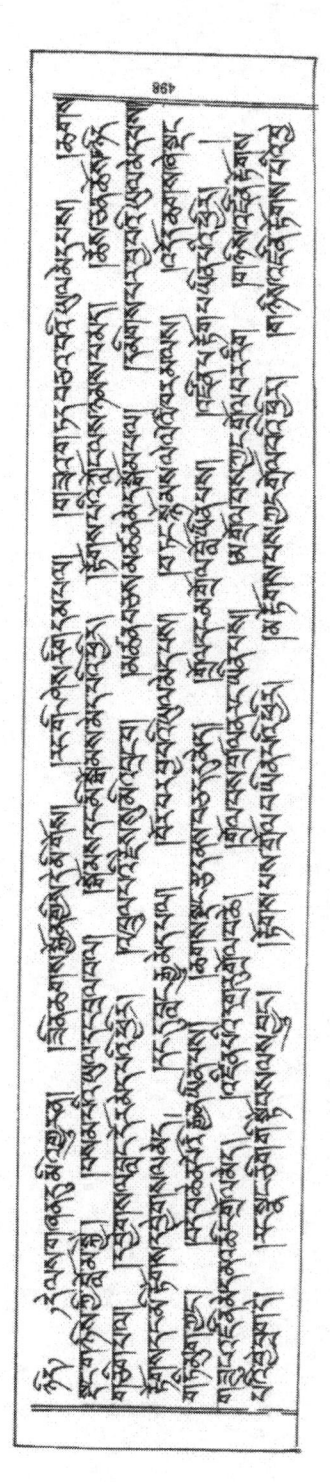

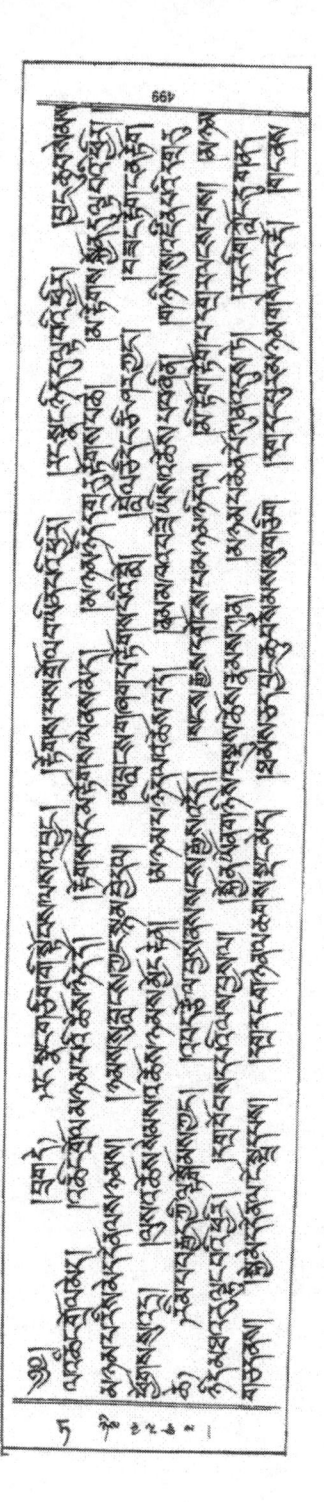

The Royal Tantra on the Brilliant Diffusion of Majestic Space

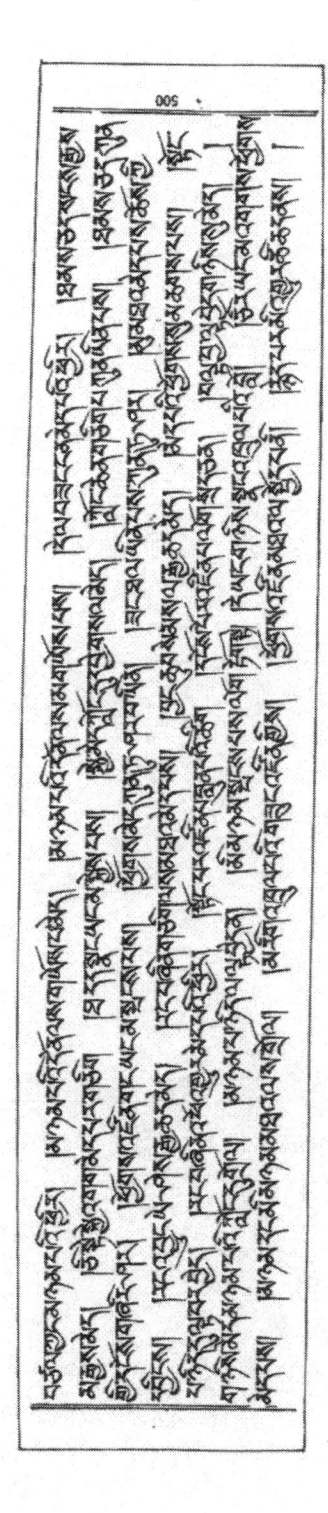

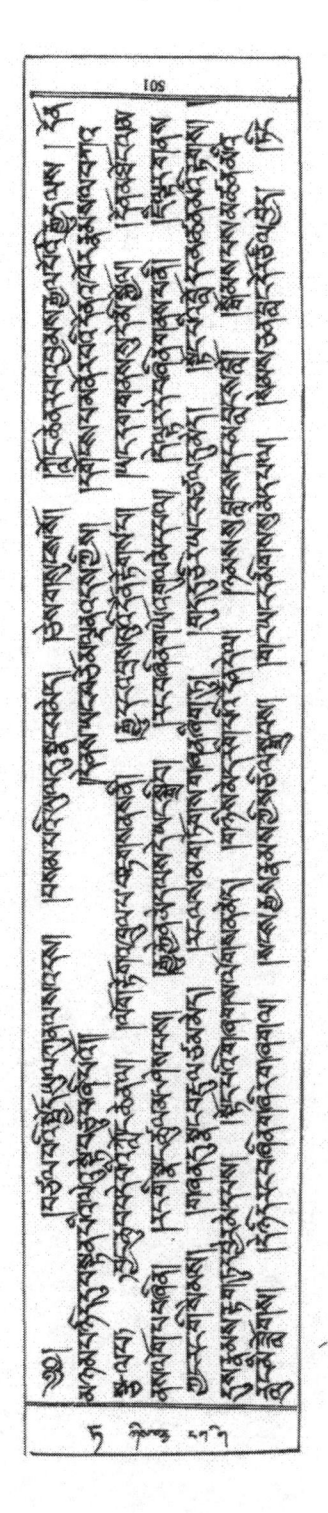

The Royal Tantra on the Brilliant Diffusion of Majestic Space

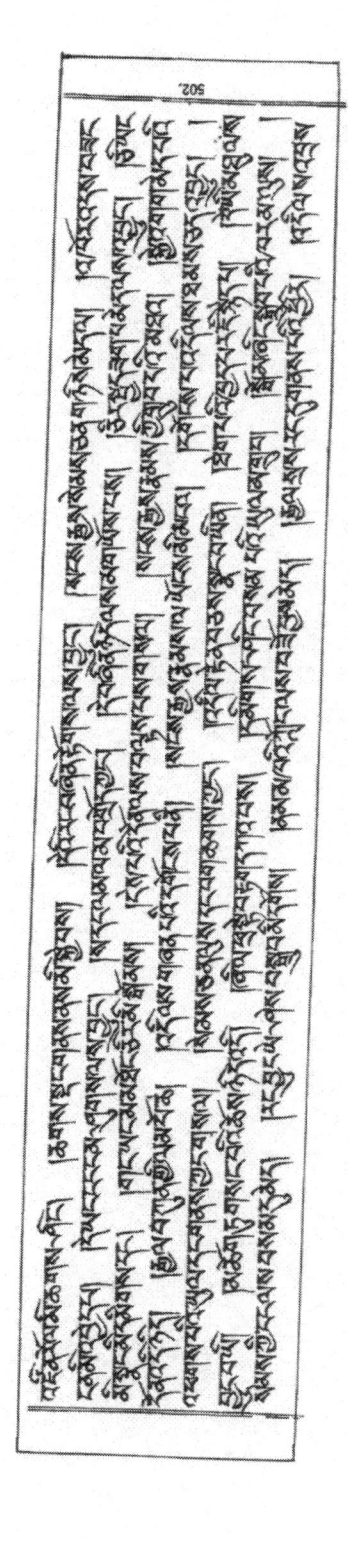

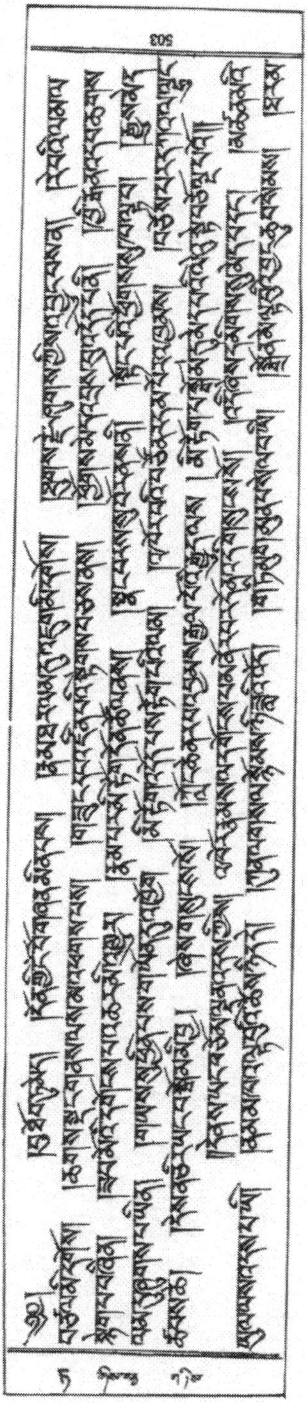

The Royal Tantra on the Brilliant Diffusion of Majestic Space

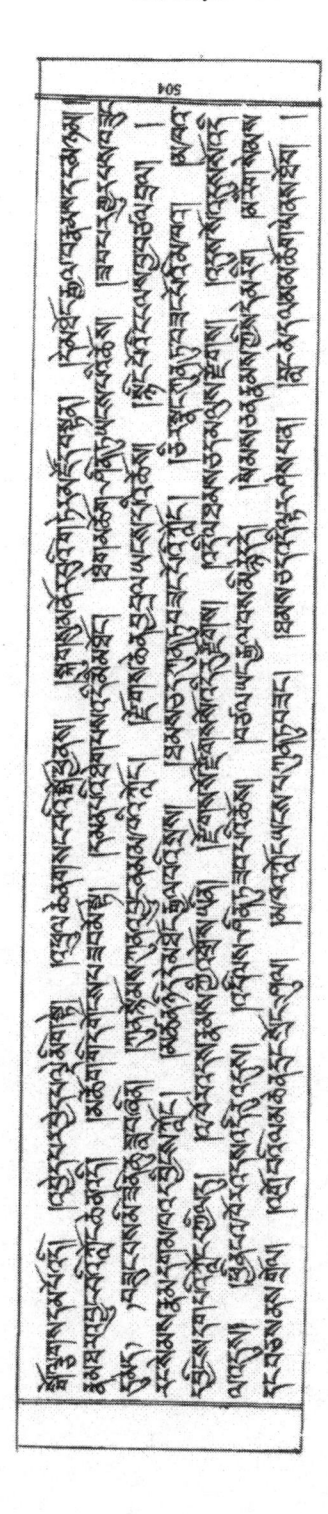

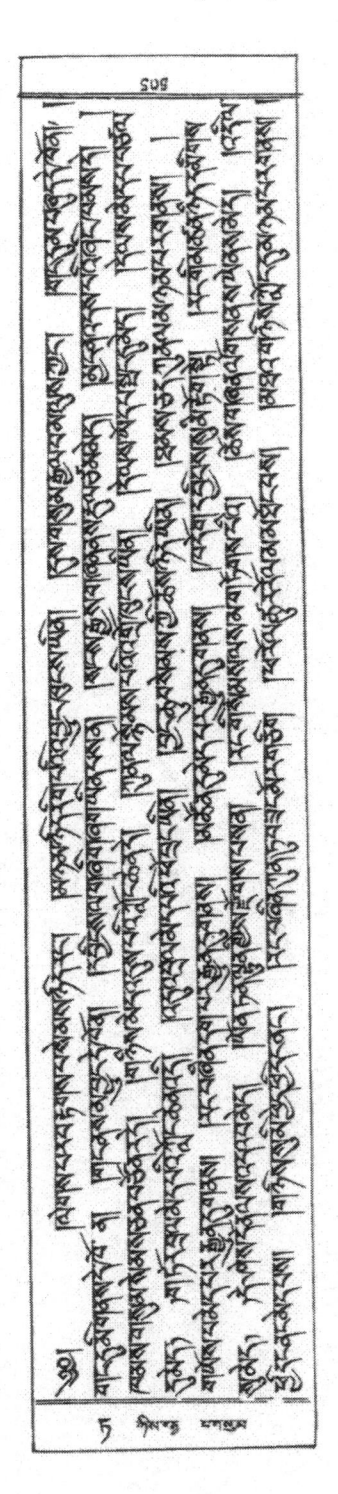

The Royal Tantra on the Brilliant Diffusion of Majestic Space

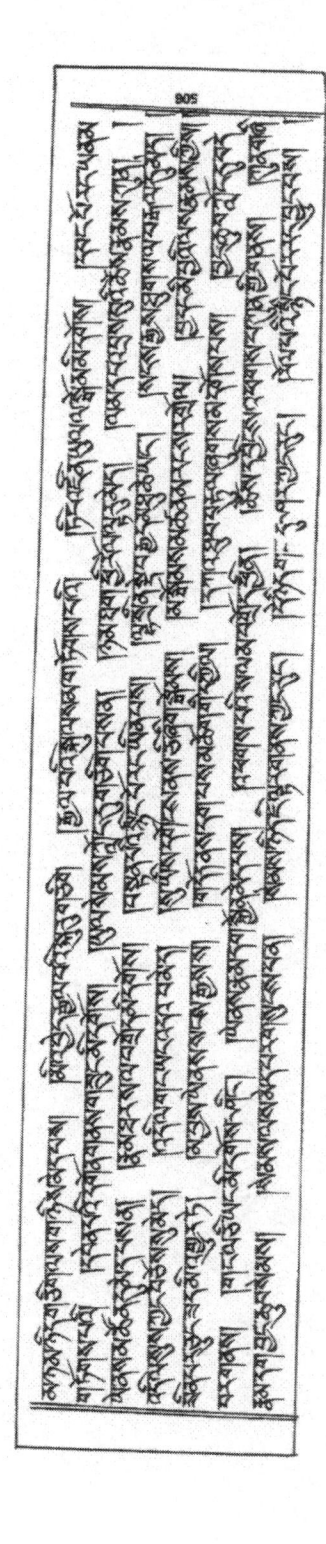

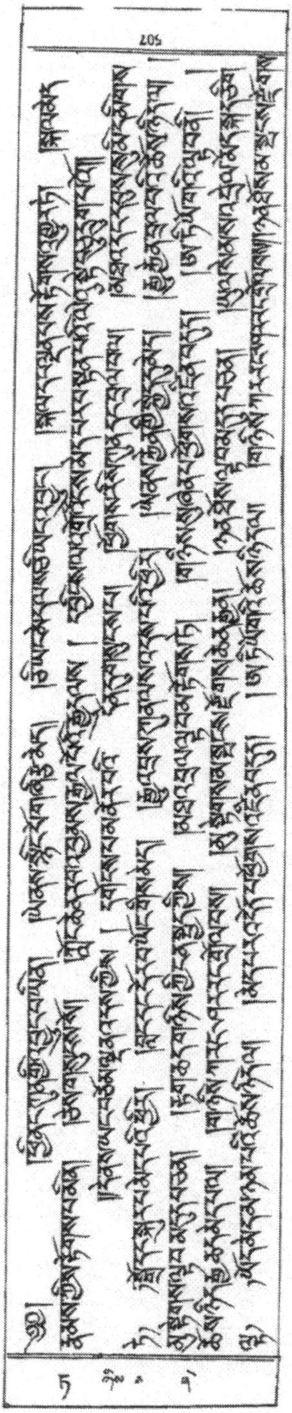

The Royal Tantra on the Brilliant Diffusion of Majestic Space

The Royal Tantra on the Brilliant Diffusion of Majestic Space

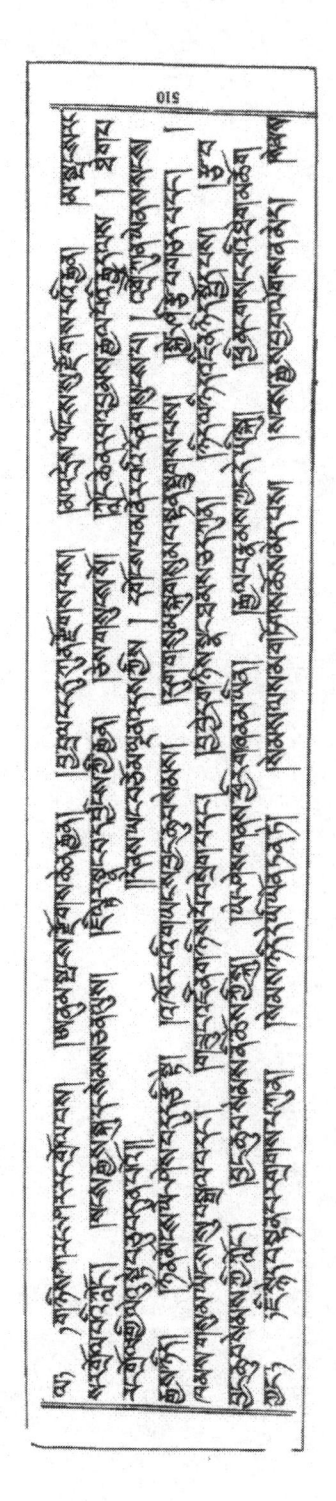

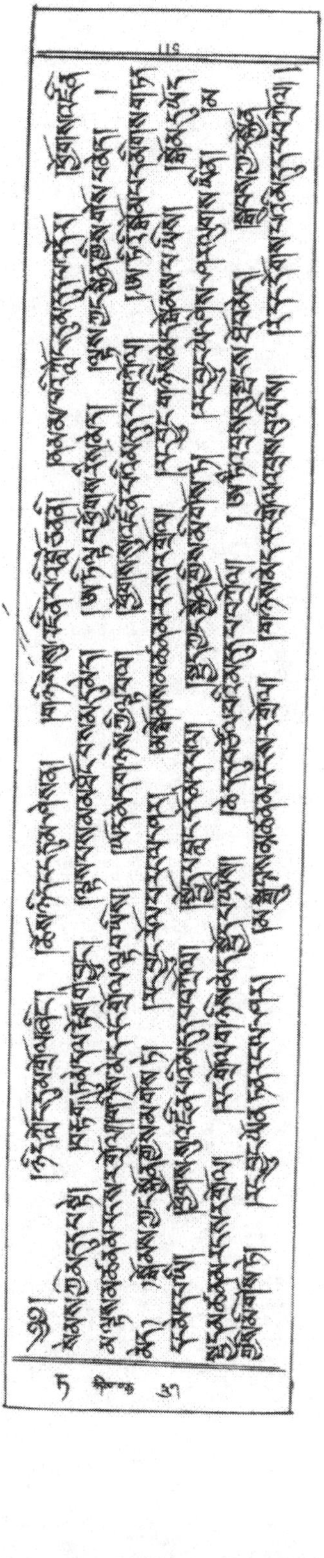

The Royal Tantra on the Brilliant Diffusion of Majestic Space

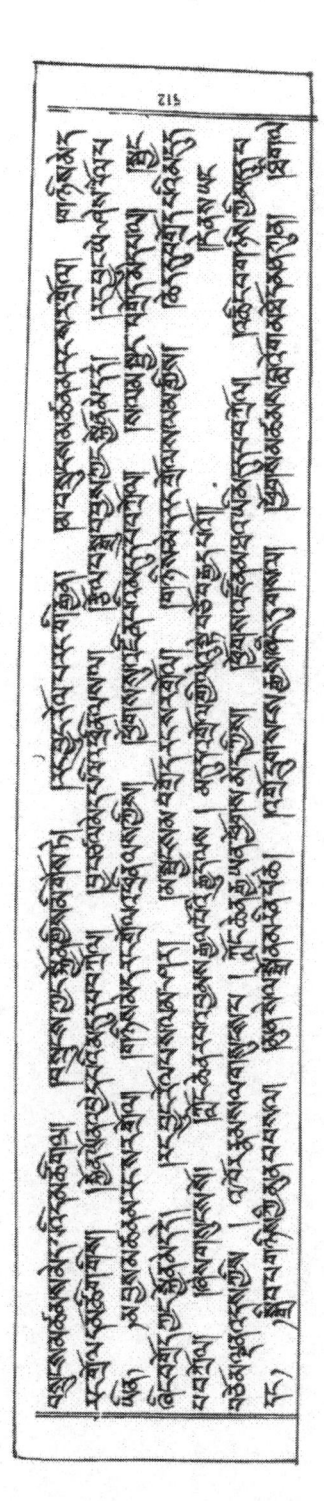

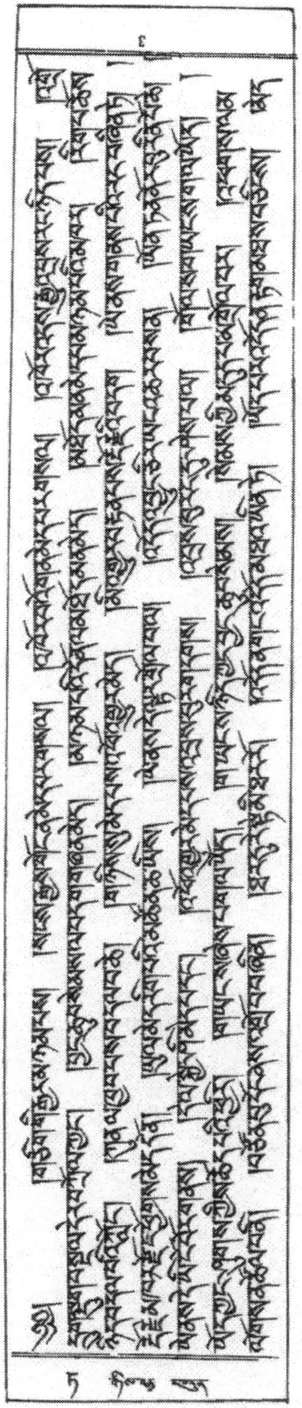

The Royal Tantra on the Brilliant Diffusion of Majestic Space

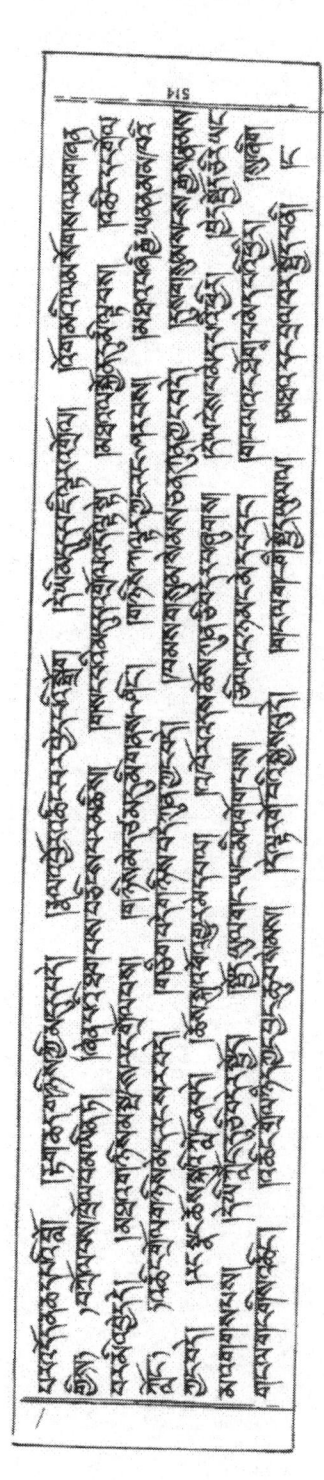

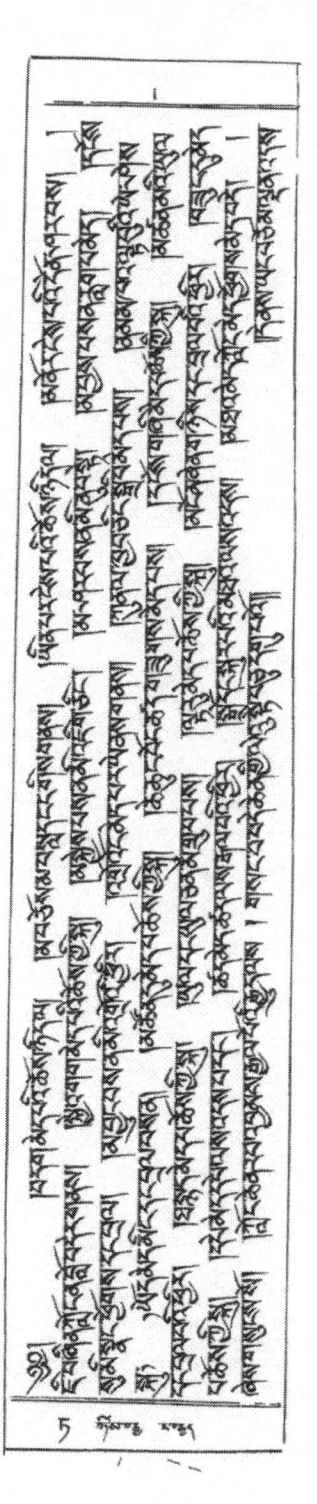

The Royal Tantra on the Brilliant Diffusion of Majestic Space

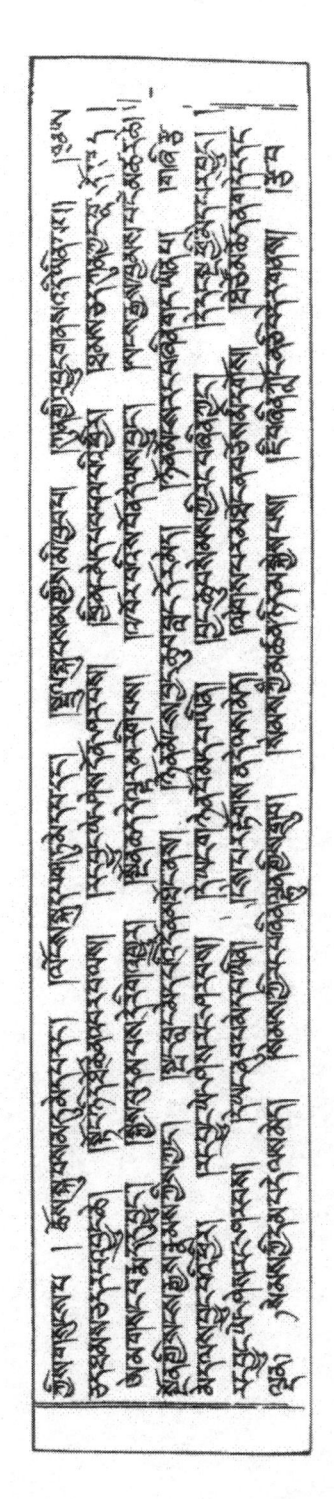

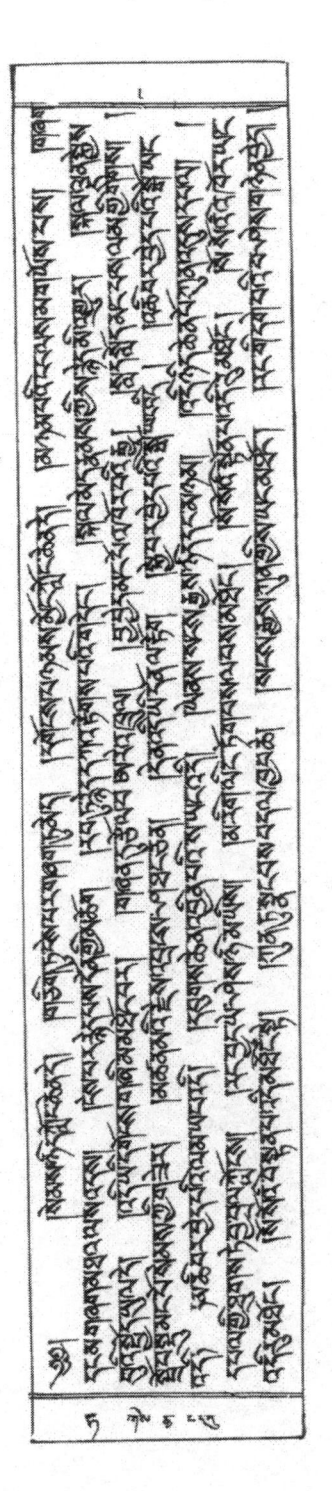

The Royal Tantra on the Brilliant Diffusion of Majestic Space

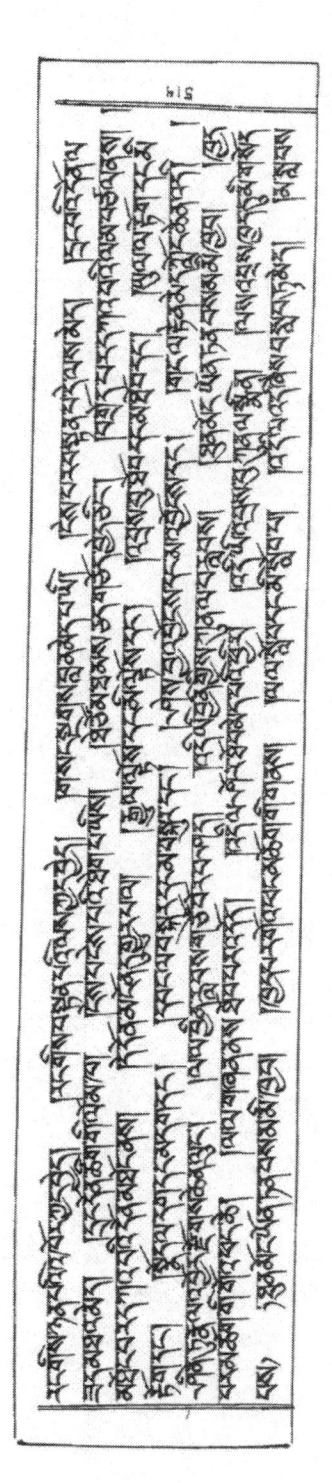

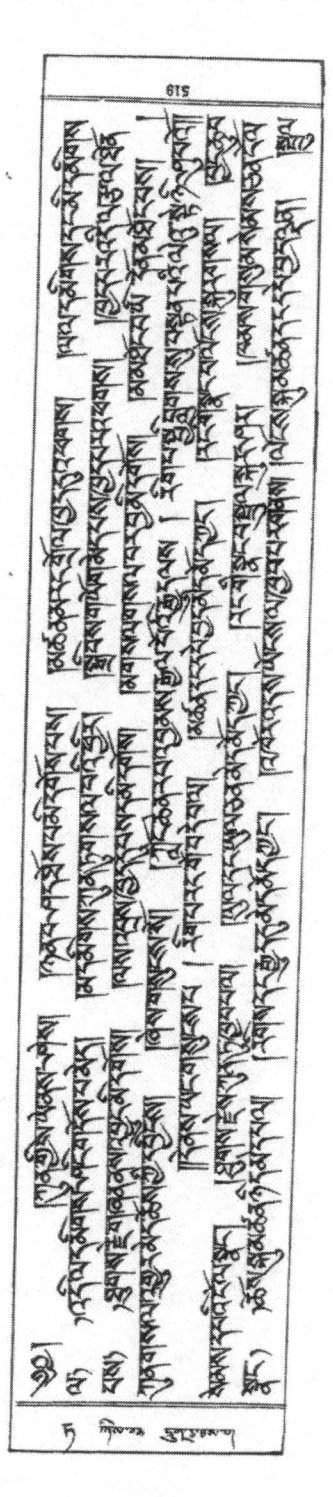

The Royal Tantra on the Brilliant Diffusion of Majestic Space

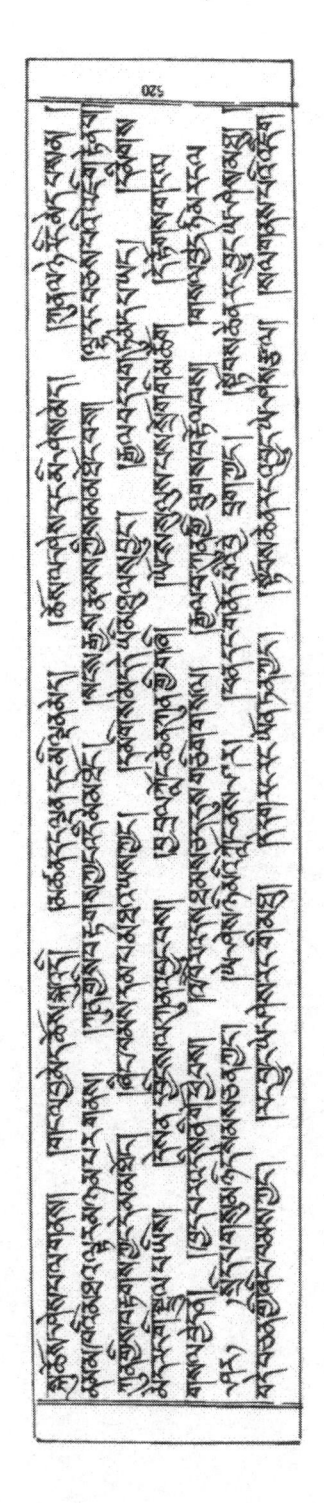

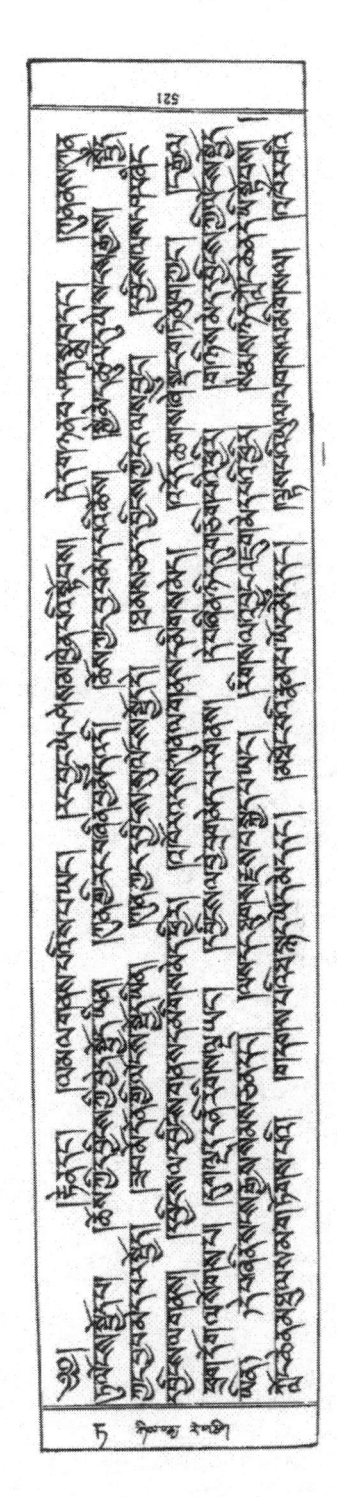

The Royal Tantra on the Brilliant Diffusion of Majestic Space

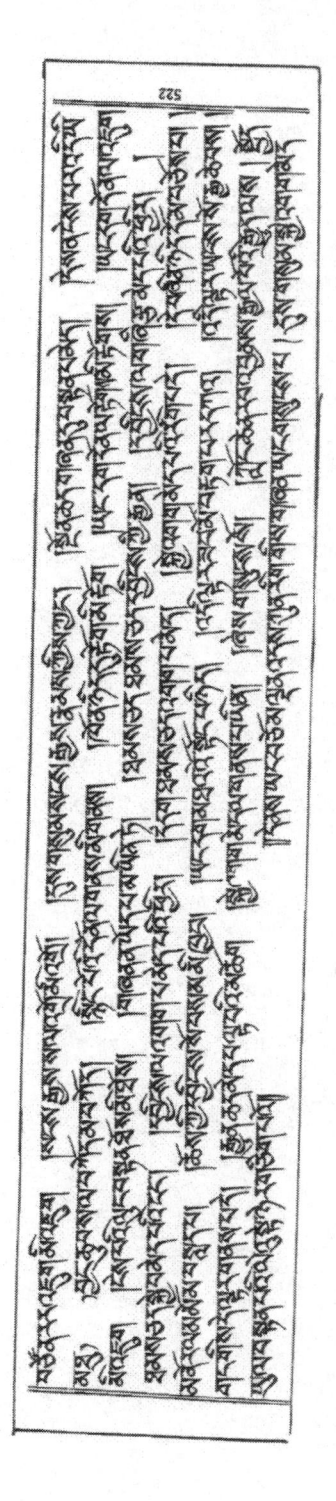

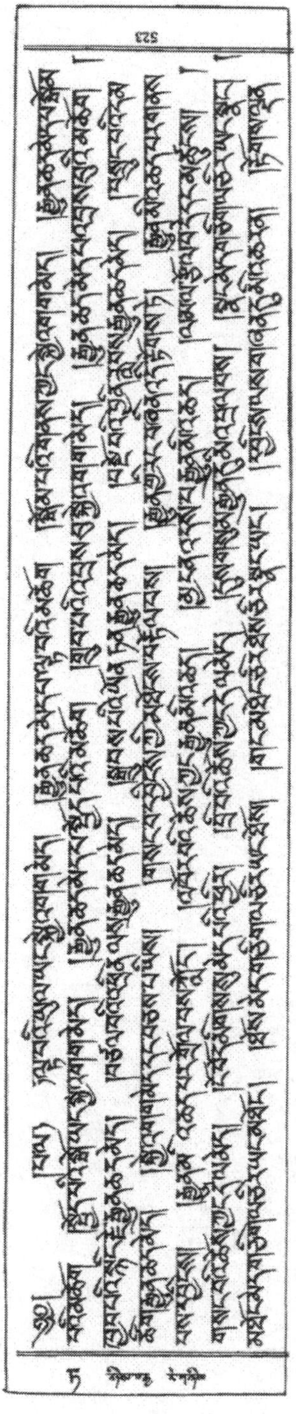

The Royal Tantra on the Brilliant Diffusion of Majestic Space

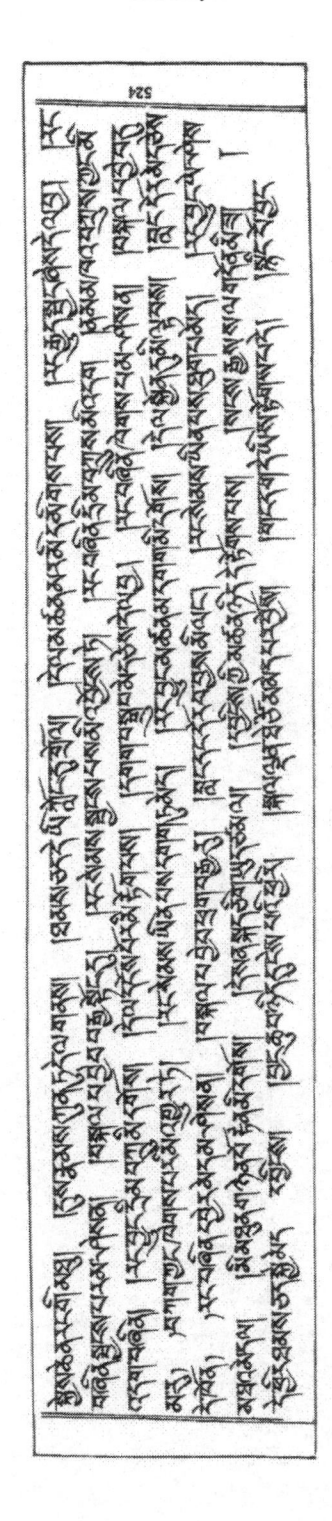

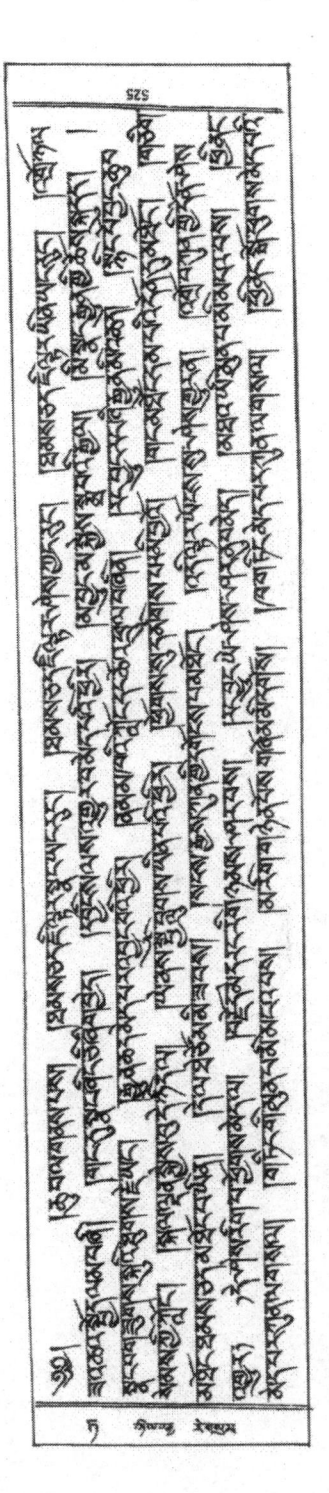

The Royal Tantra on the Brilliant Diffusion of Majestic Space

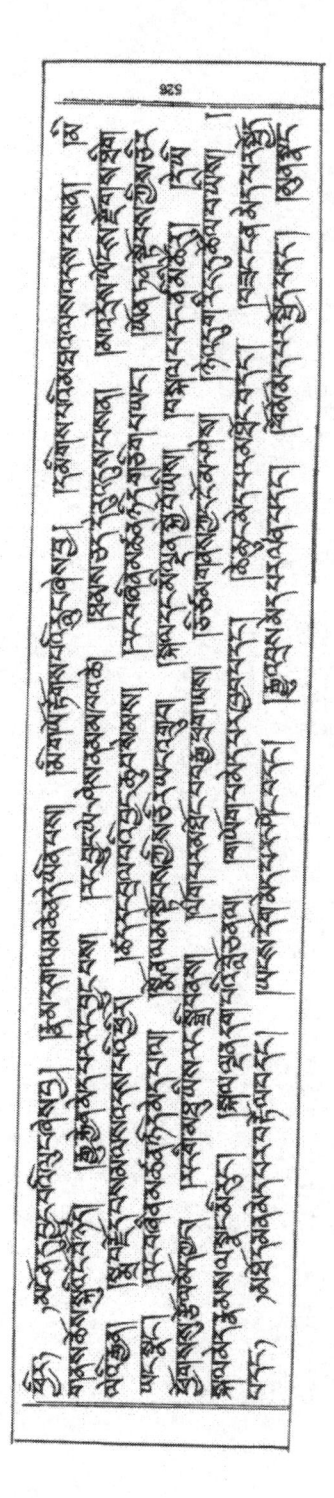

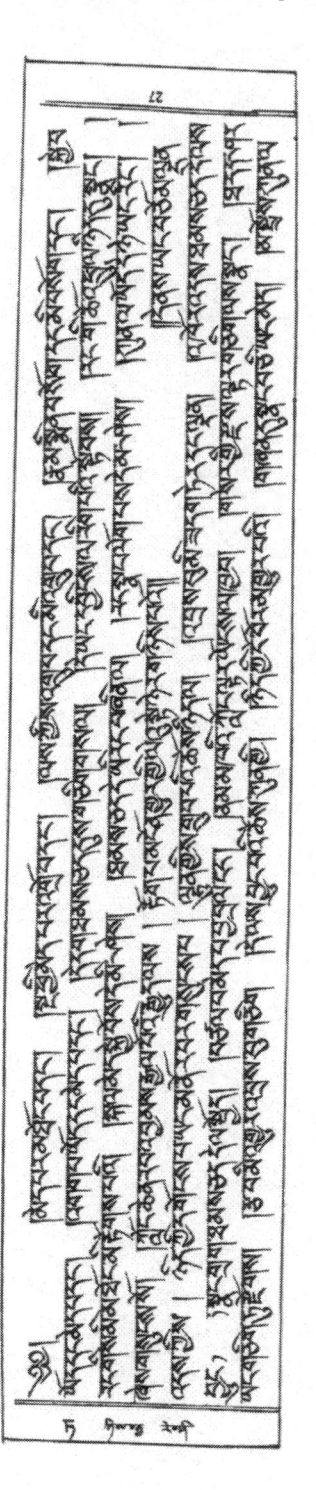

The Royal Tantra on the Brilliant Diffusion of Majestic Space

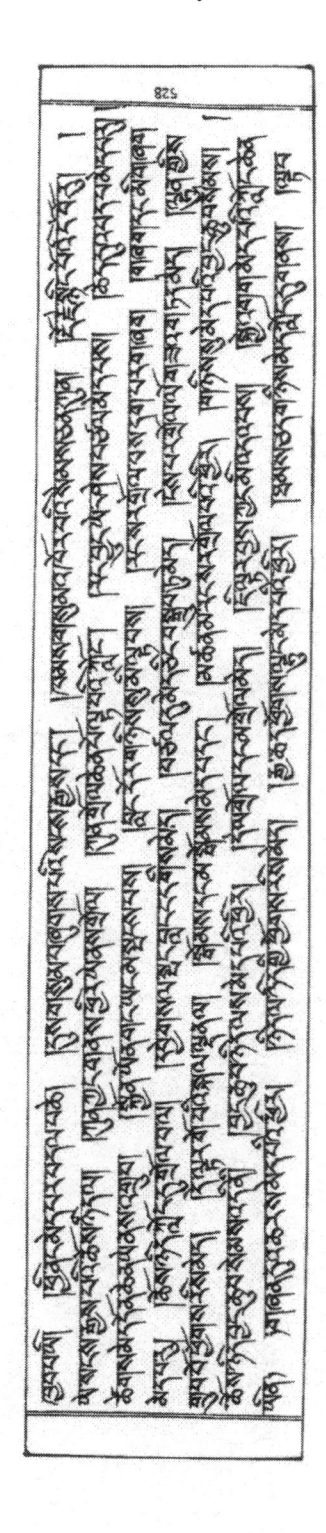

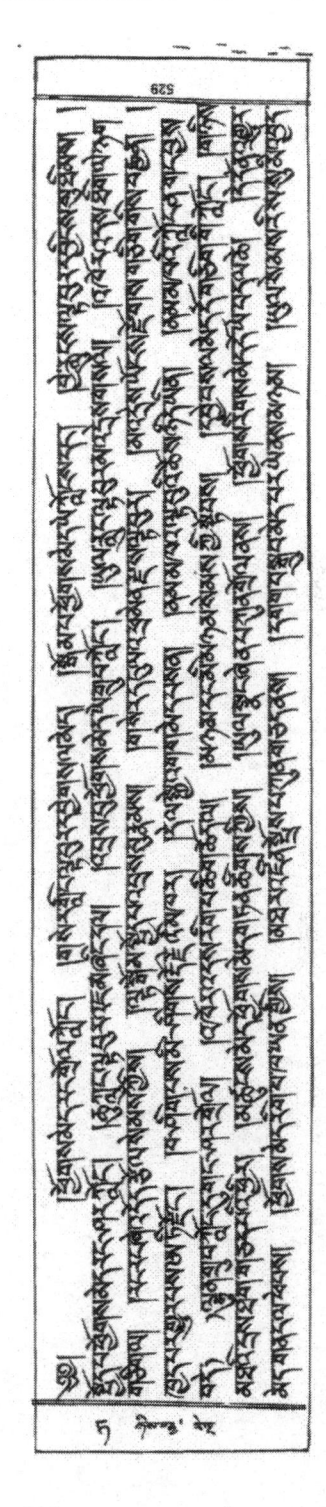

The Royal Tantra on the Brilliant Diffusion of Majestic Space

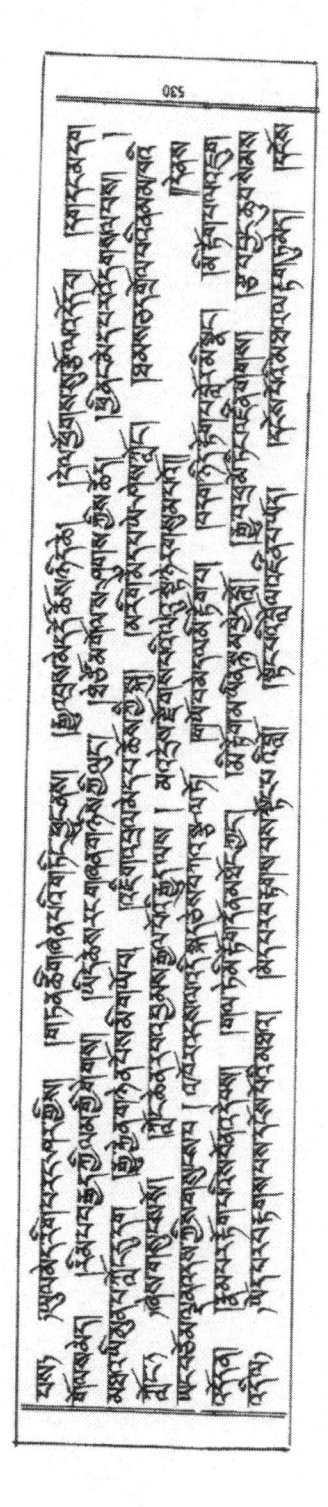

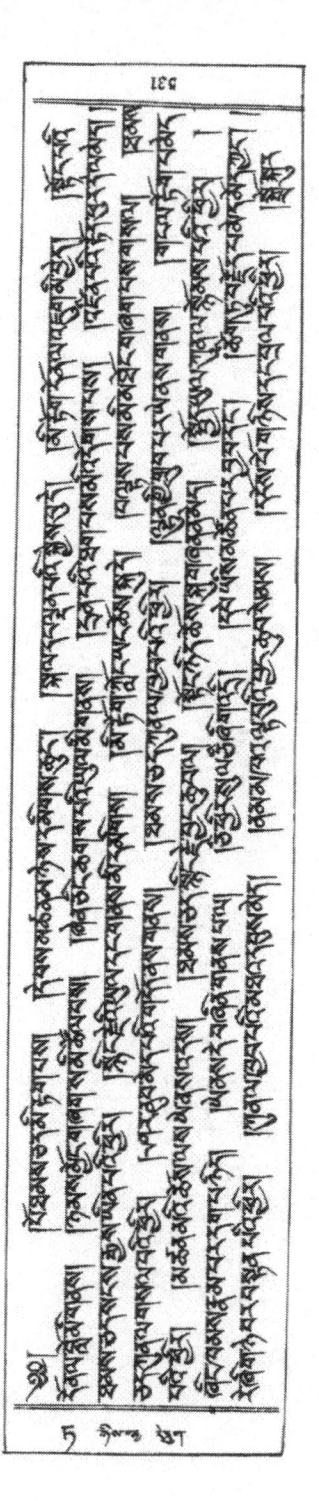

The Royal Tantra on the Brilliant Diffusion of Majestic Space

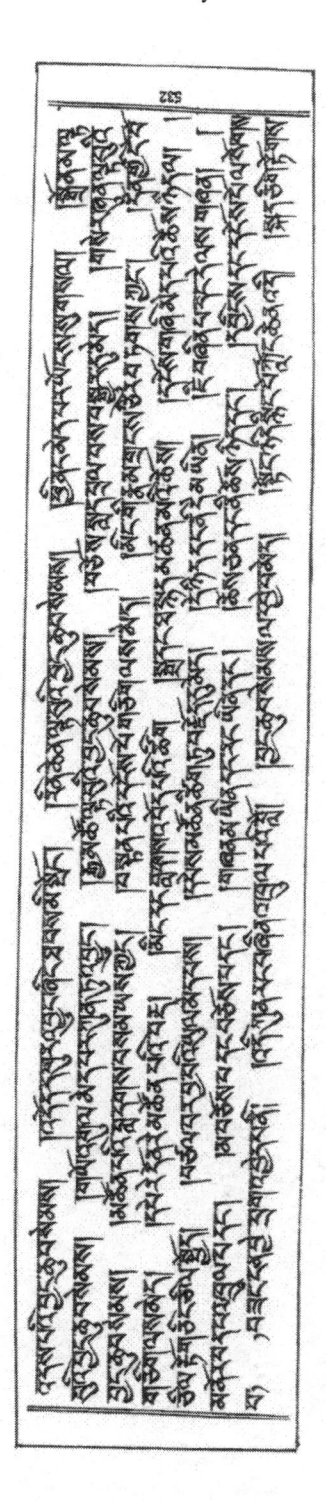

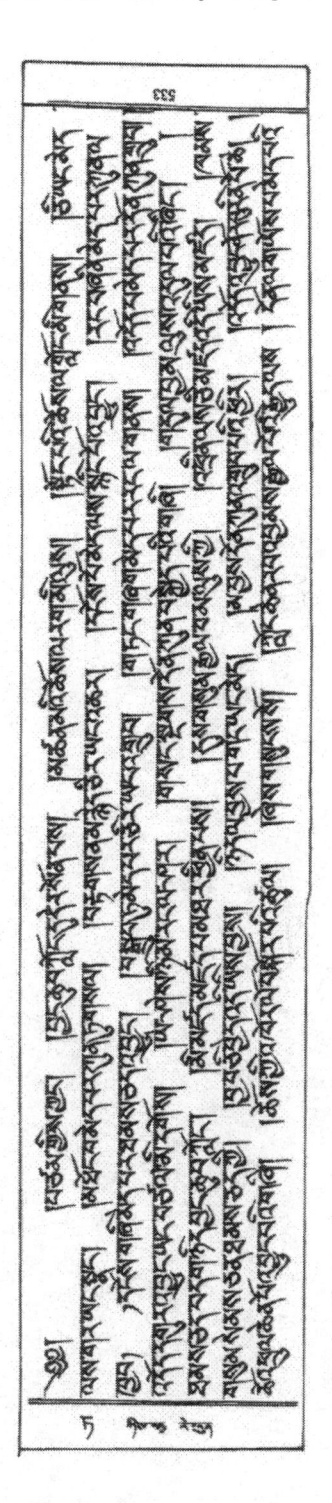

The Royal Tantra on the Brilliant Diffusion of Majestic Space

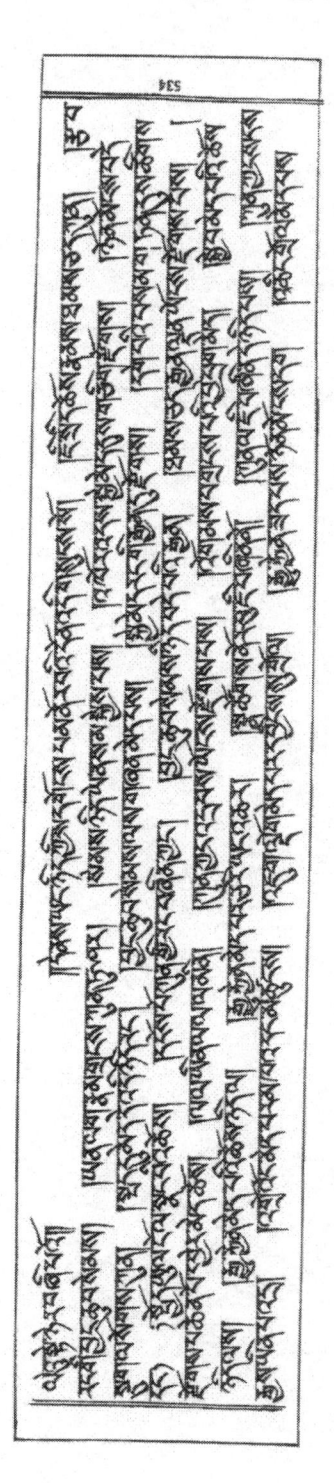

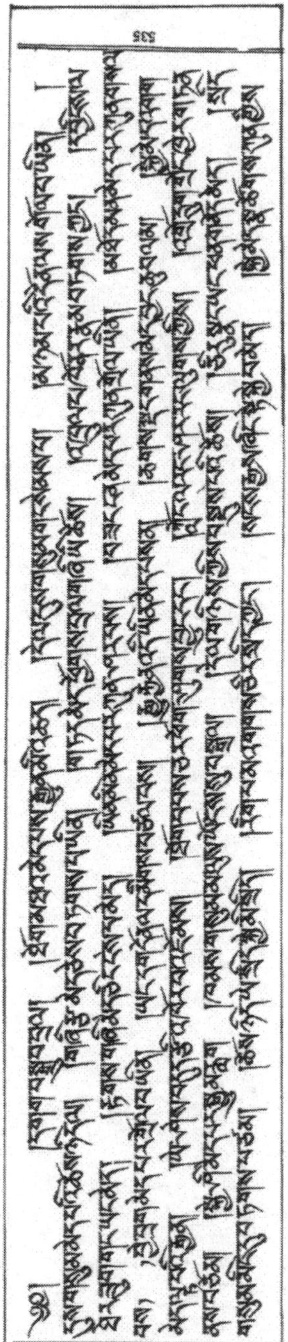

The Royal Tantra on the Brilliant Diffusion of Majestic Space

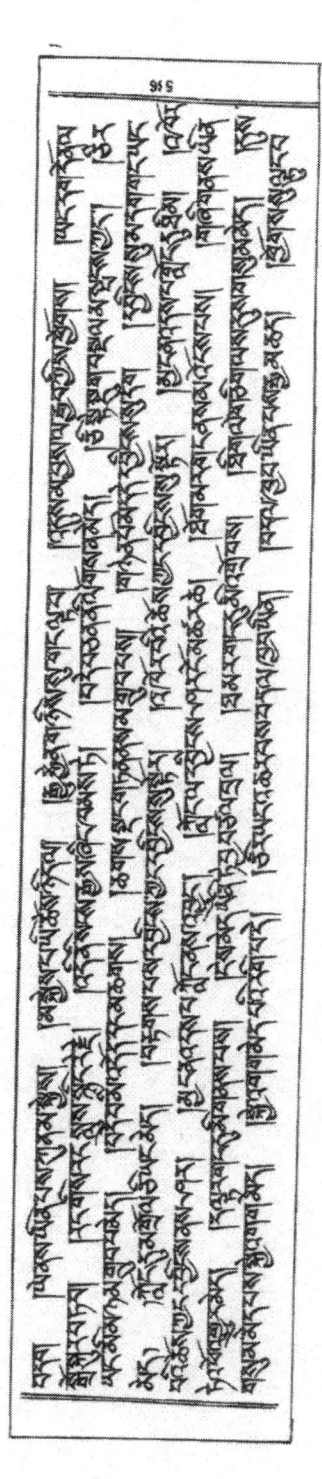

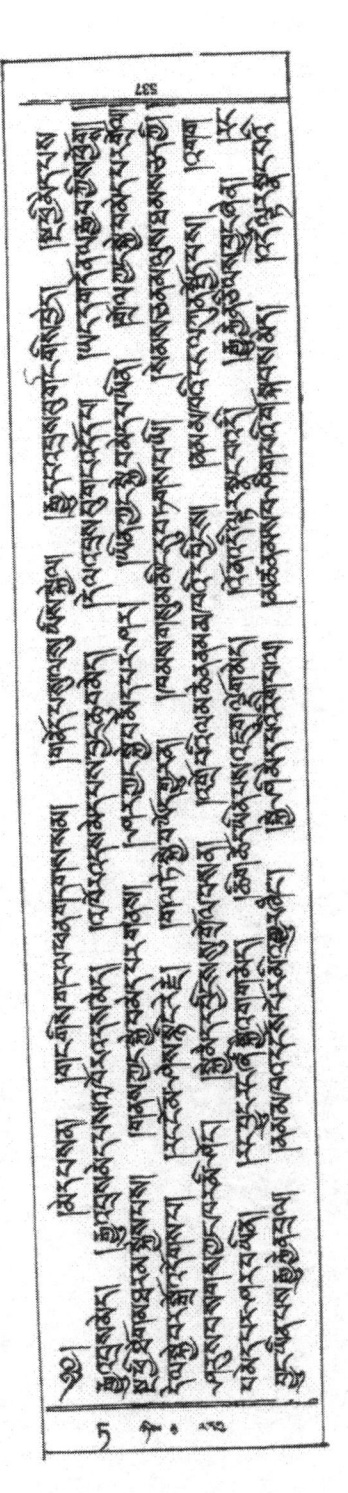

The Royal Tantra on the Brilliant Diffusion of Majestic Space

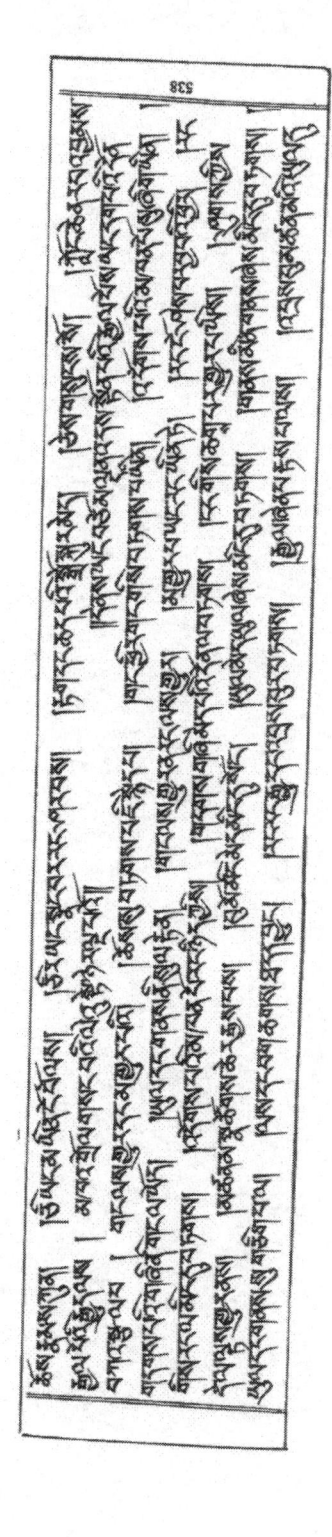

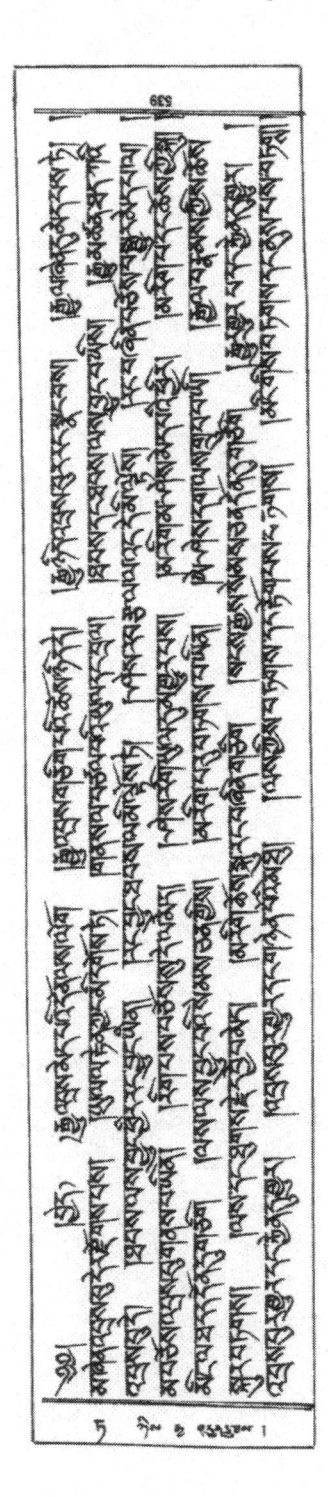

The Royal Tantra on the Brilliant Diffusion of Majestic Space

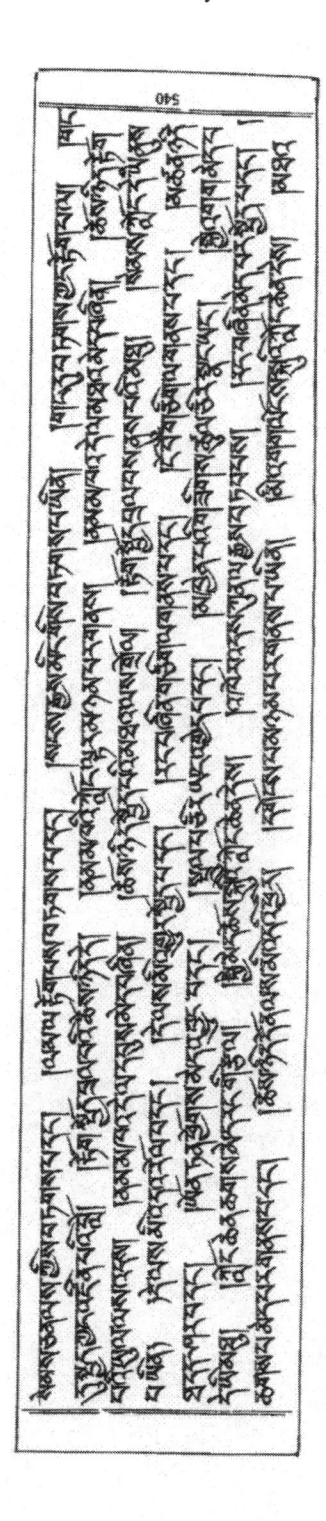

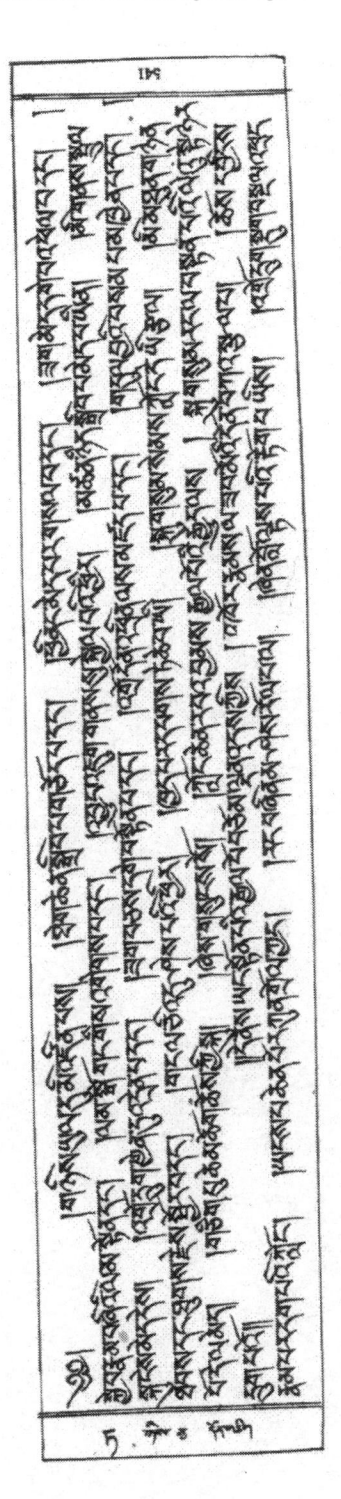

The Royal Tantra on the Brilliant Diffusion of Majestic Space

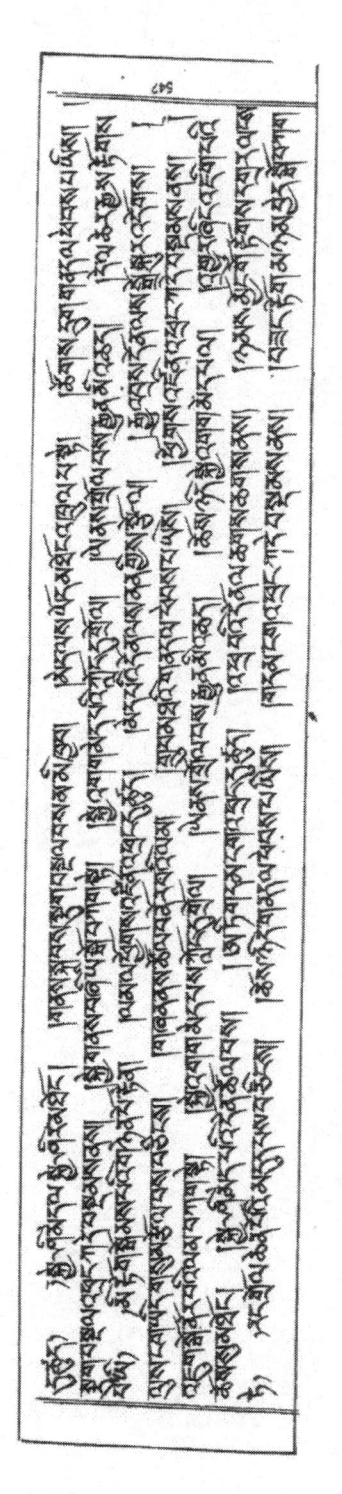

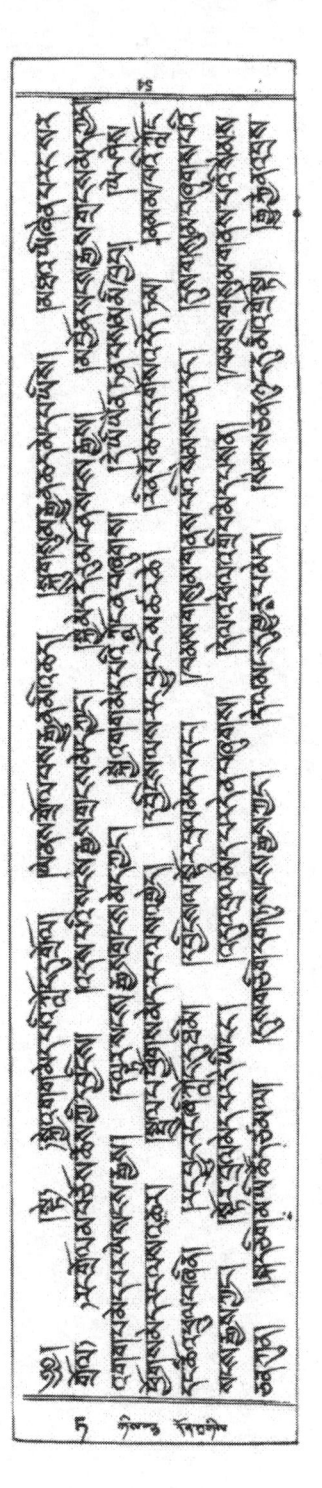

The Royal Tantra on the Brilliant Diffusion of Majestic Space

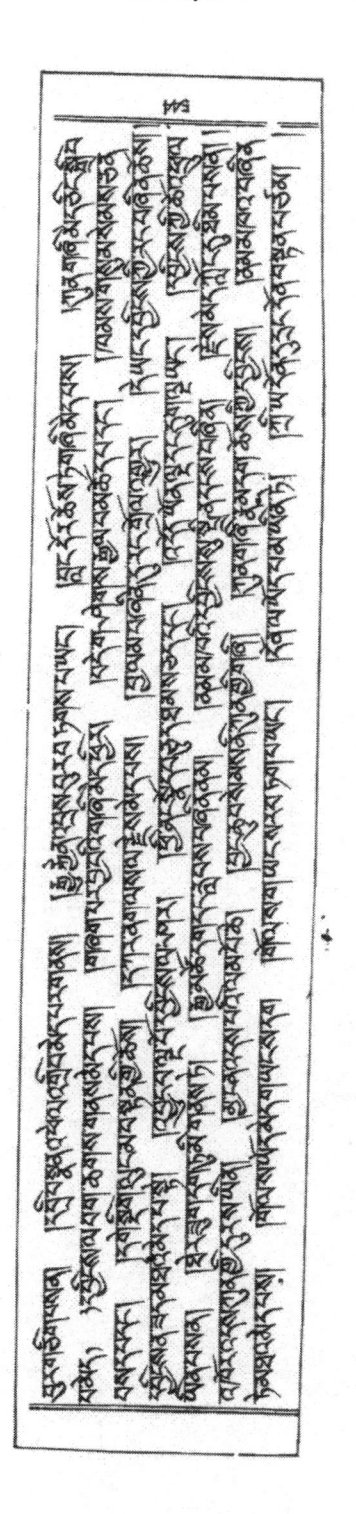

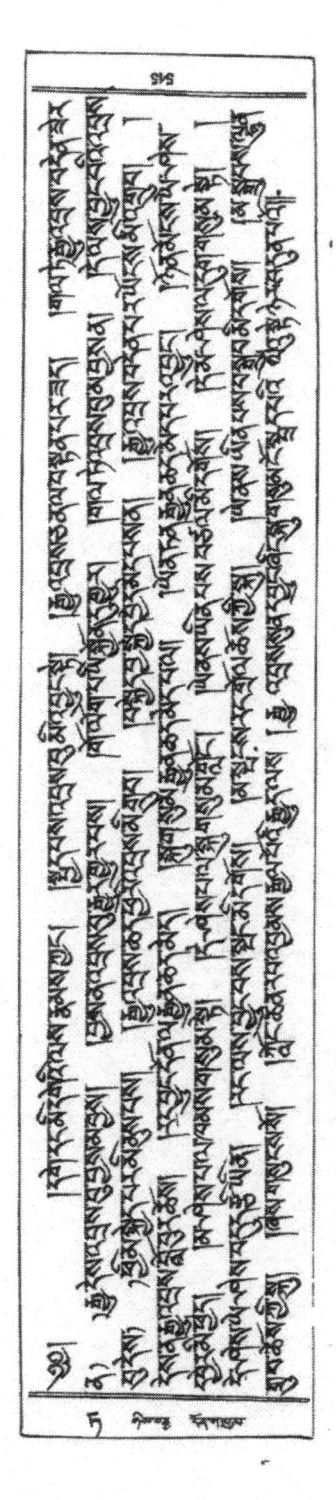

The Royal Tantra on the Brilliant Diffusion of Majestic Space

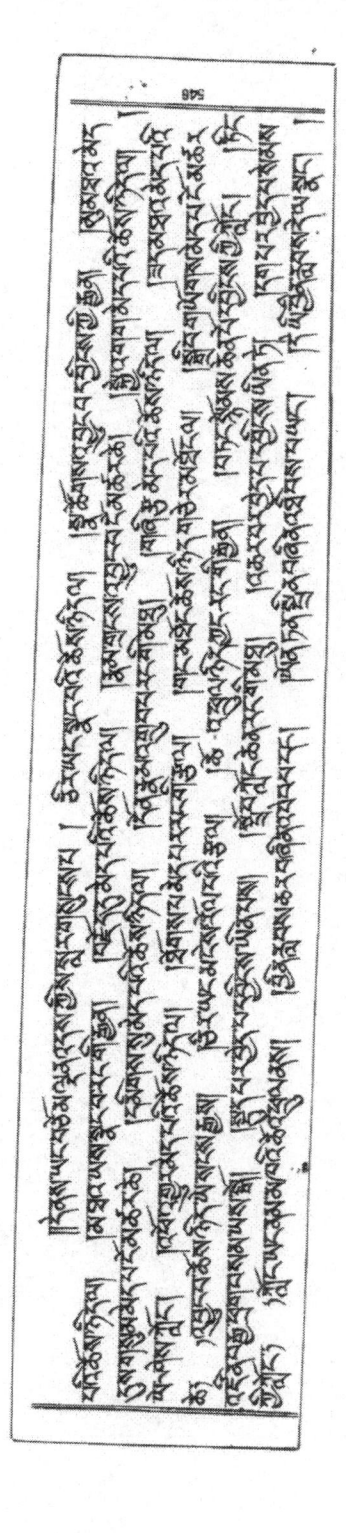

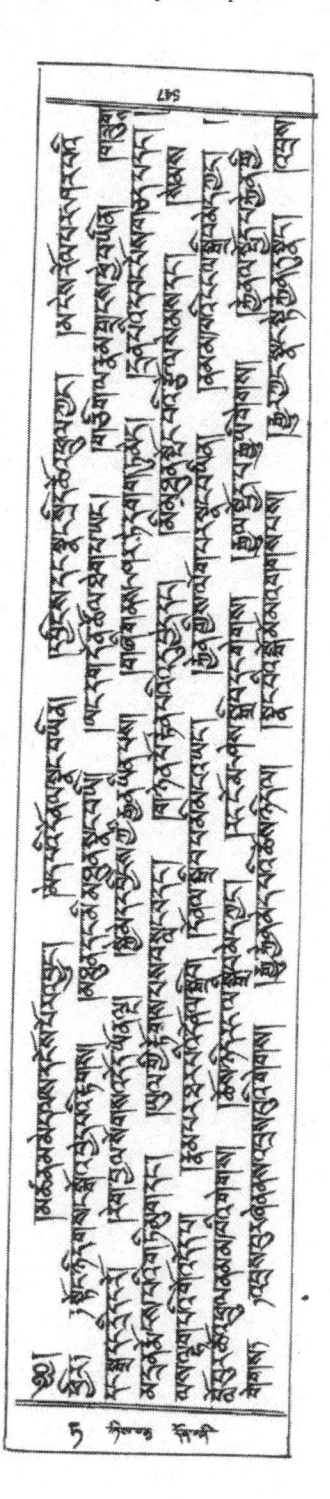

The Royal Tantra on the Brilliant Diffusion of Majestic Space

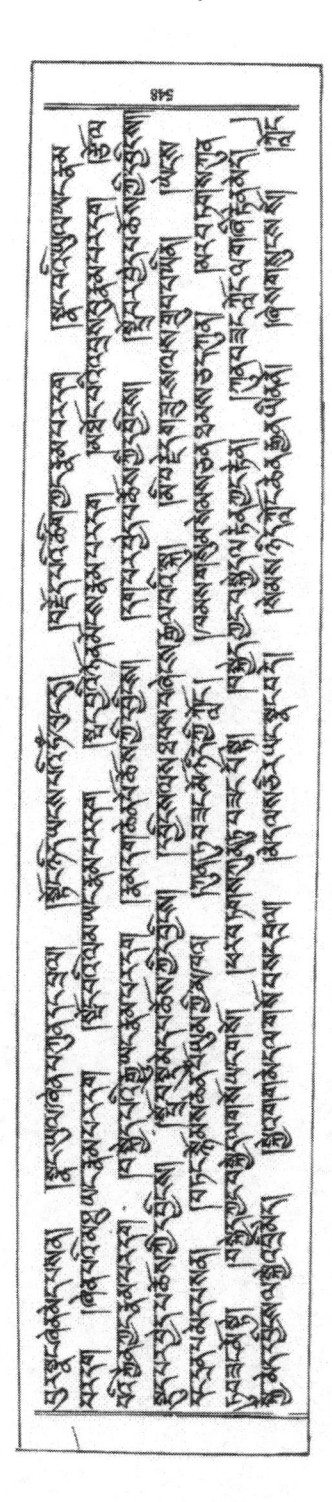

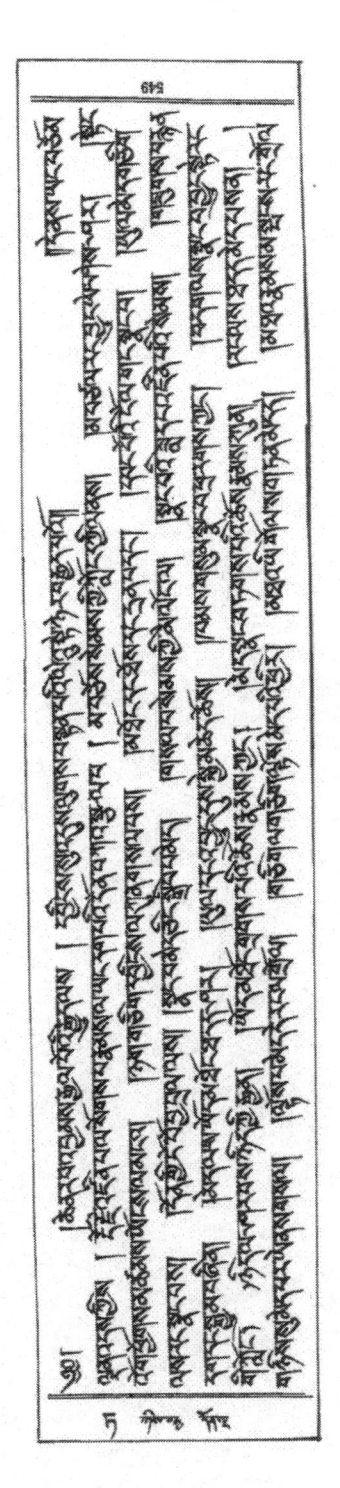

The Royal Tantra on the Brilliant Diffusion of Majestic Space

The Royal Tantra on the Brilliant Diffusion of Majestic Space

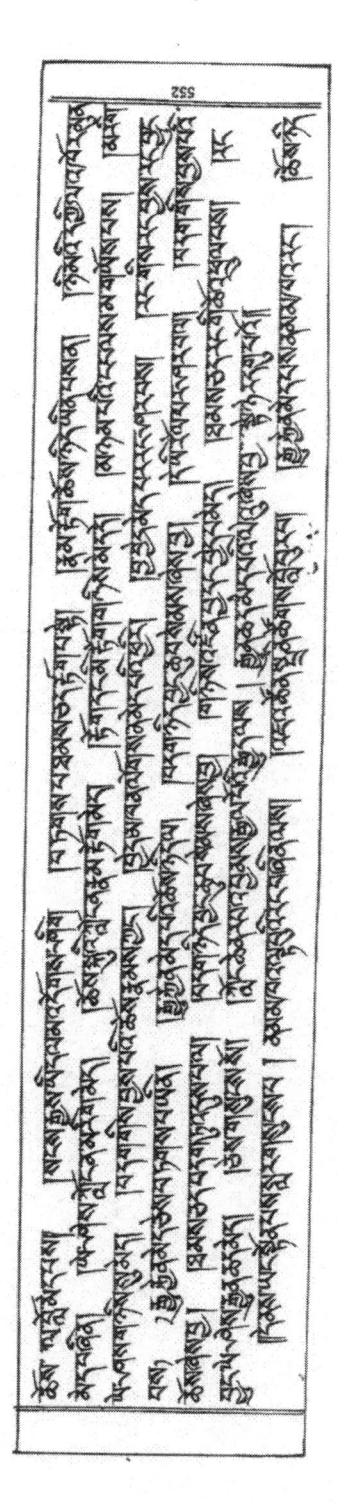

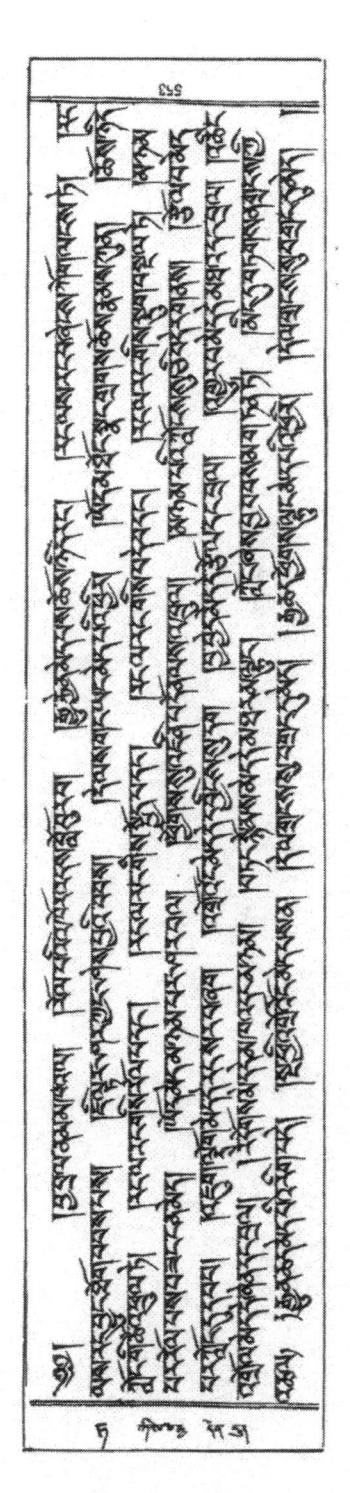

The Royal Tantra on the Brilliant Diffusion of Majestic Space

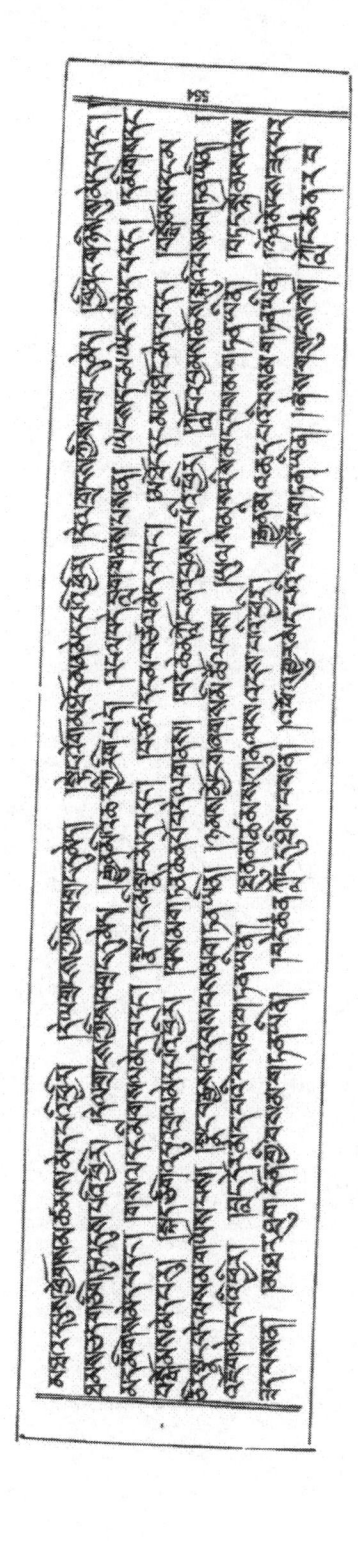

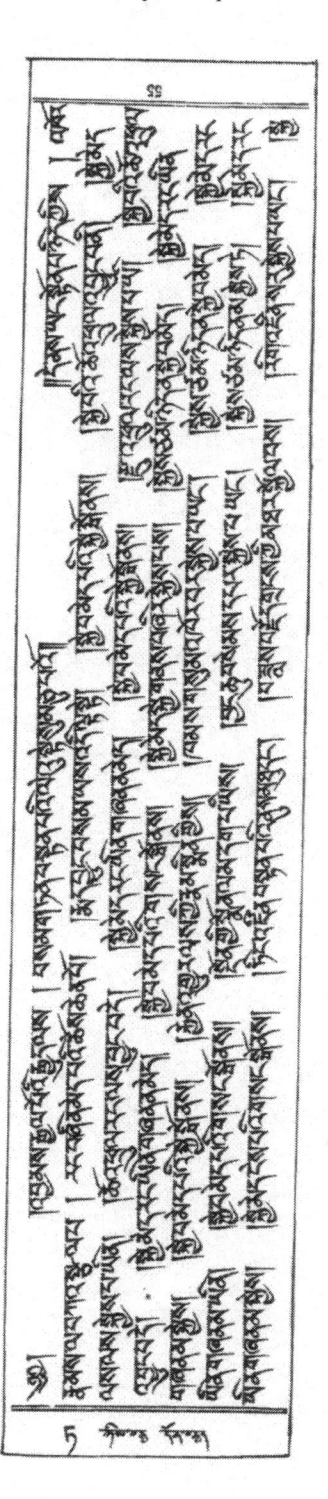

The Royal Tantra on the Brilliant Diffusion of Majestic Space

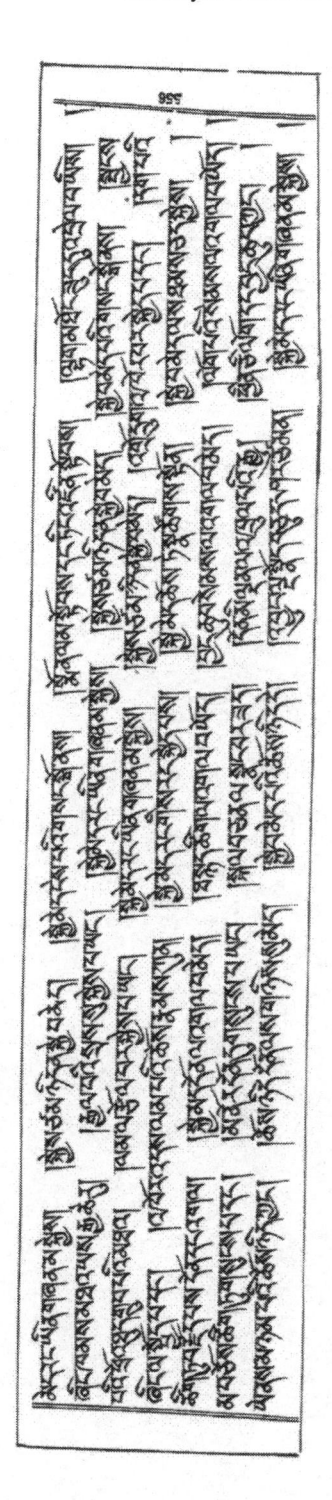

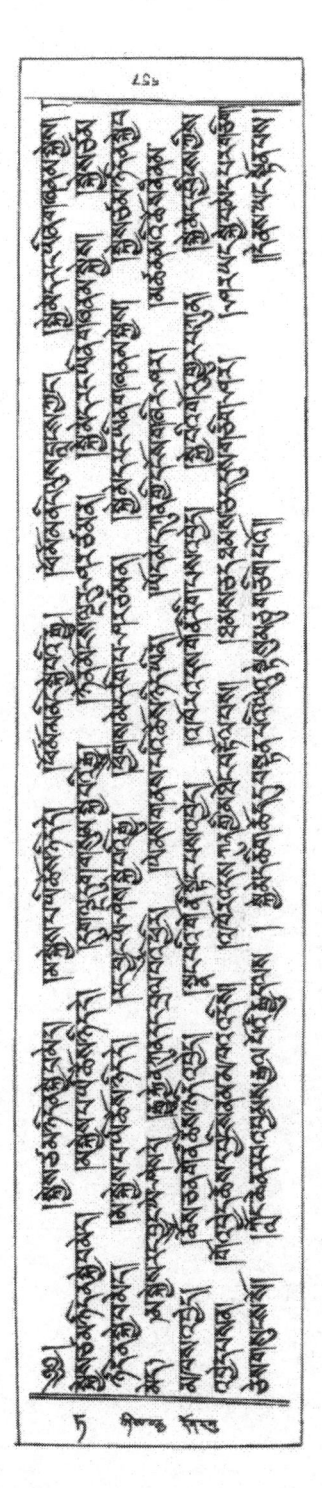

The Royal Tantra on the Brilliant Diffusion of Majestic Space

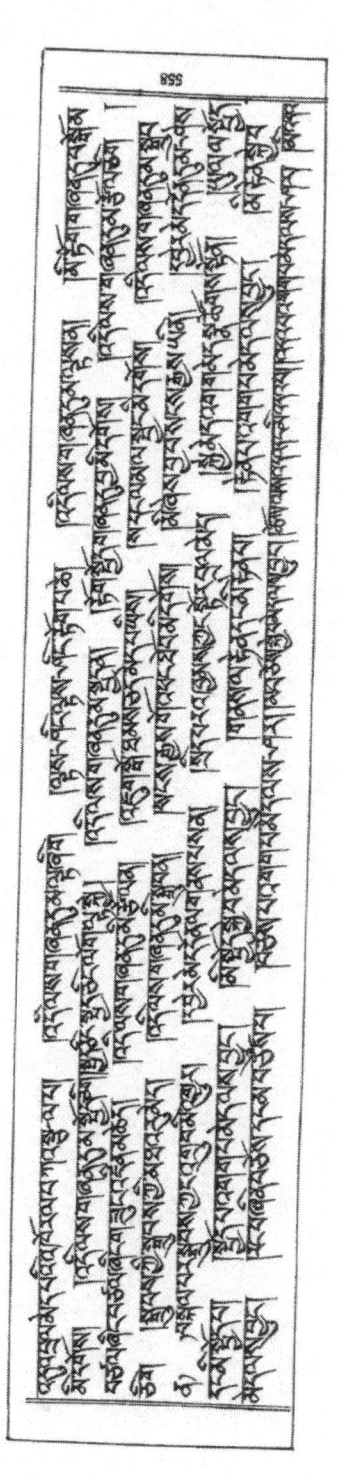

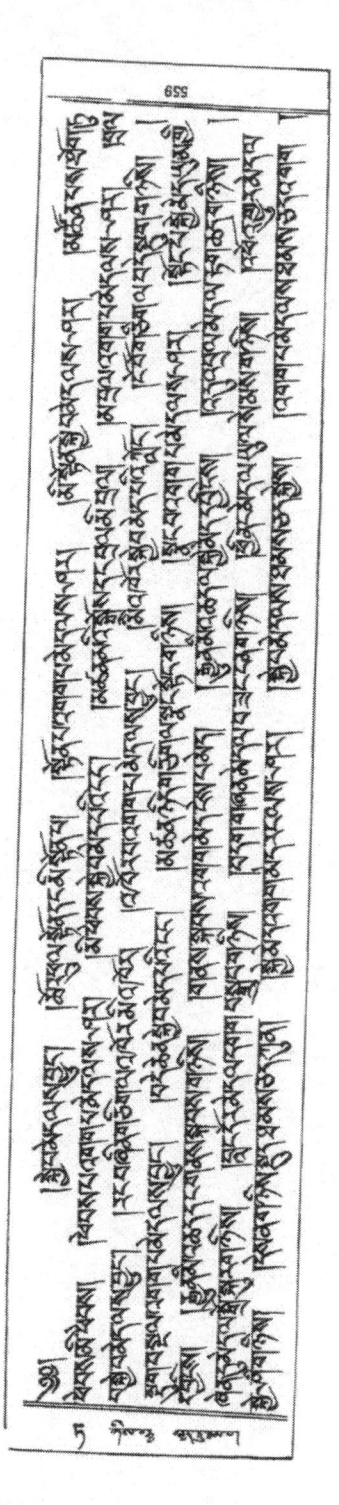

The Royal Tantra on the Brilliant Diffusion of Majestic Space

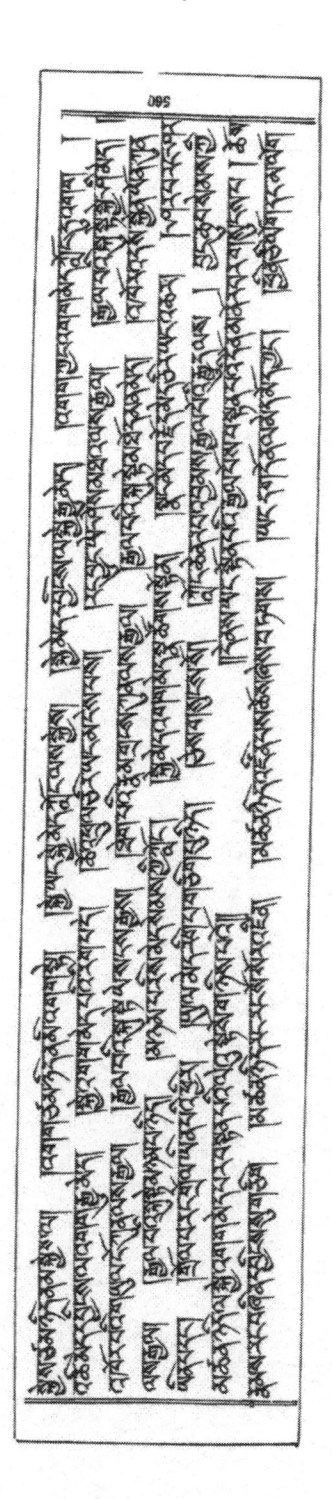

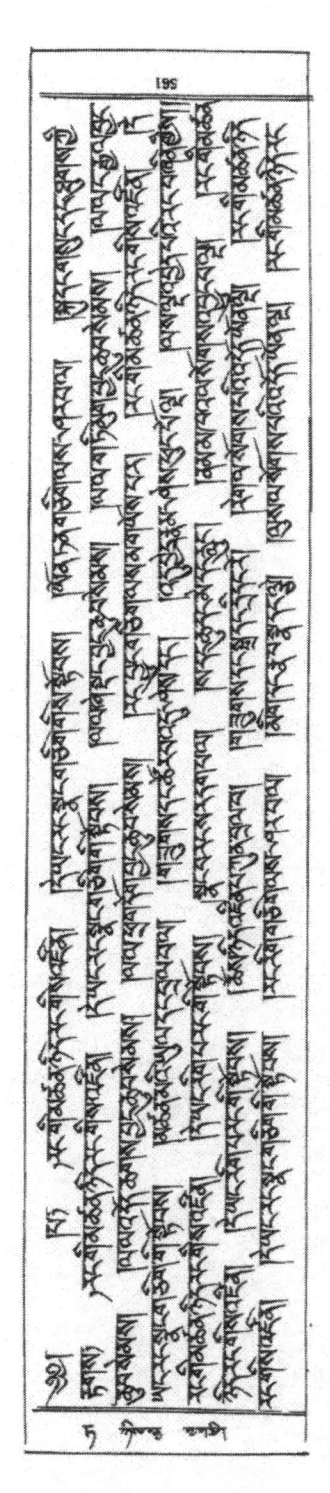

The Royal Tantra on the Brilliant Diffusion of Majestic Space

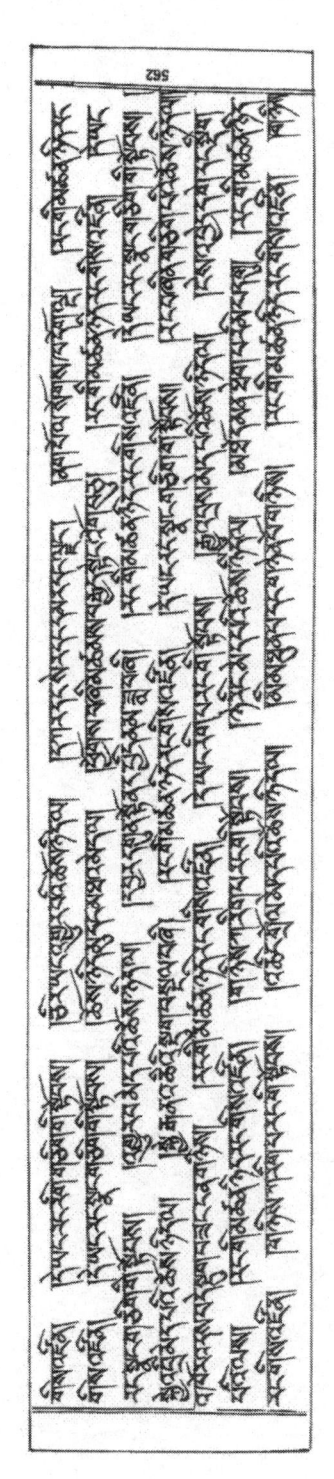

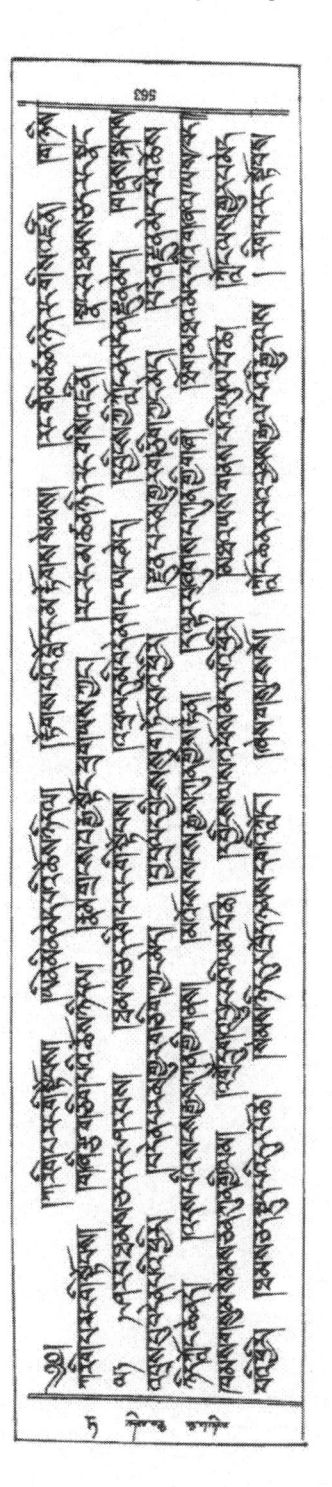

The Royal Tantra on the Brilliant Diffusion of Majestic Space

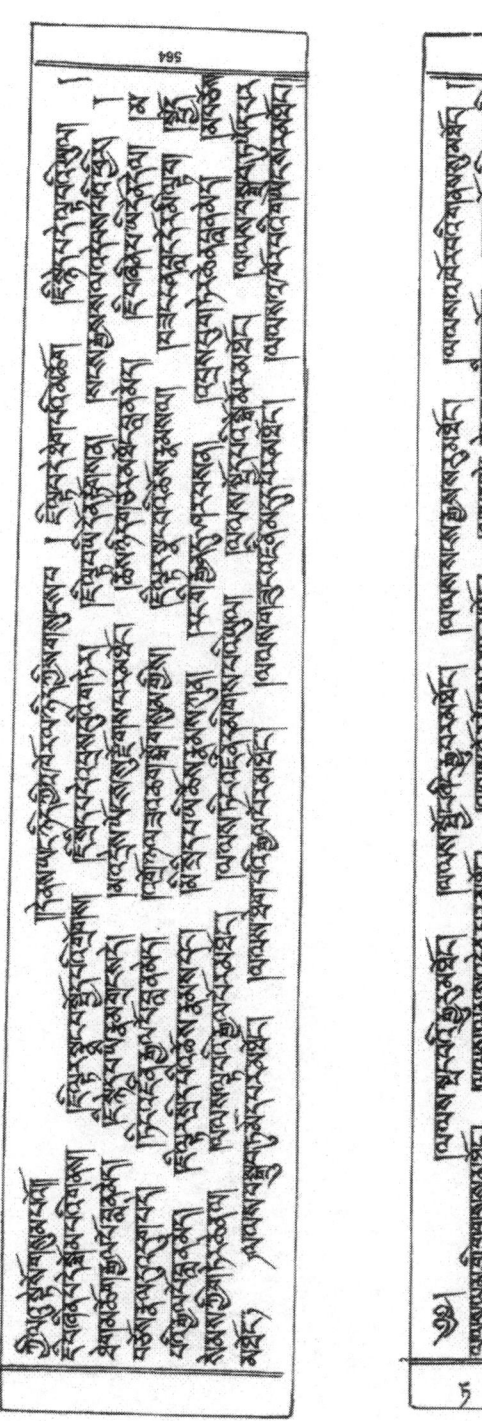

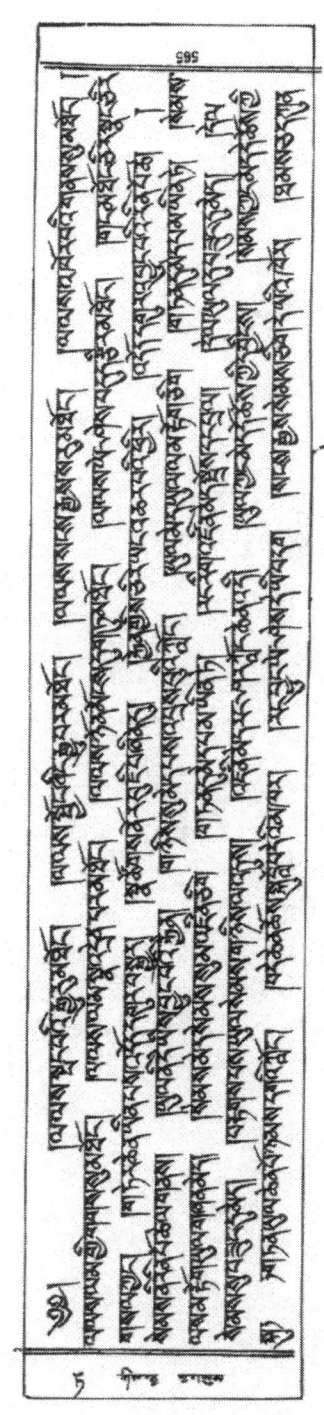

The Royal Tantra on the Brilliant Diffusion of Majestic Space

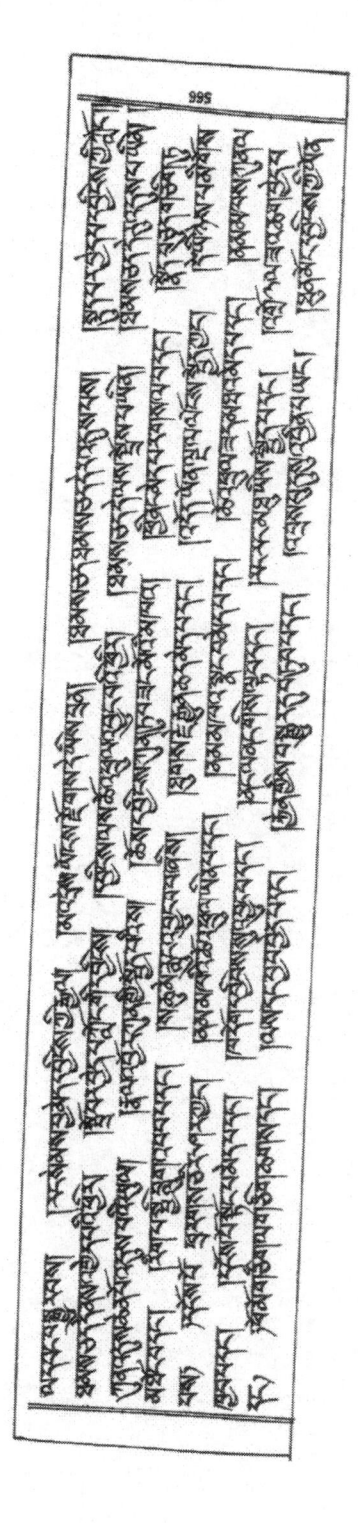

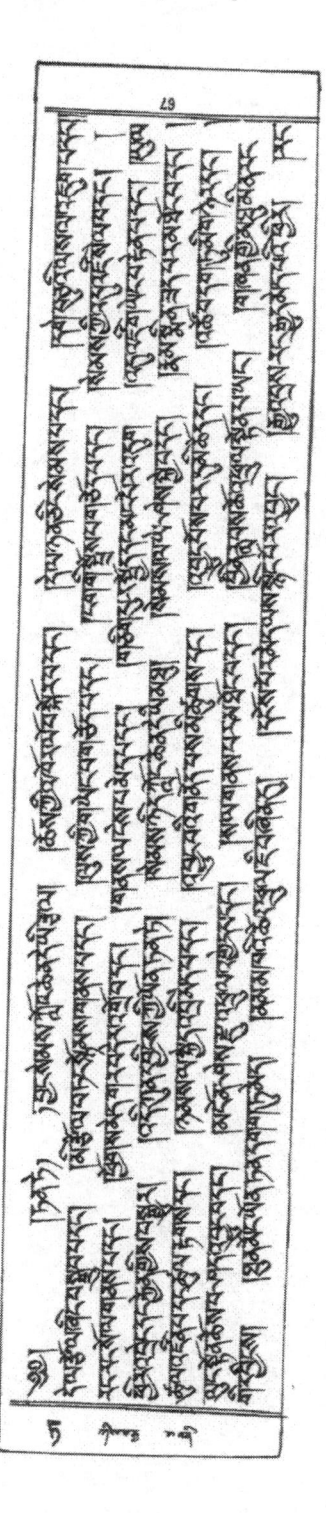

The Royal Tantra on the Brilliant Diffusion of Majestic Space

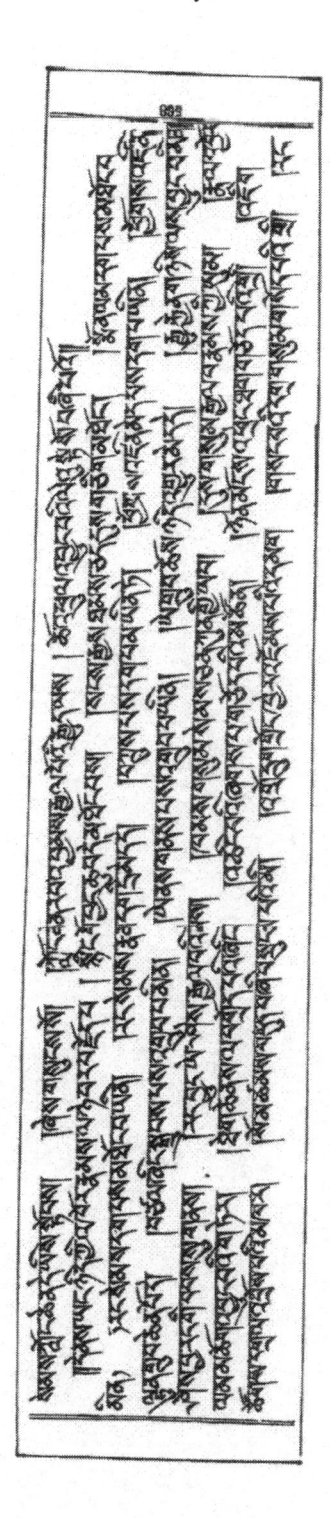

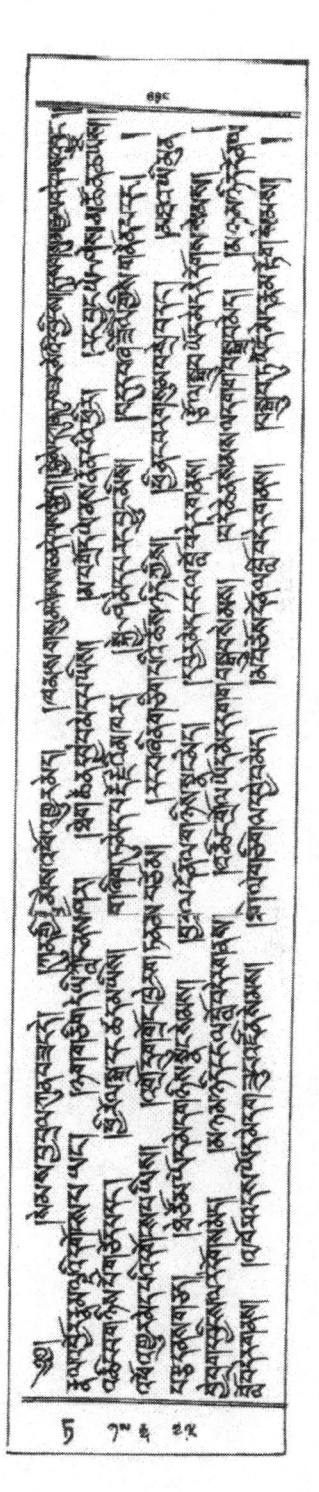

The Royal Tantra on the Brilliant Diffusion of Majestic Space

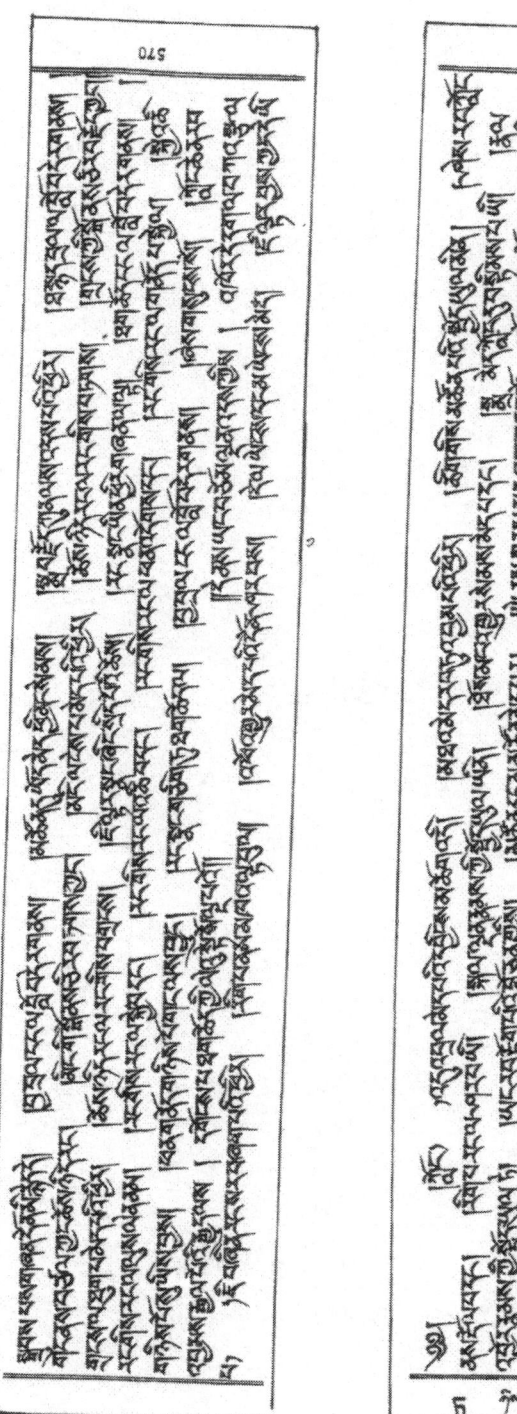

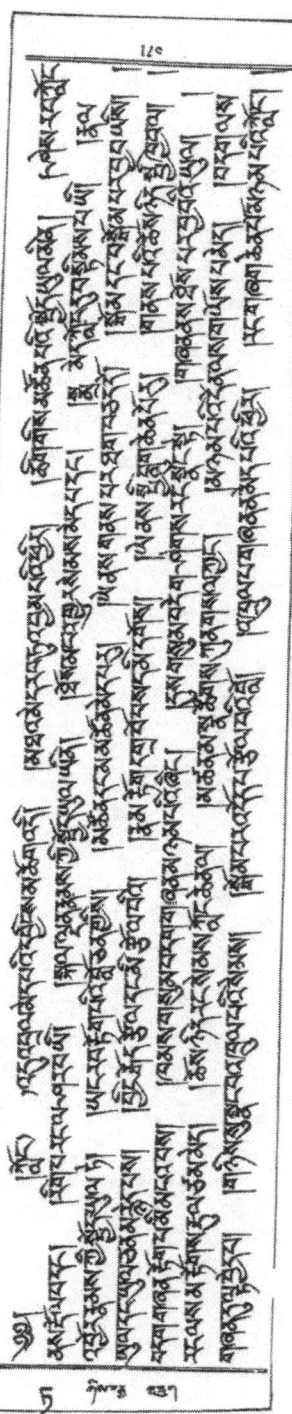

The Royal Tantra on the Brilliant Diffusion of Majestic Space

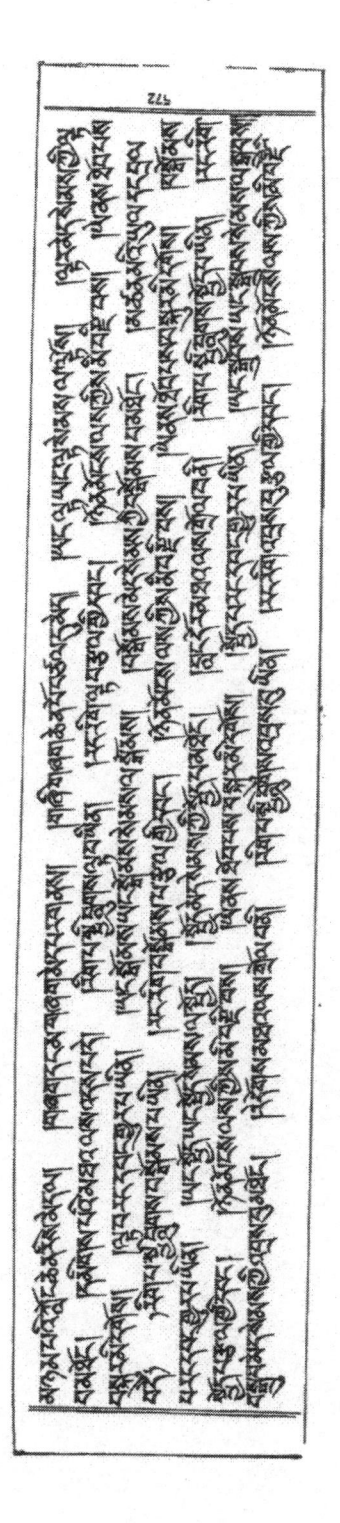

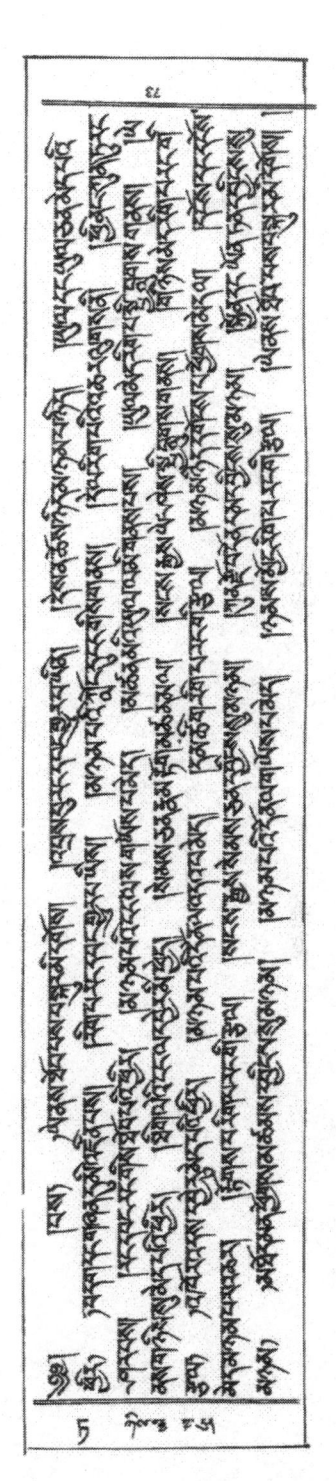

The Royal Tantra on the Brilliant Diffusion of Majestic Space

The Royal Tantra on the Brilliant Diffusion of Majestic Space

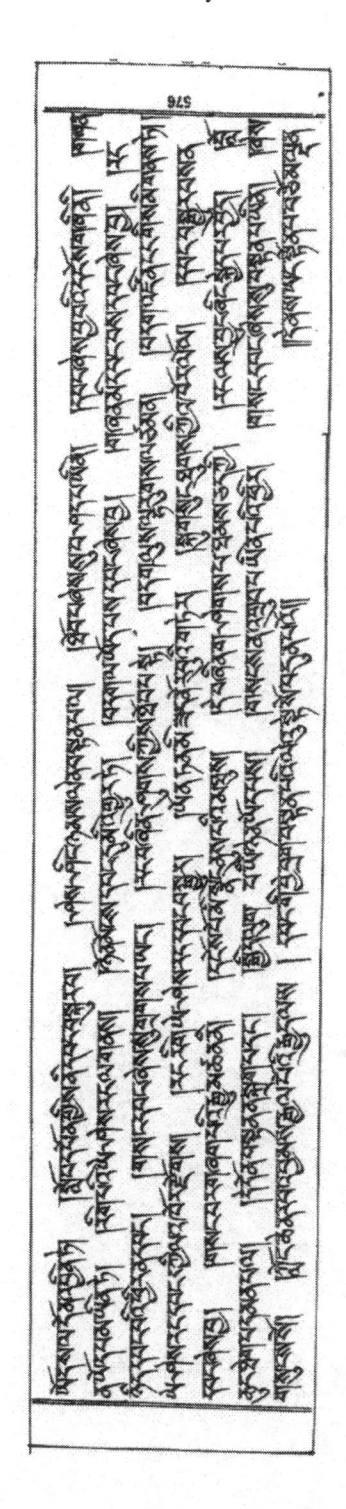

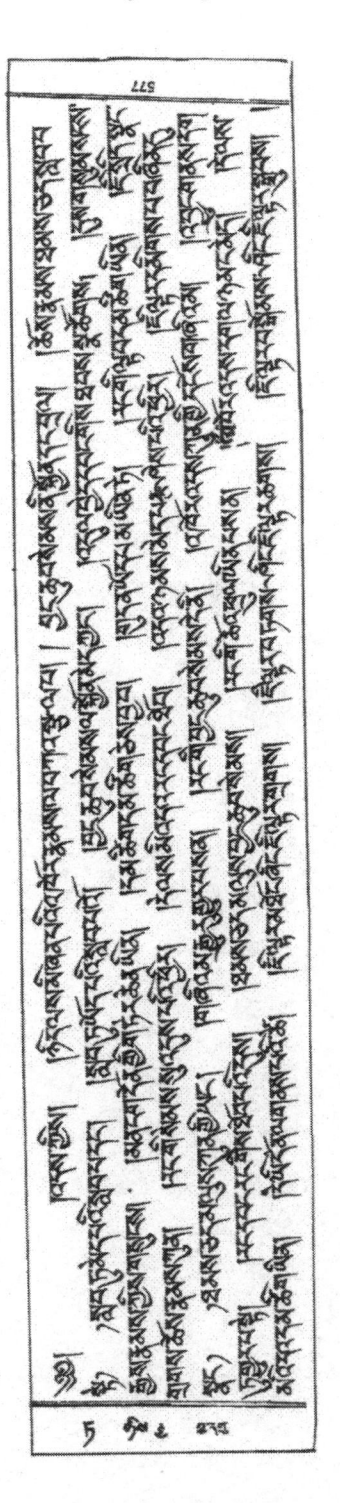

The Royal Tantra on the Brilliant Diffusion of Majestic Space

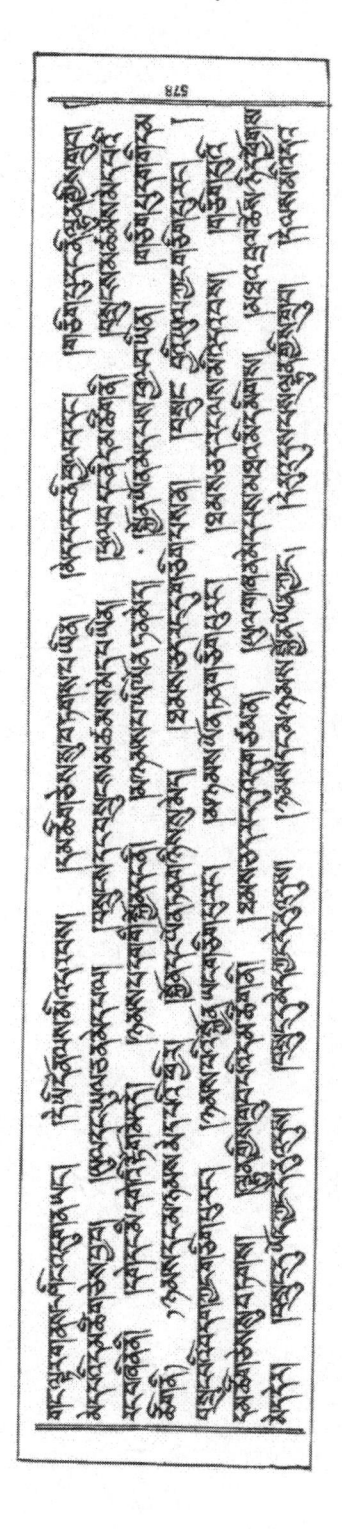

The Royal Tantra on the Brilliant Diffusion of Majestic Space

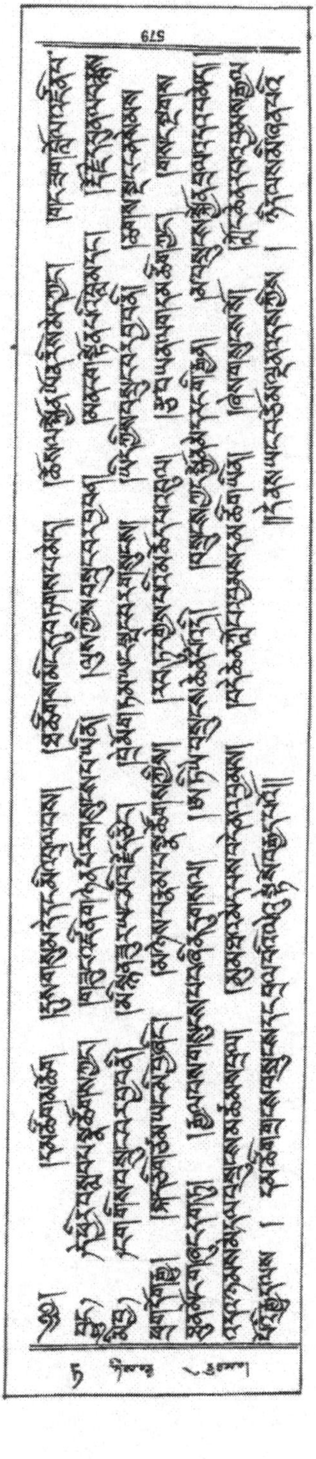

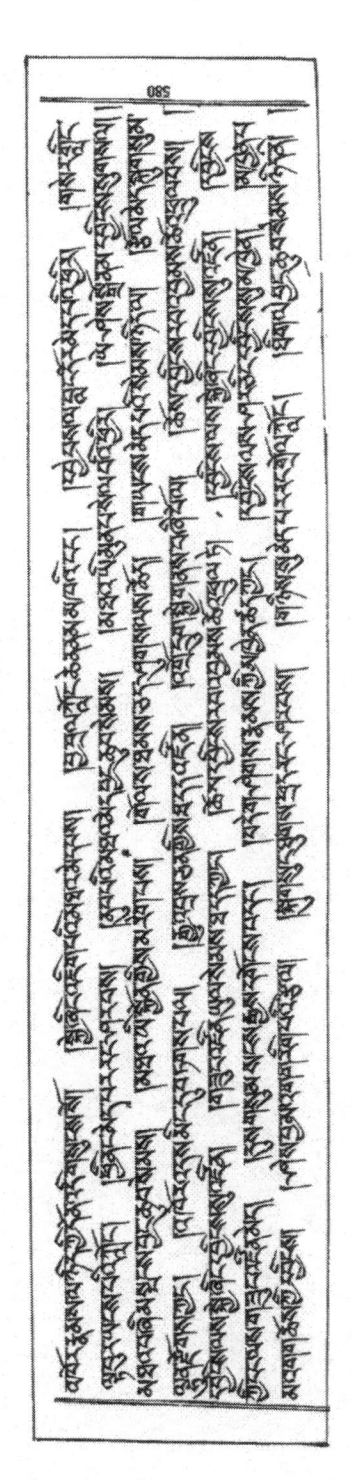

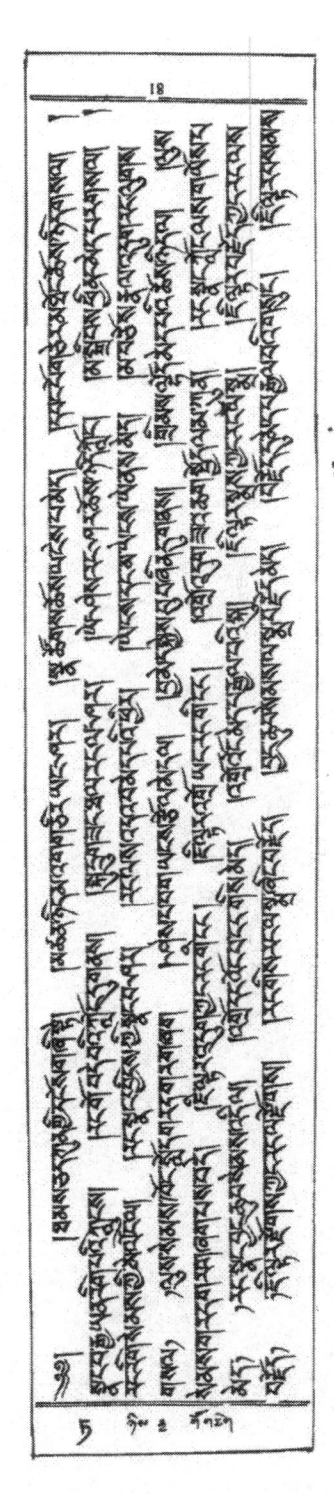

The Royal Tantra on the Brilliant Diffusion of Majestic Space

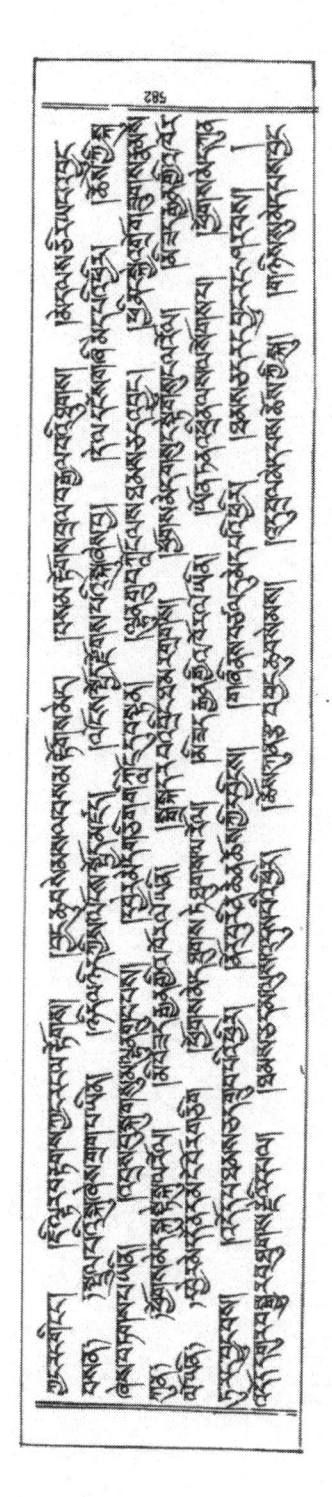

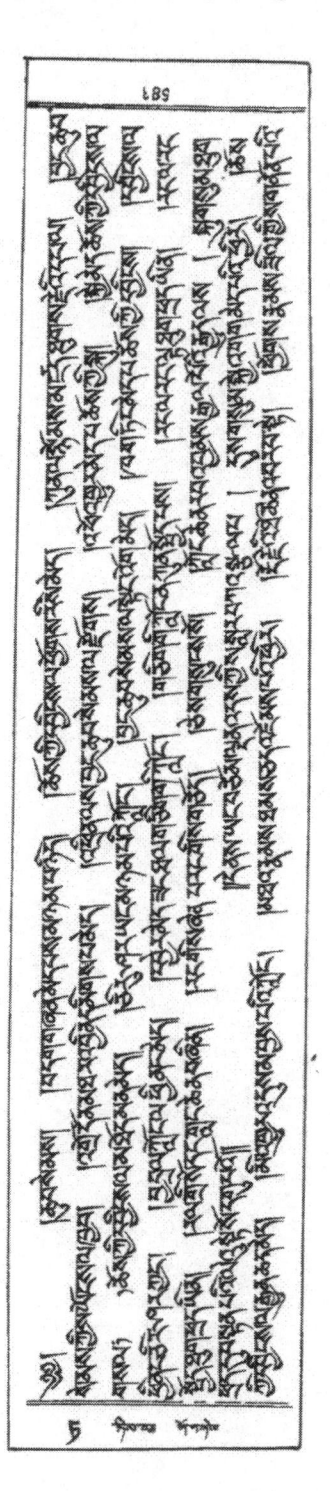

The Royal Tantra on the Brilliant Diffusion of Majestic Space

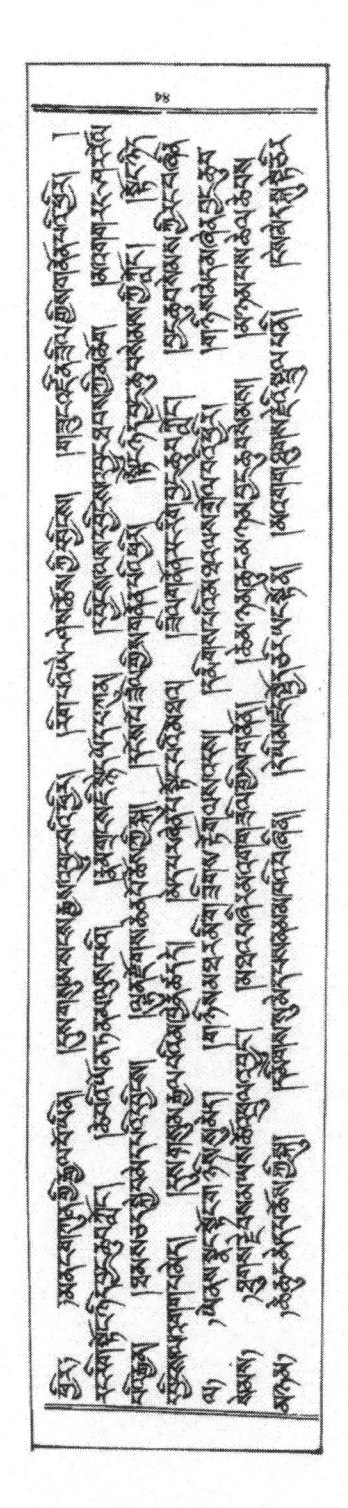

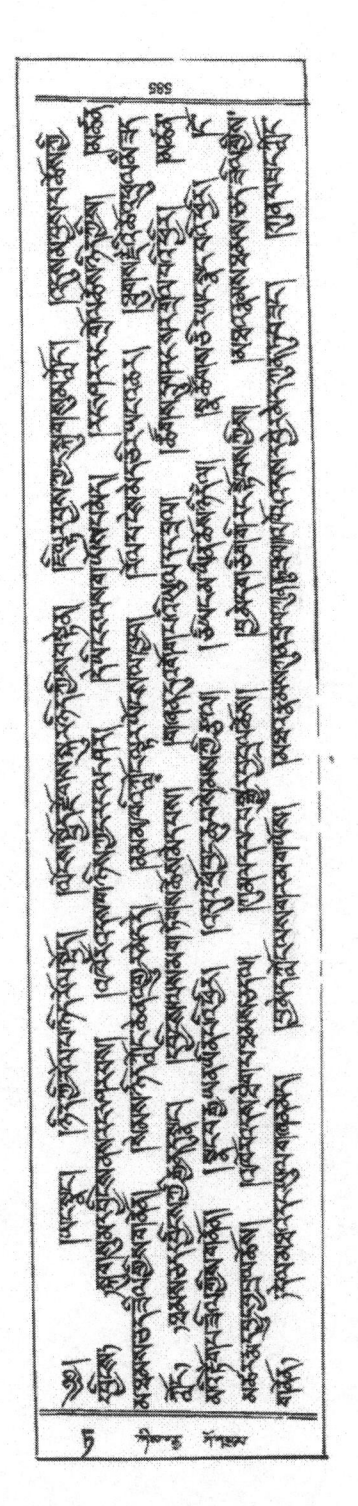

The Royal Tantra on the Brilliant Diffusion of Majestic Space

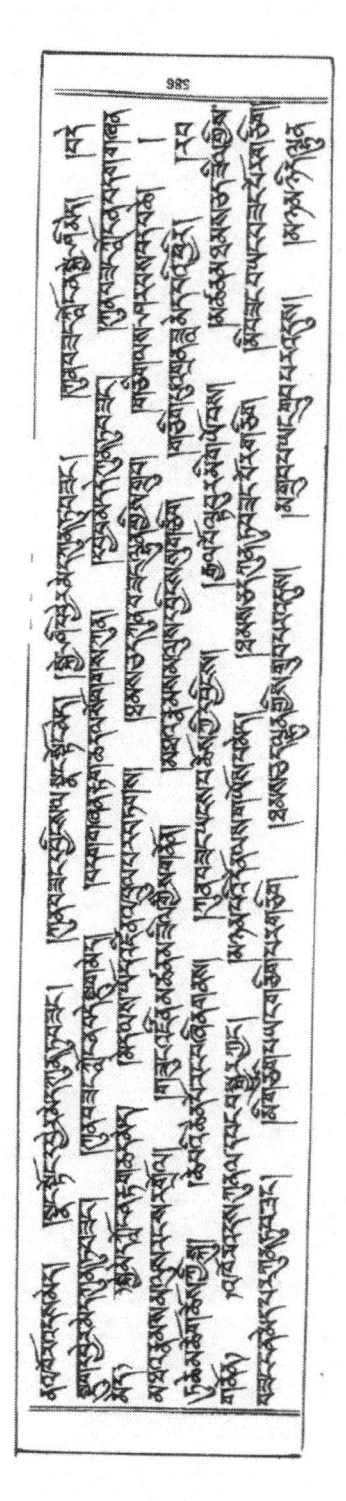

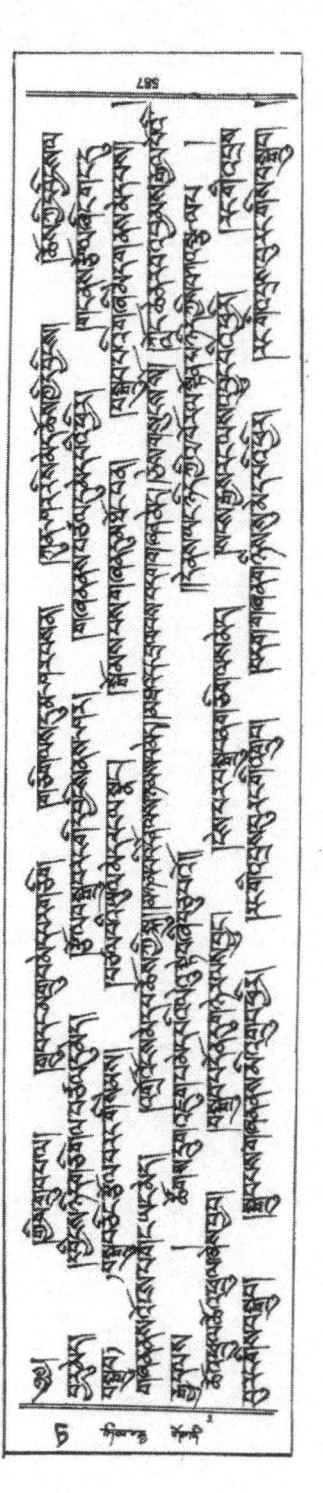

The Royal Tantra on the Brilliant Diffusion of Majestic Space

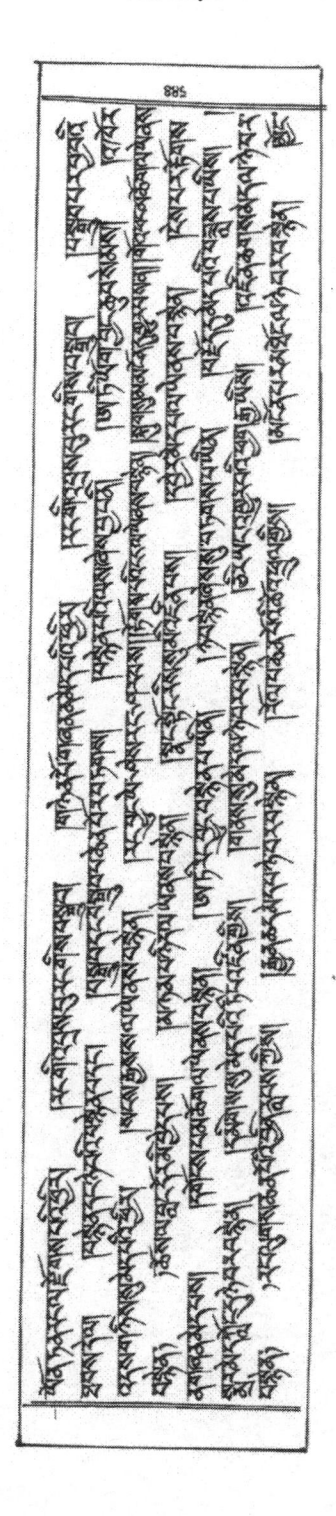

The Royal Tantra on the Brilliant Diffusion of Majestic Space

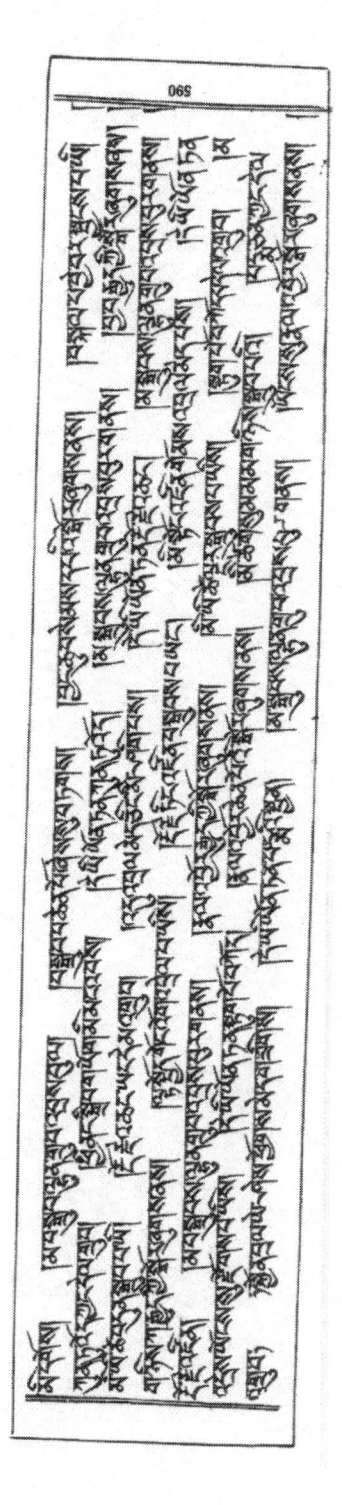

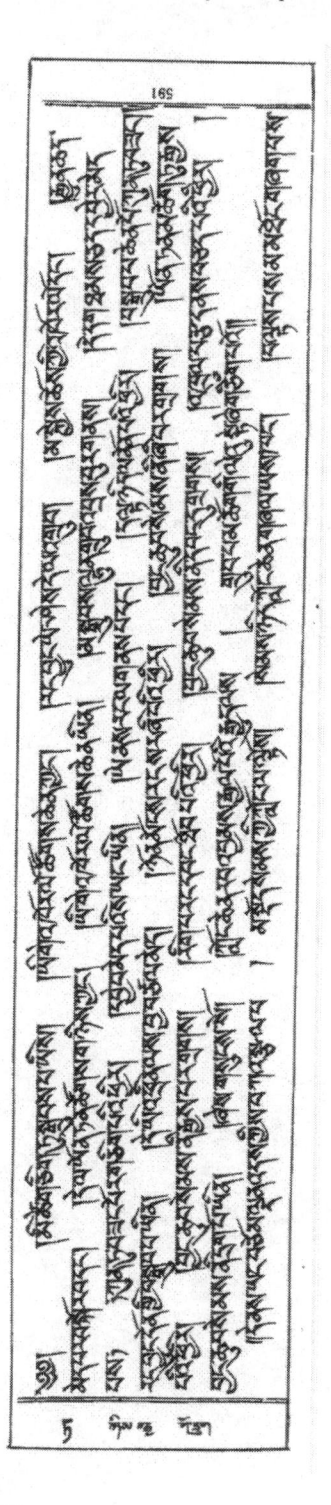

The Royal Tantra on the Brilliant Diffusion of Majestic Space

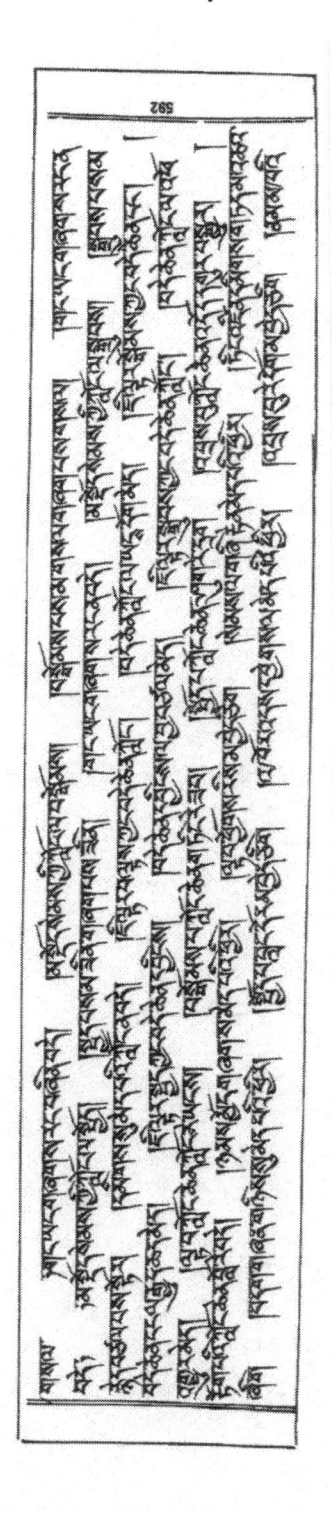

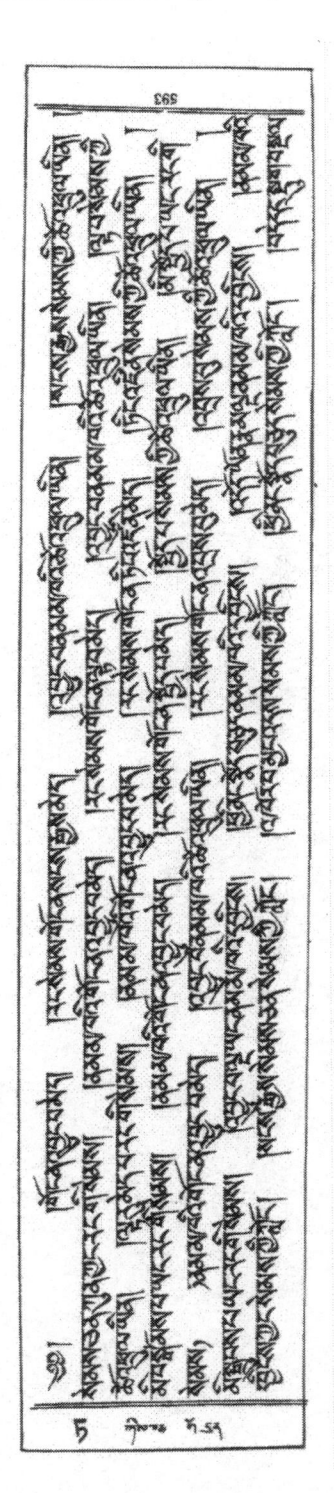

The Royal Tantra on the Brilliant Diffusion of Majestic Space

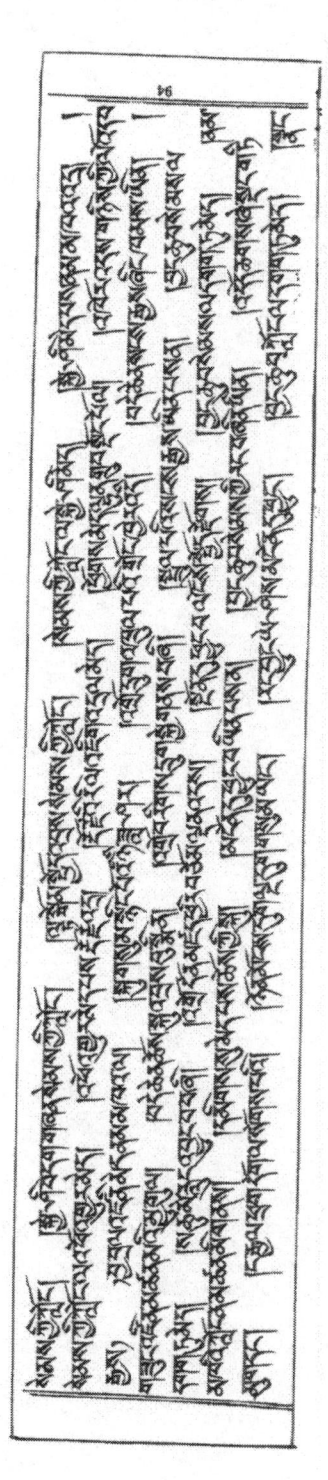

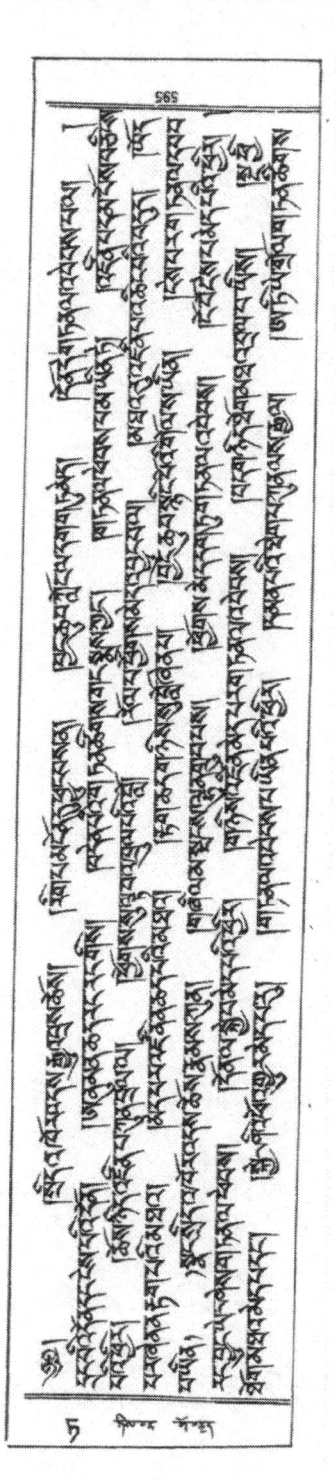

The Royal Tantra on the Brilliant Diffusion of Majestic Space

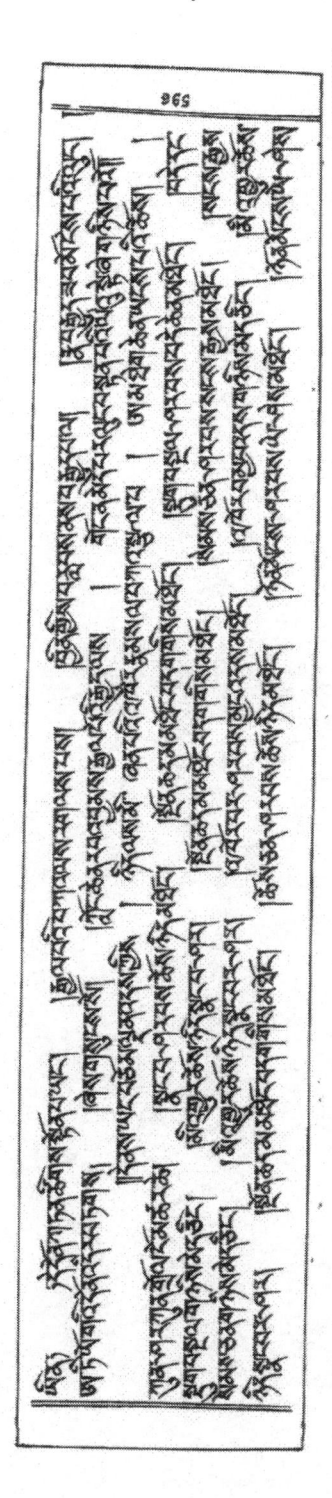

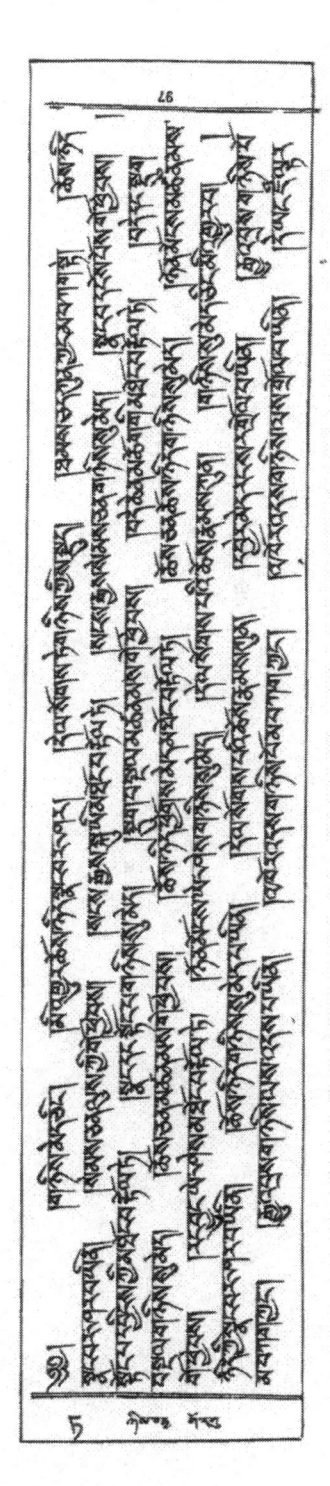

The Royal Tantra on the Brilliant Diffusion of Majestic Space

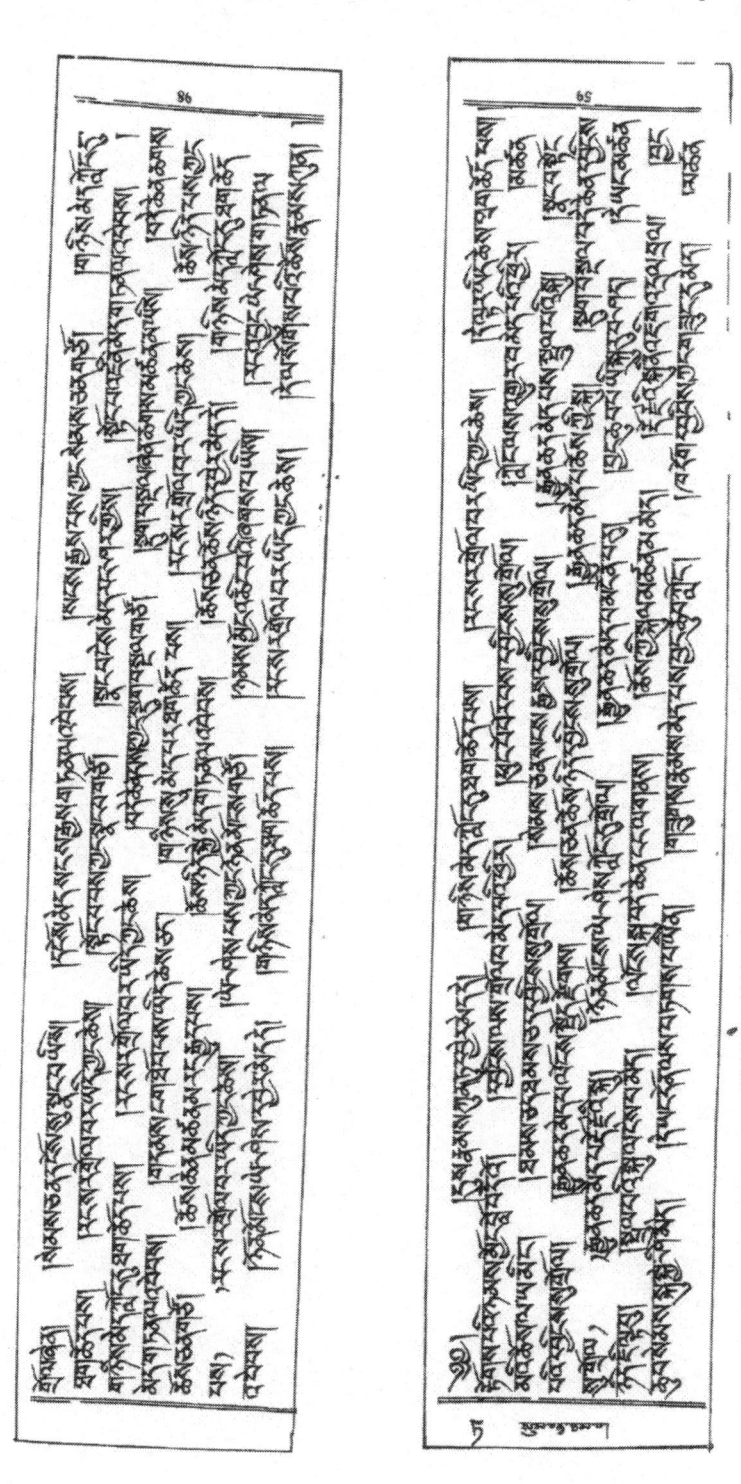

The Royal Tantra on the Brilliant Diffusion of Majestic Space

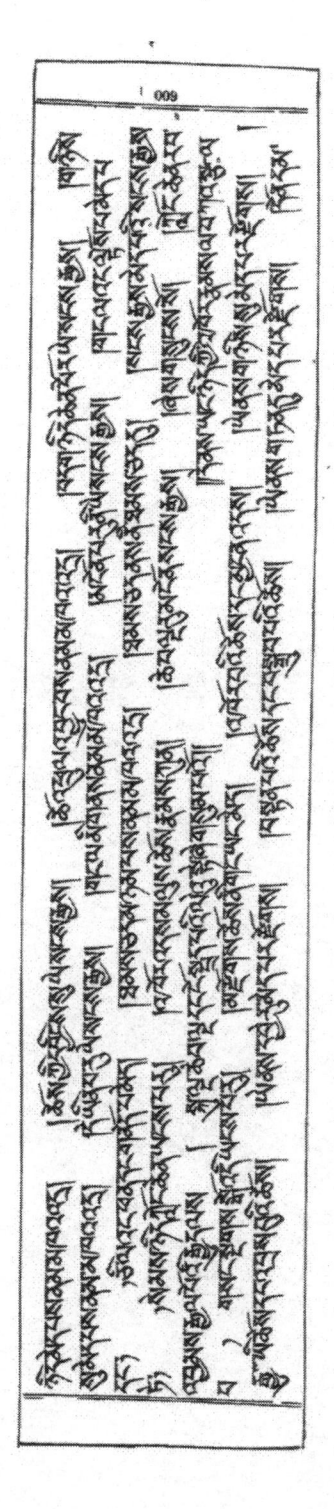

The Royal Tantra on the Brilliant Diffusion of Majestic Space

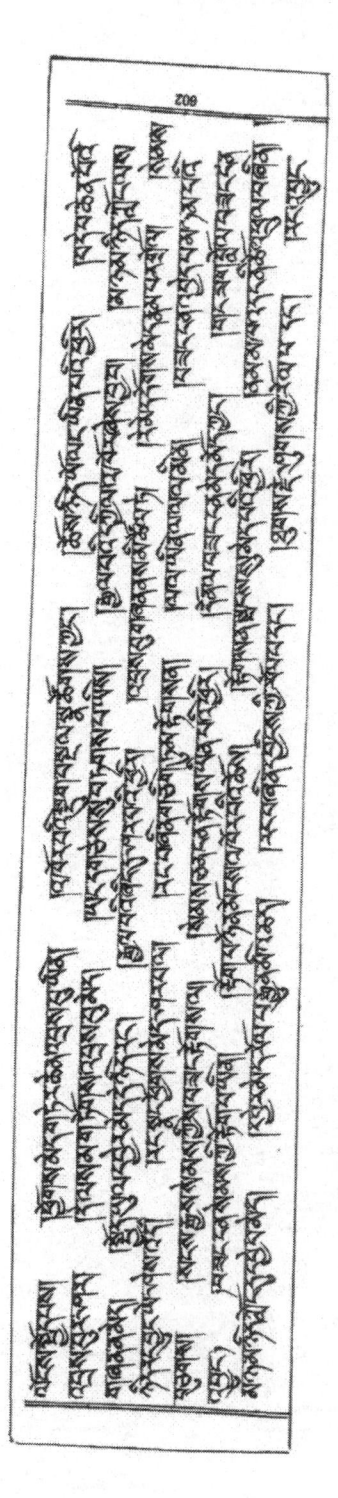

The Royal Tantra on the Brilliant Diffusion of Majestic Space

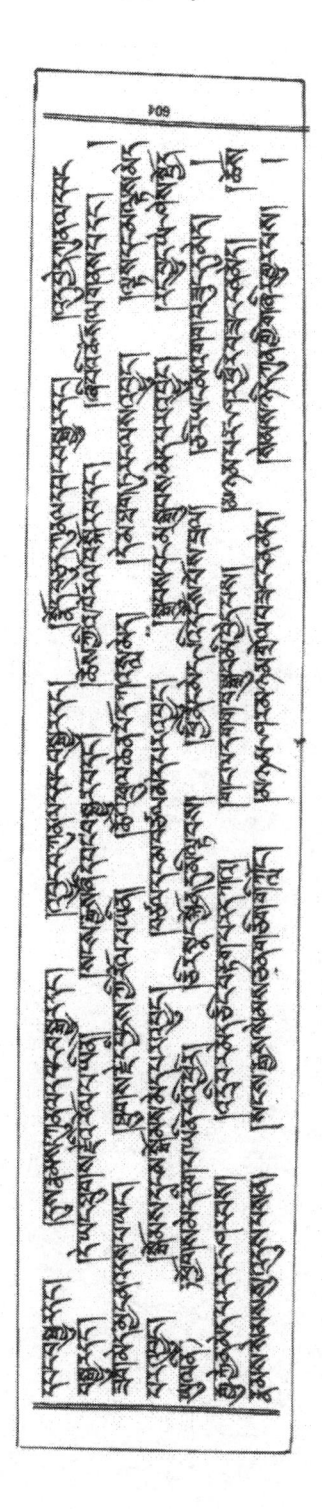

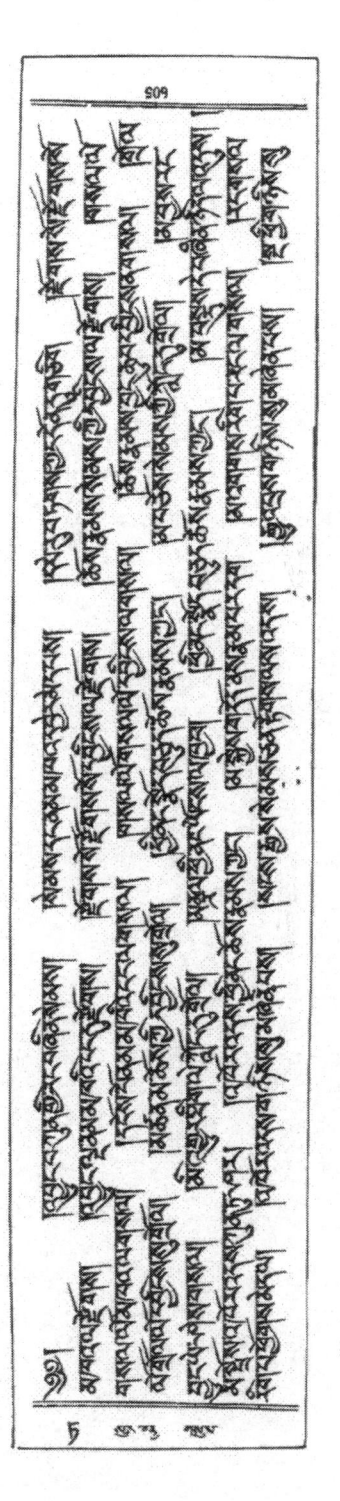

The Royal Tantra on the Brilliant Diffusion of Majestic Space

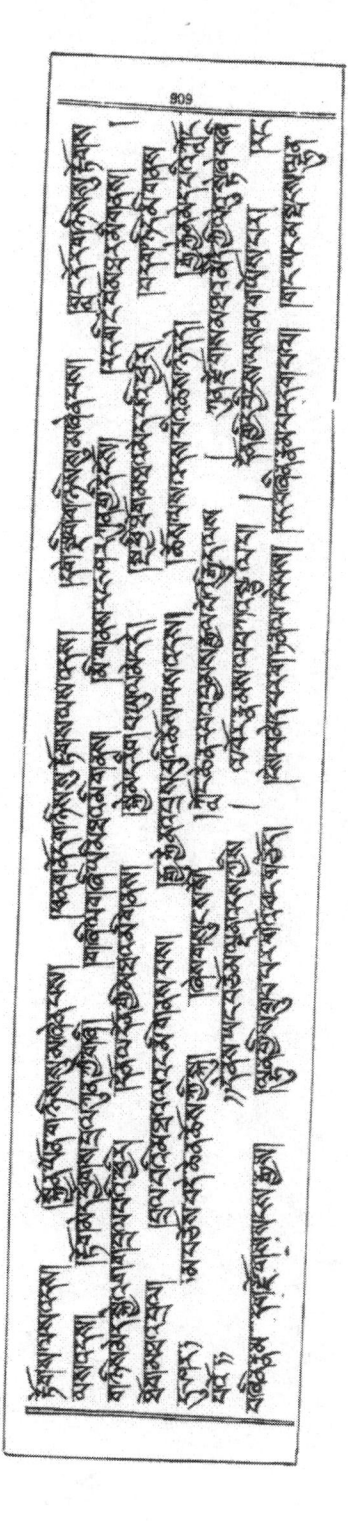

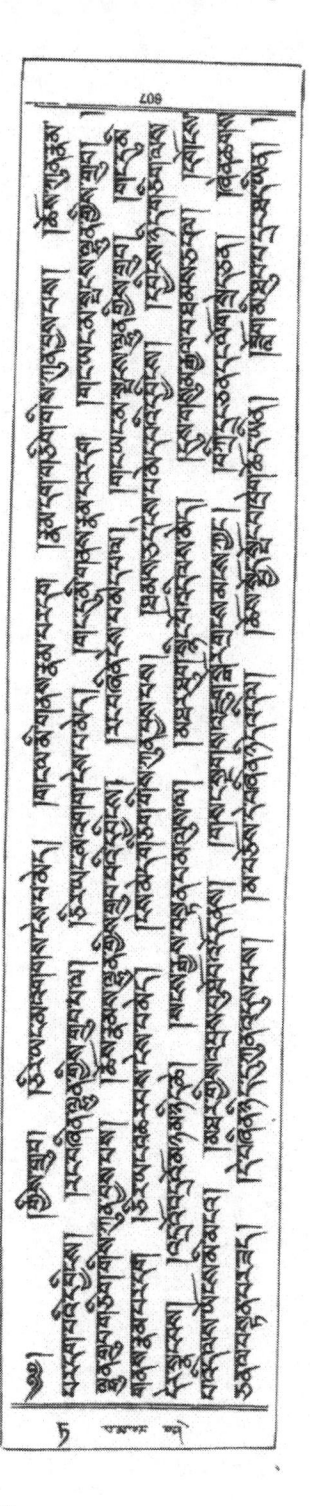

The Royal Tantra on the Brilliant Diffusion of Majestic Space

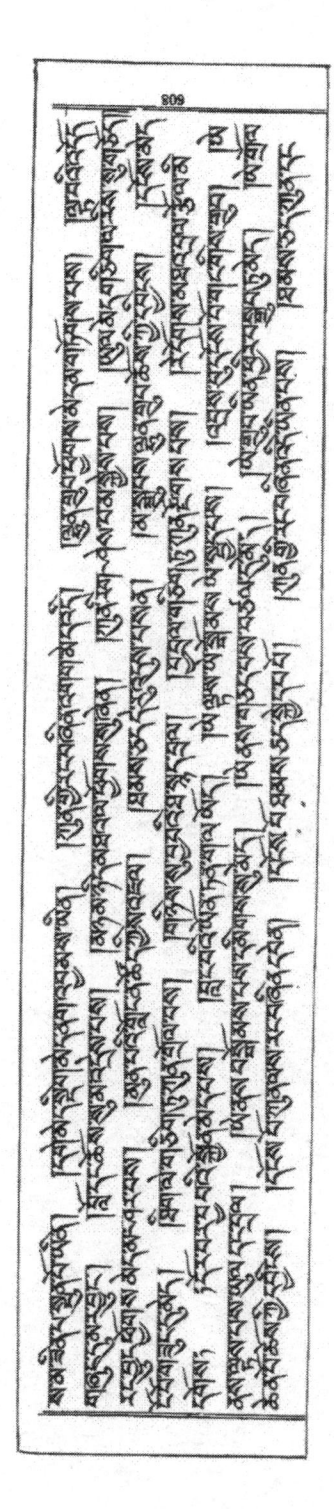

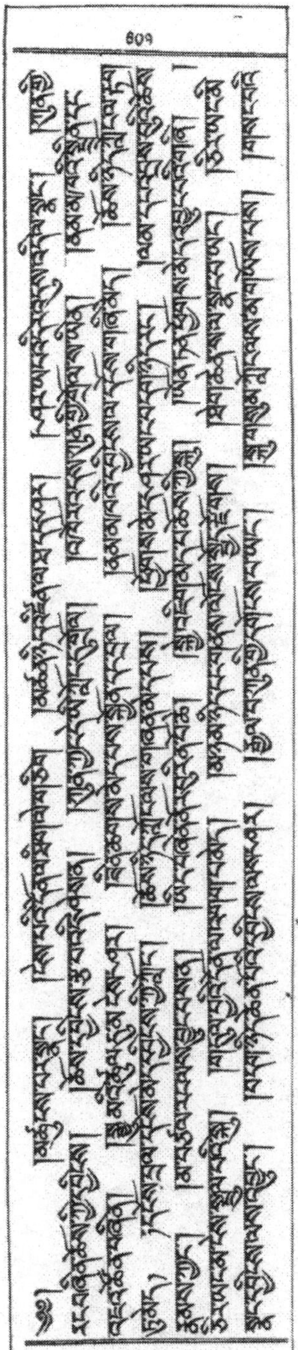

The Royal Tantra on the Brilliant Diffusion of Majestic Space

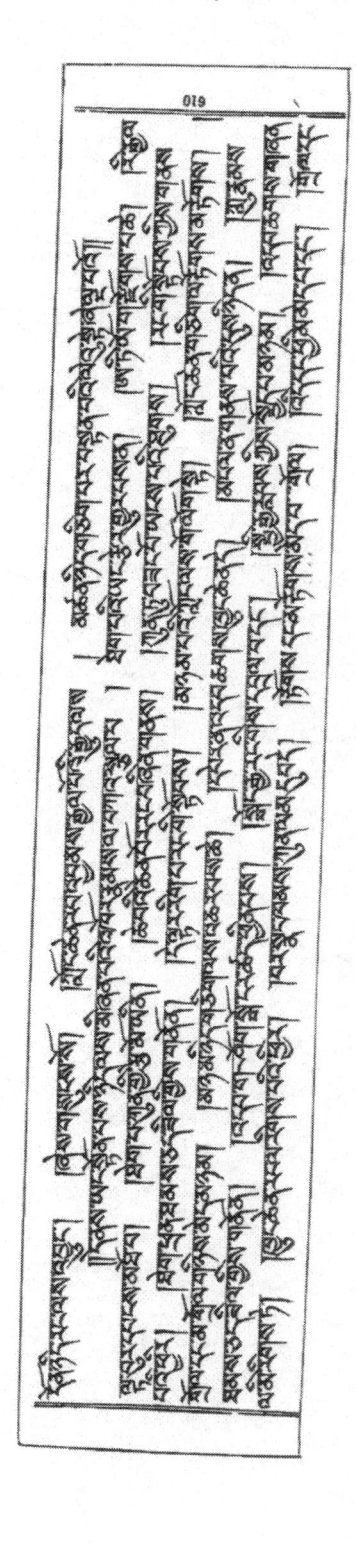

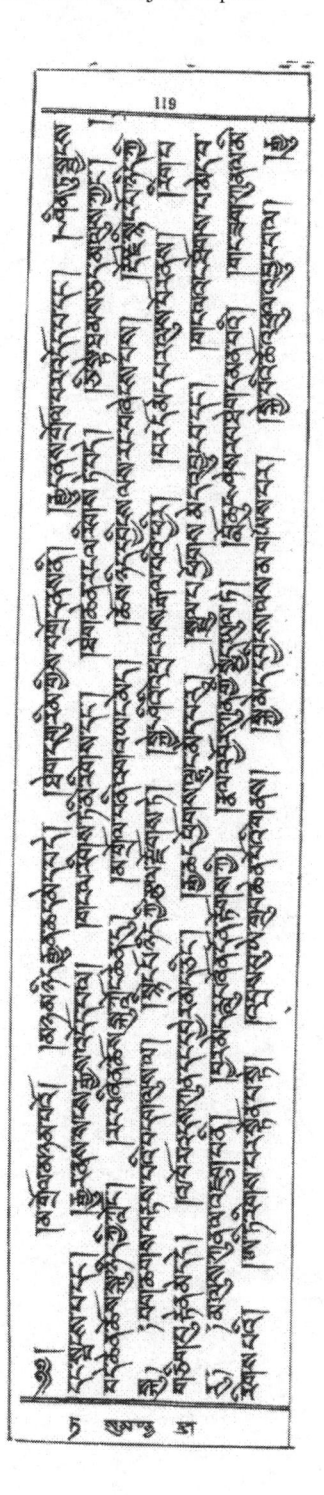

The Royal Tantra on the Brilliant Diffusion of Majestic Space

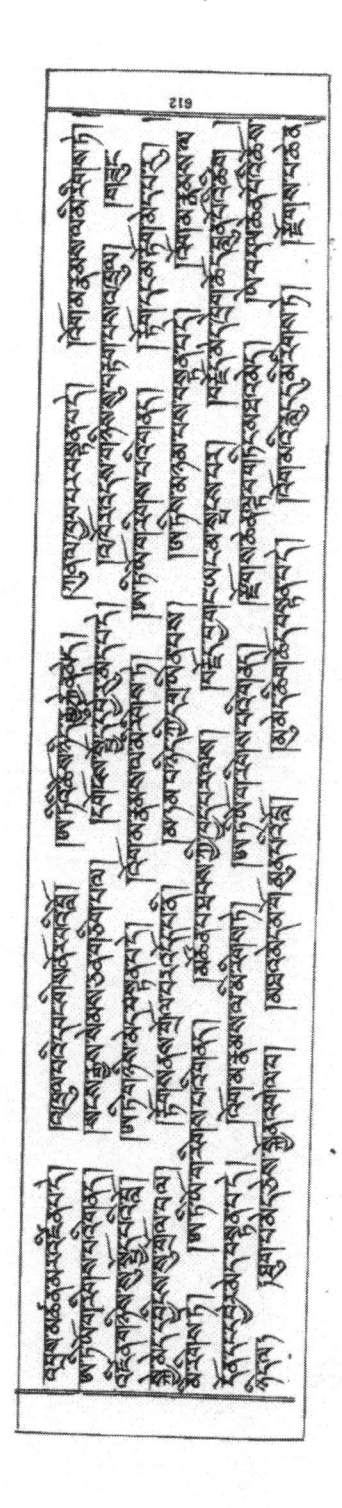

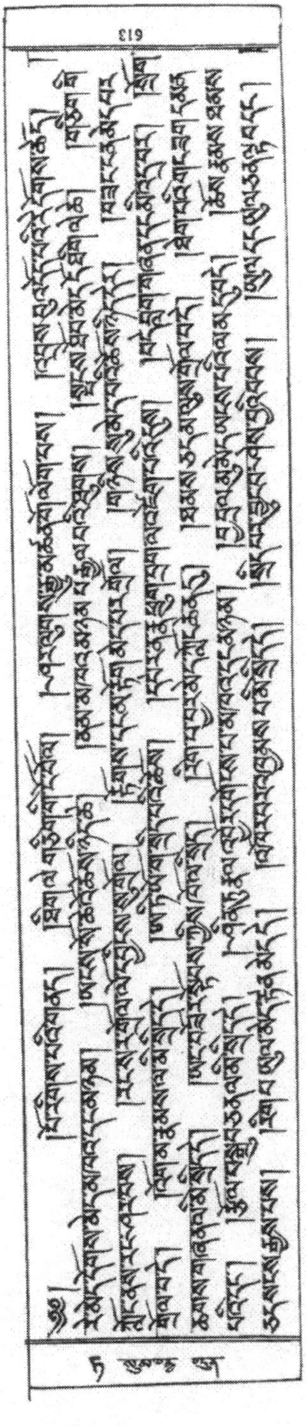

The Royal Tantra on the Brilliant Diffusion of Majestic Space

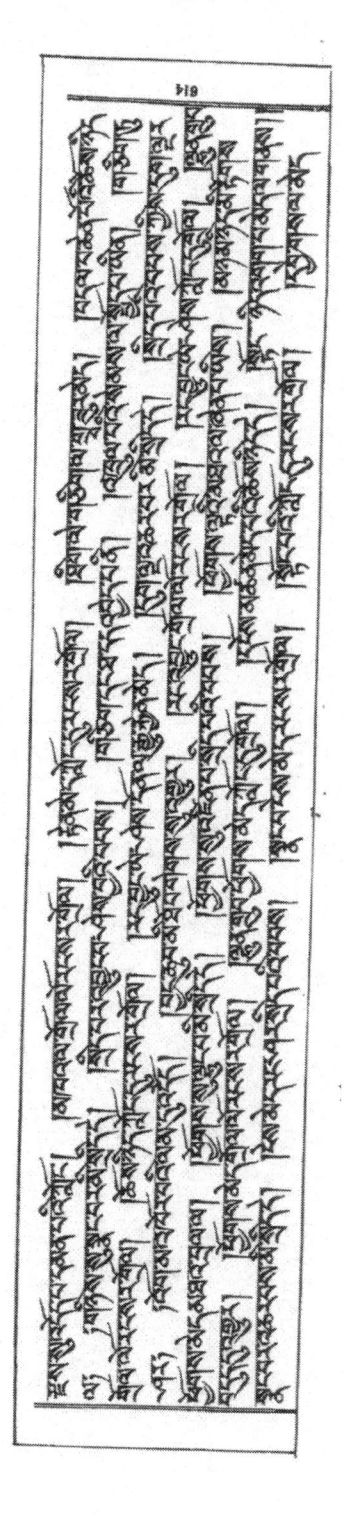

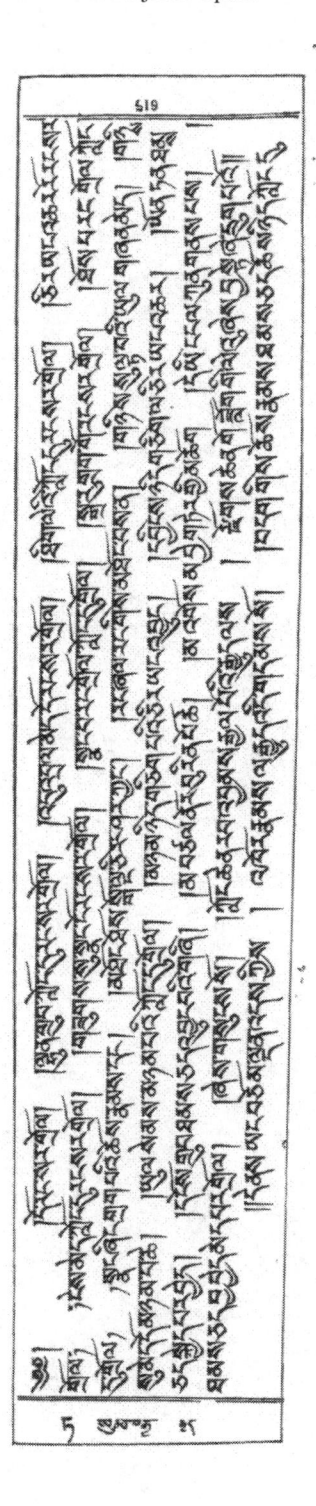

The Royal Tantra on the Brilliant Diffusion of Majestic Space

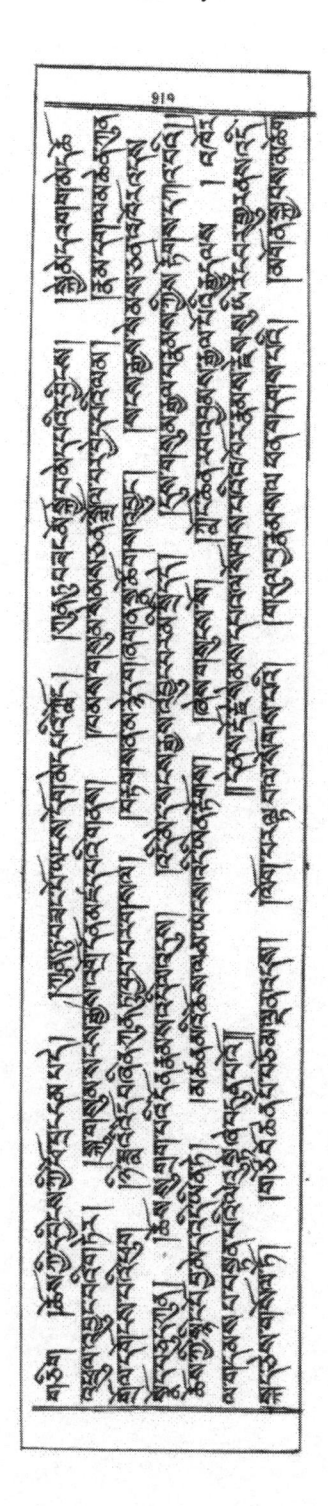

The Royal Tantra on the Brilliant Diffusion of Majestic Space

ABOUT THE TRANSLATOR

Christopher Wilkinson began his career in Buddhist literature at the age of fifteen, taking refuge vows from his guru Dezhung Rinpoche. In that same year he began formal study of Tibetan language at the University of Washington under Geshe Ngawang Nornang and Turrell Wylie. He became a Buddhist monk, for three years, at the age of eighteen, living in the home of Dezhung Rinpoche while he continued his studies at the University of Washington. He graduated in 1980 with a B.A. degree in Asian Languages and Literature and another B.A. degree in Comparative Religion (College Honors, Magna Cum Laude, Phi Beta Kappa). After a two year tour of Buddhist pilgrimage sites throughout Asia he worked in refugee resettlement programs for five years in Seattle, Washington. He then proceeded to the University of Calgary for an M.A. in Buddhist Studies where he wrote a groundbreaking thesis on the Yangti transmission of the Great Perfection tradition titled "Clear Meaning: Studies on a Thirteenth Century rDzog chen Tantra." He proceeded to work on a critical edition of the Sanskrit text of the 20,000 line Perfection of Wisdom in Berkeley, California, followed by an intensive study of Burmese language in Hawaii. In 1990 he began three years' service as a visiting professor in English Literature in Sulawesi, Indonesia, exploring the remnants of the ancient Sri Vijaya Empire there. He worked as a research fellow for the Shelly and Donald Rubin Foundation for several years, playing a part in the early development of the Rubin Museum of Art. In the years that followed he became a Research Fellow at the Centre de Recherches sur les Civilisations de l'Asie Orientale, Collège de France, and taught at the University of Calgary as an Adjunct Professor for five years. He has currently published sixteen volumes of translations of Tibetan literature, and is currently engaged in further translations of classic Buddhist literature.

Made in the USA
San Bernardino, CA
24 July 2016